The Visionary Queen

EARLY MODERN FEMINISMS

Series Editor
Robin Runia, Xavier University of Louisiana

Editorial Advisory Board
Jennifer Airey, University of Tulsa; Paula Backscheider, Auburn
University; Susan Carlile, California State University; Karen Gevirtz,
Seton Hall University; Mona Narain, Texas Christian University;
Carmen Nocentelli, University of New Mexico; Jodi Wyett,
Xavier University

Showcasing distinctly feminist ideological commitments and/or method-
ological approaches, and tracing literary and cultural expressions of feminist thought, Early Modern Feminisms seeks to publish innovative readings
of women's lives and work, as well as of gendered experience, from the years
1500–1800. In addition to highlighting examinations of women's literature
and history, this series aims to provide scholars an opportunity to emphasize new approaches to the study of gender and sexuality with respect to
material culture, science, and art, as well as politics and race. Thus, monographs and edited collections that are interdisciplinary and/or transnational
in nature are particularly welcome.

Series Titles
Eliza Fenwick: Early Modern Feminist, by Lissa Paul
The Circuit of Apollo: Eighteenth-Century Women's Tributes to Women,
   edited by Laura L. Runge and Jessica Cook

The Visionary Queen

JUSTICE, REFORM, AND THE
LABYRINTH IN MARGUERITE DE NAVARRE

THERESA BROCK

UNIVERSITY OF DELAWARE PRESS

NEWARK

Library of Congress Cataloging-in-Publication Data

Names: Brock, Theresa, author.
Title: The visionary queen : justice, reform, and the labyrinth in
Marguerite de Navarre / Theresa Brock.
Description: Newark : University of Delaware Press, [2024] | Series: Early
modern feminisms | Includes bibliographical references and index.
Identifiers: LCCN 2023014646 | ISBN 9781644533086 (paperback) |
ISBN 9781644533277 (hardcover) | ISBN 9781644533093 (epub) |
ISBN 9781644533109 (pdf)
Subjects: LCSH: Marguerite, Queen, consort of Henry II, King of Navarre,
1492–1549. Heptaméron. | Marguerite, Queen, consort of Henry II, King
of Navarre, 1492–1549—Criticism and interpretation. | Labyrinths in
literature. | Justice in literature. | Reformation in literature. |
Short stories, French—History and criticism. | French literature—
16th century—History and criticism. | Reformation—France.
Classification: LCC PQ1631.H4 B75 2024 | DDC 843/.3—dc23/eng/20230601
LC record available at https://lccn.loc.gov/2023014646

A British Cataloging-in-Publication record for this
book is available from the British Library.

References to internet websites (URLs) were accurate at the time of writing. Neither
the author nor University of Delaware Press is responsible for URLs that may have
expired or changed since the manuscript was prepared.

Printed and bound by CPI Group (UK) Ltd, Croydon, CR0 4YY

♾ The paper used in this publication meets the requirements of the American
National Standard for Information Sciences—Permanence of Paper for Printed
Library Materials, ANSI Z39.48–1992.

udpress.udel.edu

Distributed worldwide by Rutgers University Press

Contents

Acknowledgments

Unlike the typical, solitary labyrinth walker, I have benefited from the company and the wisdom of a great many people while following the path of this project. Many thanks go to the Department of French and Francophone Studies at the Pennsylvania State University, where I completed my doctoral studies and where the earliest iterations of this research took shape. I am particularly grateful to Jean-Claude Vuillemin, Bénédicte Monicat, and Christine Clark-Evans, as well as Tom Beebee in Comparative Literature, for their astute comments and encouragement, both during my PhD years and in the intervening period in which this project has evolved and unfolded. I would also like to thank Heather McCoy for her support of my professional development over this same period. I am grateful to the Department of Women's, Gender, and Sexuality Studies at Penn State for the formation it provided in modern-day feminist causes and in historical approaches to the works of women writers. A special thank-you also goes to Kit Hume, whose generosity and sage advice over the years, on matters editorial and professional, have proved invaluable to this project.

The Visionary Queen likewise derives inspiration from my time at Williams College, where colleagues and students alike sparked insights that led to a new vision for my research. I am grateful to the Department of Romance Languages, and especially to the French program, for the opportunity to develop new courses in early modern studies and to engage with the creative and highly perceptive students who call Williams home. Many thanks to Brian Martin, Kashia Pieprzak, and Sophie Saint-Just for their mentorship within French; thanks also to Jennifer French, who lent support to the formation of a research group that nourished this study. I am indebted to Pramila Kolekar and Michele Monserrati who, as part of the research group, provided important feedback on a draft of chapter 3. I also extend my gratitude to the Department of French Studies at Smith College, where I now work and where colleagues have expressed warm support for this project. I look forward to many convivial conversations in the years ahead.

This book would not exist if not for the support of Julia Oestreich and Robin Runia at the University of Delaware Press; their commitment to women writers and early modern studies breathed fresh inspiration into the project. Thank you also to the many staff members in editing and marketing whose behind-the-scenes work made the book a reality. I am likewise very thankful to my anonymous reviewers at the University of Delaware Press, whose collegiality and discernment have greatly improved this study.

Women in French Studies has generously agreed to grant permission to reprint material from volume 26 (2018), as an article I published there provides inspiration for parts of chapter 6.

Finally, I want to thank my spouse, Carl Cornell, for his enthusiastic support of my research over many years, from first steps to a winding path and now to this particular labyrinth's end. I am forever grateful to walk life's labyrinth with such a generous and insightful companion.

Introduction

Marguerite de Navarre

The Visionary Queen

Centuries ago, in the 1500s, a woman sat pondering in the wee hours of the night. Alone in her library, she contemplated relics against a backdrop of blue wall hangings, whose rich color represented both the Virgin Mary and the kings of France, one of whom was now her own brother.[1] Her seven-volume Bible featured prominently on her bookshelves and offered her solace in the face of the many problems and responsibilities to which her piles of correspondence attested.[2] Her brother's reign and policies, her family members' fluctuating health, her desire for spiritual truth, her fight for institutional justice—such troubles filled her thoughts, even in the tranquil atmosphere of the library. In this place of preoccupation and contemplation, nature motifs such as fountains alluded to the garden on the castle grounds while also conveying a desire for calm and inspiration.[3] A love of creativity likewise led this woman to acquire literary works from Italian writers.[4] Yet alongside such pleasant items, an herbal encyclopedia detailing antidotes to poisons served as a constant reminder that the life of the mind and of the spirit could not be divorced from the dangers of politics.[5] The woman who sat pondering among these books, papers, and symbolic objects was Marguerite de Navarre (1492–1549).[6]

If, as biographer Pierre Jourda has asserted, the queen of Navarre felt fully herself at her château in Nérac,[7] where this library was located, it may have been because the three key components of her life and works—politics, religion, and creative endeavor—came together there. Marguerite lived in a moment of religious and institutional turmoil that also witnessed significant developments in the arts. Her brother would later become known as France's Renaissance king due to the flourishing of Italian-inspired literature, art, and architecture under his reign. Yet despite her brother's association with new trends and ideas, the figures of authority in Marguerite's early life, such as her mother, Louise de Savoie, were products of the Middle

Ages. As Marguerite entered adulthood in the early sixteenth century, she therefore encountered great paradigm shifts and societal upheavals. From Martin Luther's 95 *Theses* (1517) onward, the Reformation called into question aspects of the Catholic Church's teaching and practices, with particular attention paid to the roles of ritual and exegesis in Christian life, as well as criticisms over the power dynamics inherent to Church hierarchy and systems of absolution. New forms of faith emerged in the years that followed, some of which favored non-schismatic, internal Church reform and others of which advocated separation. Although Luther would eventually espouse a schismatic model of reform, along with his French-speaking counterpart John Calvin, Marguerite de Navarre held onto hope that the Church could be purified from within.

Indeed, the queen of Navarre was a key figure in a non-schismatic but reform-minded group of Catholics known as *les évangéliques*. This group sought, in response to Luther's critiques, to promote greater access to the scriptures in the vernacular, printing numerous religious texts and commentaries. They also valued faith and exegesis above ritual and viewed Christian education as a crucial form of charity.[8] To promote spiritual instruction, they placed sympathetic preachers in influential positions, thanks in large part to Marguerite's proximity to the king as well as to the Concordat of Bologna (1516), which had granted extended authority to François Ier (1494–1547) over the Church within France.[9] Moreover, the évangéliques believed in a hands-on approach to reform. Individual Catholic orders were reformed under their watch. Marguerite took a keen interest in this cause, initiating and overseeing the reform of several orders herself, even writing to the pope about expelling unscrupulous religious leaders and replacing them with more upright individuals.[10] As an évangélique, Marguerite adopted an active stance on faith that was intertwined with the project of reform, a project that sought to foster justice in institutions and, as a consequence, in society writ large. Ultimately, in Marguerite we find a biblically oriented and engaged Catholic who viewed reform as a stepping stone to a better and more just society, one in which those in positions of power would harness their influence to succor the poor, the vulnerable, and the innocent.

As this brief overview suggests, the queen of Navarre lived and wrote at the intersection of institutions. Her gender, among other aspects of her identity, influenced her perception of, and involvement in, both the Church and the aristocracy. As such, it is important to examine the confluence of several factors in Marguerite's life experience, including gender, class, and religion, that intersected within her identity as a devoutly Christian noblewoman.[11] On the one hand, as sister to the king, she had considerable class-based privilege and political influence. On the other hand, her status as a woman limited the extent to which she could exercise power overtly and independently, especially given Salic law, which forbade women from ruling in France. Still, the regencies of Marguerite's mother and of her forebear, Blanche de Castille, pushed the limits of women's political power in France and gave the sense that rules could be bent under the right forms of pressure.[12] Marguerite therefore proceeded strategically, building religious and political networks composed mostly of men in order to further her vision for institutional reform and greater justice in society. Whether she had her brother's ear or collaborated with the bishop of Meaux, Marguerite found creative ways to work around the limitations that her society imposed on women.

This was true not only of her real-world endeavors but also of her literary texts. When the second edition of her controversial poem *Le Miroir de l'âme pécheresse* was published in 1533, Marguerite narrowly avoided being labeled a heretic by the Sorbonne theology faculty, a fate that her brother forestalled.[13] Even in the realm of the written word, then, Marguerite sought out strategic workarounds, couching political and spiritual reflections in lighthearted formats that seemed less threatening to men in positions of power and that drew inspiration from respected male authors. Because Marguerite de Navarre adopted such strategies, her vision and her endeavor for reform have yet to be fully appreciated. Bringing the visionary thrust of the queen's life and works to the fore is this book's aim.

In uncovering Marguerite's status as a visionary, this study contributes to ongoing efforts to rehabilitate the queen of Navarre's political agency, all while shifting the focus of that discussion. Elizabeth Chesney Zegura's book on Marguerite de Navarre's gaze provides important reflections on the queen's political endeavors, highlighting how the motif of sight in the *Heptaméron* gestures toward Marguerite's awareness of societal injustice.[14] Zegura's treatment of gender, class, and politics builds on Barbara Stephenson's analysis of the queen's correspondence and leveraging of political influence.[15] Carla Freccero's many articles and book chapters on women and governance in Marguerite's writings likewise recover her understanding of the gendered power dynamics encoded within aristocratic hierarchies.[16]

All of these analyses contribute critical components to a politically oriented portrait of Marguerite. They foreground the queen's political activities, and as such, her religious faith comes to occupy the background. *The Visionary Queen* adopts a slightly different approach, bringing the queen of Navarre's political agenda into direct conversation with her faith and putting the two on equal footing. It does so out of the conviction that we can most fully comprehend the queen of Navarre's political role and her significance to early modern Europe and to our own times when we examine the intertwining of the two major institutions in which she participated. After all, in a society in which the Church confirmed the power of monarchs and in which kings were said to answer to God, there was no separation of church and state. Any action undertaken to alter the structure or practices of the Church would, by necessity, influence the government and vice versa.

In today's Western societies, which are far more secular than those in Marguerite's time, feminisms of various kinds have often distanced themselves from formal religion, especially surrounding such questions as birth control, abortion, and familial hierarchies.[17] Religion and politics may thus seem like a difficult pairing to some modern-day feminists.[18] Yet in the queen of Navarre's case, religious engagement opened up new avenues for personal fulfillment and the betterment of society. For this reason, in Marguerite's writings, Christian faith and the empowerment of women are often interrelated. As such, treating religion and politics together enables us to fully appreciate the scope of her contribution, which I argue is far more creative and encompassing, far more visionary than we have previously realized.

Because Marguerite's visionary qualities become clearest when her faith and her sociopolitical endeavors are examined in tandem,[19] *The Visionary Queen* brings together two critical currents on the queen of Navarre: the previously mentioned political vein developed by Zegura, Freccero, and Stephenson and the rebirth of studies on Marguerite's religion, featuring insights into her crucial role among the évangéliques in her life and fictional works as well as her outlook on material goods. In this second vein, one finds such scholars as Jonathan Reid, Nicolas Le Cadet, Carol Thysell, and Catharine Randall.[20] To bring these approaches together while also highlighting Marguerite's visionary life and writing, the present volume puts her into dialogue with her male contemporaries who wrote on religious and political topics to show how her own approach to reform differed from, or dovetailed with, theirs.

In the domain of Church reform, Marguerite's writings consider similar topics as those of Erasmus (1466–1536), Luther (1483–1546), Calvin (1509–1564), her mentor, Guillaume Briçonnet (1472–1534), and one of Briçonnet's key sources of inspiration, Augustine (354–430). On politics and its overlap with gender, Marguerite's *Heptaméron* revisits genres and themes found in the works of Giovanni Boccaccio (1313–1375) and Baldassare

Castiglione (1478–1529), all while calling out the abuses of the aristocracy, especially of aristocratic men. However, her works also treat topics related to the writings of Juan Luis Vives (1493–1540), who discussed women's education and state assistance for the poor. When one considers the ways in which the queen of Navarre's life and earlier writings and especially her most mature text, the *Heptaméron*, enter into a larger discussion in which well-known male figures participated, a revised image of Marguerite emerges, one in which she is not merely a supporter of male authority figures in the Church and monarchy but a visionary and a key player in reform efforts.

In order to perceive the visionary nature of Marguerite's work, it is helpful to consider what gender and genre theorist Christine Planté calls the conventional versus exceptional binary, which has at times shaped feminist approaches to women's literature and history of earlier eras. According to Planté, this binary is reductionist since all women live and write from within patriarchy. Some are more aware of patriarchal influences than others and are therefore more overtly resistant, but no individual exists entirely outside of the patriarchal order.[21] By observing how various attitudes toward women and their lives converge in the writings of female authors, we can gain a more holistic image of their experiences and of the numerous ideologies they may have encountered within the patriarchal structures of their times.

In the same vein, we can draw attention to the contributions of women from earlier eras by considering not only their writings but also their life stories and the sociocultural contexts in which they wrote. This information can enrich our appreciation for women's literary texts when incorporated into attentive examinations of both form and content.[22] Of course, we cannot access with certainty the precise intentions of any deceased author, nor does textual interpretation depend on the author's intentions even if they were knowable.[23] The reader's thought process should certainly enter into dialogue with the text's content and form.

However, readers may end up inadvertently downplaying the significance of women's accomplishments if they base the entirety of their analyses on their modern-day concepts and life experiences.[24] Zegura therefore argues for a careful balance between reader and text and between text and historical context, contending that Marguerite was "a woman who engaged in 'social criticism,' which loses a portion of its experiential edge, and is diminished, when studied outside the context of her (gendered) life and times."[25] Placing literary texts in the context of a female author's lived experience does not, in this approach, entail an extreme limiting of interpretation in which the modern day is absent from consideration. Neither does such an approach suggest that only one reading, based fully on biography, is possible or desirable when examining an author's work with sociohistorical frameworks in mind. Instead, the stance that Zegura elaborates and that *The Visionary Queen* also adopts is one in which knowledge of a woman writer's life and historical moment informs our understanding of her creative output and enables us to identify rich new connections that might not otherwise have been possible.

This conversation between the present and the past on the topic of gender and women's writings finds echoes in Freccero's concept of the early/modern, which fosters cross-temporal dialogues that, if approached in a spirit of balance, can act as fruitful alternatives to purely anachronistic reading. This approach encourages a back-and-forth across time, as symbolized by the slash between the terms *early* and *modern*.[26] Through an early/modern approach to reading texts from the past and considering the lives of their authors, we can contemplate our own realities while also respecting the temporal and cultural difference that others' experiences represent. Instead of imposing our own standards of what constitutes theory or feminism on earlier writings in any strict or narrow way, we can ask how an author's thought proved helpful toward women in their day and what their ideas can say to us as we work through complex twenty-first-century problems.

An early/modern approach works particularly well in the case of Marguerite de Navarre, as she lived through a tumultuous era, staring down large-scale societal problems and seeking to leverage her influence for reform and thus for justice. When we talk about these endeavors, however, we need to understand that the term *justice*, for example, did not carry all of the same connotations in Marguerite's time as would arise in later centuries. "Justice" did not necessarily imply the overthrow of institutions, the elimination of social class, or radical changes to the structure of society, given the ideologies of Marguerite's day, such as the divine right of kings and the Church's confirmation of monarchical power. *The Visionary Queen* does not, therefore, propose an extreme reading of Marguerite in which she would constitute an iconoclastic figure that we might now term a radical. Rather, her concern for justice occurs within the context of her society and historical moment, which was a moment marked by reform. Within that context, her engagement is innovative, visionary, and worthy of modern attention, including for its pro-woman orientation and the resonances between her life and writings and our own concerns today.

Indeed, Marguerite's writing can be read as an exploratory space in which to develop a vision for reforming institutions and fostering justice, two objectives she pursued in her real-world engagement. To highlight the visionary work in which the queen of Navarre's writings can be said to engage, *The Visionary Queen* examines the symbol of the labyrinth, a built structure and polysemous concept in Marguerite's society that represented spiritual ideals and earthly realities, process and product, difficulty and reward. The labyrinth's ability to subsume apparent opposites within a larger coherent structure will prove crucial to understanding the visionary nature of the queen of Navarre's political, religious, and literary contributions.

I. Key Terms: Justice, Reform, Visionary, Labyrinth

While the terms *justice*, *reform*, *visionary*, and *labyrinth* will receive additional attention in the chapters that follow, a brief overview will help orient readers and clarify differences between modern-day and early modern usage. Robert Estienne's 1549 French-Latin dictionary offers insights into how Marguerite and her contemporaries would have understood such terms. In his initial entry line for "justice," Estienne provides the Latin term *justitia*,[27] which translates in modern English to "justice" or "equity."[28] Subsequent entries provide greater clarity through common phrases that contain the word *justice*, including "punir, ou faire bonne justice des malfaicteurs" (to punish or bring evildoers to justice), "la justice criminelle" (criminal justice), "le gouvernement & superintendence de toute la justice" (the direction and superintendence of justice), and "reformer la justice" (reforming justice).[29] Such expressions lend a strong judicial flavor to the word *justice* in the French of Marguerite's era, while also implying government, oversight, authority, and the need for reform.

By contrast, some common meanings of "justice" in modern English, according to *Merriam-Webster*, include "the maintenance or administration of what is just especially by the impartial adjustment of conflicting claims or the assignment of merited rewards or punishments," "the quality of being just, impartial, or fair," and "conformity to truth, fact, or reason."[30] Although such definitions allude to both the judicial system and governance, more broadly, justice as a modern concept implies both moral ideals and administrative concerns. What we can take away from this cross-temporal comparison is a common understanding of justice as both practical and moral, with the pragmatic questions of governance appearing to weigh a bit more heavily in Marguerite's context. These two meanings would have been familiar to Marguerite not only due to her involvement in government but also through her study of scripture, which foregrounds justice both as a practical matter (notably, in Old Testament law) and as a moral one (e.g., in Jesus's treatment of the poor, sinners, and Gentiles, which models mercy as a component of a righteous attitude toward others).[31] Balancing the two ideals would have been a central concern for an individual such as Marguerite, who operated in governmental and religious circles simultaneously.

Yet another concept with implications for both governance and religion in the queen of Navarre's era, marked by the Reformation, is that of reform. Estienne's dictionary provides an entry for the verb form "reformer," as opposed to the noun. He offers the Latin definitions "reformare" (to reform) and "vertere in meliorem statum" (to change into a better state),[32] which suggest a process of reshaping and improvement. Other entries include the nouns *reformation, reformations,* and *reformateur,* which imply the unfolding process of the verb *reformer* as well as the agent that enacts this process. All of these entries cast reform as an active endeavor, one that requires power and agency.

In modern English, an active stance is also present, with *Merriam-Webster* foregrounding definitions of *reform* as a verb. A few examples include "to put or change into an improved form or condition," "to amend or improve by change of form or removal of faults or abuses," "to induce or cause to abandon evil ways," and "to become changed for the better." As a noun, *reform* is defined as "amendment of what is defective, vicious, corrupt, or depraved" and "removal or correction of errors or of an abuse or a wrong."[33] These modern-day definitions of *reform* underscore the themes of morality, correction, and justice. Reform, then, intersects with justice as part of a larger process of transformation in both our own times and the sixteenth century.

Another key term that enters into dialogue with justice and reform in this book is *visionary.* What does it mean to call someone a "visionary," and how might our comprehension of that term differ from that of earlier eras? For modern readers, a visionary is someone "having or marked by foresight and imagination."[34] However, there are numerous other possible definitions in the present day, such as "one whose ideas or projects are impractical" and "one who sees visions." A fourth definition brings the term into closer contact with the root word *vision*: "of, relating to, or characterized by visions or the power of vision." Still, this gesture is not as helpful as one might hope since the word *vision* also has multiple meanings, from "the act or power of seeing" to "something seen in a dream, trance, or ecstasy" to "a thought, concept, or object formed by the imagination" to "the act or power of imagination."[35] When we consider definitions of both "vision" and "visionary," we discover tensions between abstract and literal understandings. Which of these are in play in *The Visionary Queen* and why?

Interrogating how earlier eras challenge our assumptions regarding the faculty of sight, compared to the conjuring up of images in the mind, proves helpful to establishing relevant meanings. Looking back at Marguerite de Navarre's life and works,[36] we see that multiple notions of "vision"—some literal, some figurative—inform the relationship between human realities and spiritual ideals. The *Heptaméron*, for instance, is littered with sights of ugliness and injustice and features frequent allusions to seeing, as Zegura demonstrates.[37] At the same time, in many works by Marguerite, we see a more creative model of vision. In *Dialogue en forme de vision nocturne* (1533) and *La Navire* (published posthumously in 1896), Marguerite depicts mystical, dreamlike visions in which she mourns departed loved ones, such as her young niece Charlotte and her brother, François Ier. She uses these literary texts as a space in which to imagine what insights her niece and brother might offer from an eternal perspective, especially when it comes to living as a Christian in the world.

A spiritually oriented sense of vision likewise figures in *La Comédie de Mont-de-Marsan* (1548), which analyzes varying approaches to Christian faith in Marguerite's lifetime, from orthodox Catholicism with its many rituals, to a biblically centered religious practice, to a mystical experience of the divine, with this last tendency embodied by an enraptured shepherdess in the play. In *Mont-de-Marsan*, mystical vision combines with the notion of imagination that we more commonly associate with the term *visionary* today since the text shows the need for creative thinking and the envisioning of new possibilities for the Church's role in society.[38] Questions of leadership and of far-reaching, imaginative vision coexist with acknowledgments of sin and suffering in these and many of Marguerite's writings. Considering just a few examples, we can infer that for Marguerite de Navarre, the term *vision* incorporates elements of sight, imagination, and revelation. Around the concept of vision, the tensions between earthly and spiritual experiences coalesce. This confluence of ideas proves unsurprising, given that in Estienne's dictionary, all three meanings of vision are reported.[39]

We see, therefore, that the queen of Navarre's literary production and practical reform efforts affirm sight, revelation, and imagination as part of "vision," but it is important to note that Marguerite's life and works also diverge from some commonly accepted understandings of the term *visionary* today. Marguerite's reform work and her writings suggest, for example, that she was not interested in unachievable or utopian dreams. On the contrary, in her faith tradition, the fallen world would only be fully restored upon Christ's return. Her understanding of justice was anchored in the real world, with all its pain and complexity, and she took concrete steps to promote the future she desired. We can say with confidence, therefore, that she is not "one whose ideas or projects are impractical." Neither is there historical evidence that Marguerite ever had a mystical, supernatural vision, even if her writings suggest a desire to possess this faculty and to thereby achieve greater closeness to God and to departed loved ones.[40]

Did she possess foresight? The individuals we often consider to possess foresight today are those who reject the prevailing trends of their times and strike out in a totally different direction whose value can only be perceived at a later date. The queen of Navarre's brand of foresight does not resemble that model. She did not abandon the ideals or institutions of her era. However, one might argue that her support for non-schismatic church reform suggests her awareness of the violence that would ultimately follow a more divisive program of religious change. In the sense of political acumen, then, Marguerite does seem to have possessed foresight and to have played what we might now call the long game in her approach to institutional change.

What truly marks the queen of Navarre as a visionary, however, is the last definition that *Merriam-Webster* offers, as her real-world activities and her literary texts underscore "the power of vision" in its physical, spiritual, and imaginative senses. Vision, here, is not limited to the sense of sight, although that does factor into Marguerite's treatment of injustice. Instead, vision encompasses imagination and faith all at once since for the évangéliques, Christians should live by faith as opposed to reason or sight alone. This is because the eyes and mind, left to their own devices, can be deceived by tricks of the light, misinterpretations, or deliberate acts of dishonesty by others. For Marguerite and her fellow évangéliques, scripture was the lone source of truth, and believers were expected to interpret the world through its lens. Indeed, the bishop of Meaux, who for years served as the queen of Navarre's spiritual mentor, advocated this approach through an Augustinian model of exegesis in which all visible phenomena— whether written or concrete—ultimately revealed divine love and charity when viewed from the angle of faith.[41] Faith thus took precedence over sight in Marguerite's relationship to vision.[42] Although the act of seeing does help to reveal problems in society, it nevertheless constitutes the first step in a larger process of working toward new realities. It is the second part of the reform equation—namely, the development of a vision for justice and positive change—that *The Visionary Queen* addresses.

The complicated process of envisioning change points toward our last key term: *labyrinth*. As this study will show, the labyrinth serves as a meaningful symbol for the visionary orientation of Marguerite's life and work, highlighting how her political activities, faith, and creative endeavors combined in complex ways that sought to edify and inspire admiration.[43] Given the prevalence of both physical labyrinths and labyrinthine literature in Marguerite's time, I employ the idea of the labyrinth—both as a structure and as a collection of metaphorical meanings—to show how Marguerite's writing can be read as an exploratory space in which to develop a vision for reforming institutions and fostering justice. A detailed account of the labyrinth's meanings and history, both in the queen of Navarre's era and in the present day, will unfold over the course of this book, with the early modern history of this structure coming in chapter 1. But for now, an overview of connections between the labyrinth and other key terms such as justice, reform, and visionary will lay vital groundwork.

The labyrinth is a polyvalent symbol that encapsulates two phenomena that moments of change can provoke: chaos and the desire for order. The labyrinth has marked Western thought since Greco-Roman times, taking on particular significance during the Middle Ages and early modern era and enjoying resurgent interest in the twenty-first century, especially amid a search for spiritual meaning and connection in a divisive and turbulent world. As such, the labyrinth fosters an exchange between past and present, much as Freccero describes via her concept of the early/modern. Indeed, because Marguerite de Navarre's culture and historical moment integrated the labyrinth's symbolism into architecture, horticulture, religion, and literature and because the labyrinth continues to inspire creative works, feminist thought, and spiritual reflection today, it serves as a multifaceted symbol that points out resonances across time, all while respecting the historical specificity of each individual's time and place.

In the queen of Navarre's time, the labyrinth existed in both ecclesiastical and courtly settings and had manifold meanings. From the twelfth century onward, stone labyrinths could be found in the floors of numerous cathedrals, including in Chartres, as well as Reims, where Marguerite accompanied her brother at his coronation in 1515, and Amiens, where she spent time during François's military campaigns.[44] Such labyrinths, termed *unicursal*, featured a single pathway and were usually circular in shape.[45] Their structure might surprise modern-day readers, who might initially imagine a structure with conflicting paths, dead ends, and hedges. In reality, the multipath or multicursal labyrinth gained in popularity after Marguerite's lifetime. In her era, the unicursal labyrinth was the widespread form, and it recalled numerous Christian concepts, which were linked to notions of justice and transformation. These include the fallen world, God's sovereignty, Christ's harrowing of hell, the divine order of creation, and the believer's arduous pilgrimage through life.[46] Because unicursal labyrinths were commonly located in the naves of churches, the faithful had to pass by them to proceed into the sanctuary and toward the altar. Situated in the portion of the church that symbolized the world, the labyrinth served as a visual symbol that encouraged the faithful to divest themselves of worldly mentalities and enter into a space of spiritual contemplation.[47] It is important to note that we do not possess historical documentation from Marguerite's era of laypeople walking church labyrinths, as is the practice today.[48] We only have written evidence that the clergy used them for dance rituals at Easter.[49] However, we do know that for the queen of Navarre and her peers, church labyrinths held symbolic and visual value.

As labyrinths were appearing in church settings in twelfth-century Europe, they also began spreading to aristocratic estates. Like the labyrinths found in cathedral floors, garden labyrinths likely retained a unicursal form.[50] Early garden labyrinths appeared in Ardres in 1195 and at Hesdin in 1338, and they may have been "constructed of fencing or plant-supporting trelliswork."[51] The first reference to a French garden labyrinth composed of hedges dates from 1431, when a hedge was removed from the Hôtel des Tournelles in Paris, where François Ier would later provide a residence for Louise de Savoie.[52] Louise possessed a garden labyrinth of her own as early as 1513,[53] most likely at her château in Romorantin, where she had a vast park and where Leonardo da Vinci was working on plans to reenvision the site as well as the surrounding town.[54] Moreover, in 1520, François Ier had a garden labyrinth at the Château de Cognac, where he and Marguerite had lived during their childhood and received their education.[55] Given that Marguerite was extremely close to her brother and mother—so much so that her contemporaries referred to the three of them as "the trinity"—and given that Marguerite had spent time at both Cognac and Romorantin, she would certainly have seen such structures in person, just as she witnessed the pavement labyrinths at several cathedrals.[56]

The main differences between labyrinths found on aristocratic estates and those located in churches at this time were that garden labyrinths were constructed of low hedges and carried connotations of courtly love and intrigue in addition to the spiritual meanings associated with the ecclesiastical setting.[57] Moreover, in the French context, people often referred to garden labyrinths as "maisons de Dédalus" in the sixteenth century, thereby alluding to the architect Daedalus. In Greco-Roman mythology, Daedalus builds an intricate labyrinth to contain a horrible beast, the Minotaur, which King Minos's wife had illicitly conceived. One also sees the association between lust and garden labyrinths in paintings from Italy and the

Netherlands, which suggest romantic dalliances occurring in these structures. However, such works of art date from the 1540s, toward the end of Marguerite's life, and as such, it remains unclear whether she knew firsthand of their being used in that way.[58] As in the case of church labyrinths, we are left to wonder about the precise use of such structures while remaining assured of their complex symbolic and visual value for the queen of Navarre and her contemporaries.

When discussing the complexities of the labyrinth in Europe during the Middle Ages and the early modern era, it is important to underscore what Penelope Reed Doob calls the labyrinth's duality, meaning its polysemous character and ability to contain seemingly opposite connotations—such as sin and redemption, order and chaos, good and evil—within a larger, coherent whole.[59] Although a labyrinth's location in either a cathedral or an aristocratic garden inflected its connotations, the larger concept of the labyrinth transcended the specificities of location or of the unicursal or multicursal design and instead functioned according to a dual set of meanings, termed *in bono* and *in malo*. These designations explain how the individual twists and turns of the labyrinth's design create disorientation and strife, even as the structure, when taken as a whole, conveys order, with the many parts converging to form an intricate work of art. This tension between part and whole means that the labyrinth contains such a complex assortment of associations, some positive and some negative, that the viewer can interpret it as conveying either good or evil depending on whether the viewer perceives the labyrinth from within or from an external perspective that enables a complete picture to emerge.[60] The duality of labyrinths holds together both immanent experience and transcendent truth, both confusion and enlightenment, with the in malo interpretations representing process and the in bono readings pertaining to the end product of engaging the labyrinth—namely, an enlightened perspective marked by admiration at both intricacy and order.

The notion of duality frames the labyrinth not only in terms of its symbolic meanings but also in terms of its manifestations in medieval and early modern culture. Indeed, the labyrinth has existed over the centuries as both a built structure and a metaphorical concept in literature that has informed the thematic contents and formats of written texts.[61] Because the labyrinth has influenced both literature and the visual arts and could thus appear in either tangible or textual forms, Doob advocates for an analysis of the larger "idea of the labyrinth" and not merely of the physical labyrinths located in church naves or in the gardens of the wealthy.[62] *The Visionary Queen* likewise explores the reality of physical labyrinths and what they meant for those who encountered them, while also examining the ways in which the symbolic connotations of these structures and the experience of engaging with them informed literary output during the medieval and early modern eras, two periods that shaped the life and thought of Marguerite de Navarre.

II. Overview of Chapters

By foregrounding the difficult process of working through societal problems while simultaneously retaining faith, creative vision, and a belief in coherence in the midst of that process, Marguerite's works, and especially her *Heptaméron*, can be read as combining the labyrinth's in malo and in bono symbolism. That symbolism subtends the search for justice and reform that we see reflected in Marguerite's real-world activities and literary texts. Because the labyrinth, as a multivalent symbol, helps elucidate the visionary quality of the queen's life and works, it constitutes a common thread that runs throughout this book's chapters. It joins together the many twists and turns of Marguerite's life and writing, marked by intersecting facets of her identity, including gender, and by themes pertinent to both the early modern world and the present day, such as justice, creative vision, and reform.

Part I examines how the idea of the labyrinth inflected Marguerite's attempts to shape Church reform and aristocratic mores, as well as her understanding of hermeneutics, a point that merits special attention given the évangéliques' enthusiasm for scripture and their dissemination of sacred texts in the vernacular. Chapter 1 contributes to these goals by developing an overview of the labyrinth's medieval and early modern history, the numerous interpretations of the labyrinth over time, and the ways in which the "idea of the labyrinth" influenced literary production. Although no single chapter could hope to offer a complete history of labyrinths during the medieval and early modern eras, chapter 1 highlights the most crucial information on labyrinths for Marguerite and her contemporaries who wrote in both religious and literary contexts. The chapter also considers the ideological and literary history with which texts can be said to engage when they emulate aspects of the labyrinth's structure or symbolism. Chapter 1 thus equips the reader with the information to parse how *The Visionary Queen* engages with the labyrinth in all of the remaining chapters.

Chapter 2 employs the trope of the labyrinth, with its in bono and in malo connotations and its combination of worldly and spiritual influences, to recount Marguerite de Navarre's life story. Much as with chapter 1, no individual chapter could relate everything about the queen's biography. Instead, chapter 2 foregrounds Marguerite's political, religious, and literary endeavors and reveals how the labyrinth's symbolism frames all three. The chapter begins with an analysis of the most significant ways in which religion, politics, and artistic creation overlapped in the queen of Navarre's life, then brings these themes to the fore as part of the larger objective of valorizing the visionary and labyrinthine nature of the queen's life and works. Her brand of vision blends the pragmatism of politics with the hope in transformative potential that her faith promoted. This account prepares an analysis in the following chapter of how the trope of the labyrinth followed Marguerite the diplomat, non-schismatic reformer, and author from her real-world activities into the domain of textual interpretation, an important topic for the évangéliques.

Chapter 3 thus explores the queen's understanding of interpretation, an activity that entails both literal sight and creative vision and that thereby harkens back to the labyrinth's symbolism as process and product, part and whole. It begins by examining Marguerite's correspondence with her spiritual mentor, Guillaume Briçonnet, the bishop of Meaux. Through her correspondence with Briçonnet, the queen of Navarre learned an Augustinian approach to interpreting scripture and the larger text of creation. Briçonnet encouraged Marguerite to read words and real-world phenomena as signs that point beyond themselves to the love and charity of God. In so doing, he taught her to perceive the literal and the figurative simultaneously, with the figurative holding greater meaning. This treatment of Augustinian hermeneutics opens up to a larger discussion of exegesis and pilgrimage in Marguerite's time and how labyrinthine symbolism encompasses both topics for writers such as Calvin, Luther, and Erasmus. The symbolism of the labyrinth, with in malo and in bono aspects, orients an analysis of scriptural hermeneutics, a topic that, like the labyrinth, intersects with the theme of pilgrimage in ways both figurative and literal, as we see in the prologue to Marguerite's *Heptaméron*. The chapter concludes by differentiating notions of reading in Marguerite's time from reception theories today, thus preparing readers to embark on an analysis of the *Heptaméron* in part II that will require them to hold both past and present hermeneutical models in mind.

Part II builds on the considerations in part I to dissect the labyrinthine nature of the *Heptaméron* and demonstrate how the text reflects not only the sights of injustice and sin that characterize the fallen world but also an active process of working-through in which the queen's visionary brilliance shines. Both sights of sin and imaginative vision are present throughout the

Heptaméron's frame and its seventy-two short stories, narrated by aristocratic men and women who debate the moral of each tale, drawing on their understanding of scripture and their exposure to social ideologies. The collection, with its complex structure and ideological influences, functions as a kind of textual labyrinth with in malo and in bono facets. To appreciate these labyrinthine elements of the text, one must perceive both product and process. The chapters in part II therefore combine analyses of individual tales with an additional component: a bird's-eye view of the text. This aerial view considers statistical trends in the work—namely, the types of injustice, and responses to wrongdoing, seen across the corpus of tales and the frequency with which they appear—alongside the genre-based elements that make up the text's structure. Because Marguerite's magnum opus is a dense, rich text, we can best appreciate its complexities via an approach that blends an analysis of larger tendencies with commentary on individual tales and debates.

Chapter 4 begins that process by examining how the in malo symbolism of the labyrinth underlies sights of sin and injustice in the *Heptaméron*'s tales. Such in malo themes as earthly trials, the fallen world, and sin undergird the *Heptaméron*'s depiction of the two major institutions in the queen of Navarre's day: the Church and the aristocracy. Chapter 4 shows how the *Heptaméron*'s tales reorient the labyrinth's in malo components toward protofeminist ends. While one key element of the labyrinth in malo is lust—specifically, the lust that Pasiphae felt for a bull and that produced the Minotaur in the legend of Theseus—the *Heptaméron* ascribes that lust not to women but rather to men and to corrupt male-dominated institutions. Whereas in the tale of Theseus it was a woman whose lust engendered a monster that threatened society, in the queen of Navarre's text, it is the predation men engage in that threatens female sexuality and the social order along with it. After all, Marguerite's society was founded on marital alliances and the assurance of lineages, both of which depended on women's sexuality and inviolability. Chapter 4 shows how, in recurring scenes of sexual predation in the text, the tales hold up this reality as a mirror to male institutional representatives. In so doing, the *Heptaméron* draws on the *miroir* genre to persuade influential men that they should be as concerned about sexual wrongdoing as women are. Marguerite practiced the miroir genre in her controversial poem *Le Miroir de l'âme pécheresse*, so the chapter considers how the *Heptaméron* builds on that treatment, as well as on Augustine's *The City of God*, yet another famous miroir and one with particular importance for those who practiced Augustinian exegesis. The chapter employs concepts from reception theories, such as Umberto Eco's model reader, as well as a combination of commentaries on individual tales and statistical analyses of the larger corpus of stories to make its case.

Chapter 5 moves beyond the sights of injustice treated in chapter 4 to consider the numerous approaches to redressing corruption that can be found throughout the *nouvelles*. These approaches figure the process of envisioning paths toward reform. As readers wander down the paths that the various tales provide, they come to recognize that the characters in the stories demonstrate myriad responses to wrongdoing. Some responses align with Christian morality; others do not. Some prove effective; others have no impact on corruption. When it comes to the visionary work of reform, the *Heptaméron* thus resembles a multicursal labyrinth, inviting readers to tread and retread its conflicting paths in the search for the way out. Statistical analyses reveal just how varied and multiple the possible reactions to wrongdoing are in the text, thus providing a useful complement to examinations of individual tales and demonstrating how the individual stories, or parts, fit into the larger whole of the *Heptaméron* as intricate textual labyrinth. Because the *Heptaméron* prompts readers to engage in a difficult interpretative process, it can be said to foster a form of education that seeks to inspire a desire for certainty and that points toward the need for a higher perspective. This education unfolds through the *Heptaméron*'s engagement with, and divergence from, Erasmus's *The Education of a Christian Prince* (1516) and Juan Luis Vives's *On Assistance to the Poor* (1526). Unlike these texts, Marguerite's magnum opus posits that successful reform must entail women's inviolability and that reform efforts require female participation in order to succeed.

Chapter 6 investigates the role of women in reform efforts in greater detail by examining the *Heptaméron*'s frame and the character Oisille's function in it. The frame underscores the in bono interpretations of the labyrinth, such as divine sovereignty, order, product, and elaborate work of art. Indeed, the chapter contends that this frame operates as an alternative source of meaning toward which the model reader can look when the tales themselves refrain from identifying an obvious path toward reform. In this way, the frame participates in the model reader's education, redirecting attention away from the labyrinth's component parts and instead providing an aerial view that conveys how the parts interact to form an intricate whole. The frame can be read as proposing faith as the way out of the labyrinth: Christ-Theseus offers to lead the model reader on a singular path of truth and salvation, thereby revealing a unicursal walkway superimposed on what appeared at first to be a multicursal maze. Oisille emerges as the female figure whose instruction guides readers toward this path of faith, both in her morning Bible study sessions and in her oversight of the debates in which the storytellers participate upon hearing each tale. The *Heptaméron*'s foregrounding of a female educator represents a divergence from the frames, nouvelles, and debates found in Boccaccio's *Decameron* and Castiglione's *Book of the Courtier*. Indeed, chapter 6 contends that the *Heptaméron* can be read as revising important elements of frame and genre in Boccaccio's and Castiglione's texts, furthering protofeminist and reform-oriented objectives. The chapter utilizes theories of genre and reception to elaborate its analysis.

The concluding chapter takes up questions of reception in an early/modern vein, interrogating the possible responses that twenty-first-century readers might have to Marguerite's sixteenth-century text. As in the other chapters, the labyrinth figures the difficulties of interpretation and the rewards of endurance over time, including when it comes to working toward greater justice in society. The conclusion therefore reflects on the resurgent interest in labyrinths in our own times, notably in the work of reverend and therapist Lauren Artress, who has led an international ministry promoting the labyrinth as a way to revalorize what she considers feminine aspects of spiritual and psychological experience in the midst of our deeply troubled world. This discussion leads into an overview of social justice causes led by women in the twenty-first century and how interpretation and the labyrinth's symbolism factor into those movements as well. The conclusion explores how readers of the *Heptaméron* today, familiar with such causes, can find inspiration to fuel their own vision for justice and reform by opening up dialogues across time.

Part I

Labyrinthine Motifs in Marguerite's Era,
Endeavors, and Spiritual Outlook

1

The Labyrinth as Structure and Symbol

From Experience to Writing in the Medieval
and Early Modern Contexts

In Chartres, France lies one of the world's most well-known labyrinths. Embedded in the stone floors, the labyrinth at Chartres Cathedral invites walkers into a circular structure with a single, undulating path. Not long after entering, the walker must follow the path down a series of sharp turns, moving to the right or to the left only a handful of paces before abruptly reversing course. This process continues until the walker reaches the rosette in the center. Yet shortly thereafter, the walker must reembark on the same disorienting endeavor, following the twisting path toward an eventual egress.

Despite being based on one of the world's most iconic pathways, this description likely diverges from the image that many modern readers generate in their minds when they encounter the word *labyrinth*. After all, few today have contact with labyrinths as built structures, and those who do have such access might not be fully aware of how people have viewed or engaged with labyrinths over the centuries. To this point, the very practice of walking the labyrinth is a relatively modern phenomenon. In the Anglophone world, one might also conflate the terms *labyrinth* and *maze*. Indeed, *Merriam-Webster* defines the term *labyrinth* as "a place constructed of or full of intricate passageways and blind alleys," "a maze (as in a garden) formed by paths separated by high hedges," and "something extremely complex or tortuous in structure, arrangement, or character."[1] It is important to understand that a maze is a structure with multiple conflicting pathways and dead ends and therefore constitutes a multicursal labyrinth. As the labyrinth at Chartres attests, however, not all labyrinths are multicursal, and the multipath format, much like the practice of labyrinth walking, evolved over time. Moreover, the Chartres labyrinth, like most church labyrinths, is constructed of stone and incorporated into the floors. It is not, as some people might assume today, composed of hedges or located outdoors. All of this is to say that the labyrinth as a concept requires disambiguation, especially given the prominent role of the labyrinth in *The Visionary Queen*, which uses this symbol to demonstrate the visionary nature of Marguerite de Navarre's life and works.

This chapter therefore provides an overview of the labyrinth as structure and symbol in the medieval and early modern eras, the two periods of interest when it comes to the queen of Navarre. A single chapter could never hope to summarize all of the information on labyrinths during this time, but this one will nevertheless highlight key elements of how labyrinths were understood, utilized, and represented in literature in the era leading up to Marguerite's birth and also during her lifetime. The labyrinth boasts a long history with many connotations, blending Greco-Roman mythology, Christian theology, and aristocratic pastimes. It is precisely the labyrinth's polysemous character that renders it a useful symbol for complexity, arduous processes, and dazzling finished products. The sections that follow seek to elucidate the labyrinth's many facets, beginning with the forms and uses of labyrinths as built structures and then moving on to an examination of the labyrinth's impact on literary and religious writings.

I. Physical Labyrinths in Medieval and Early Modern Europe

In order to better understand the different types of labyrinths and the experiences they have promoted across time, we must first separate out our modern understandings of labyrinths from those that people from previous centuries would have held. On this point, it is important to understand that prior to the seventeenth century, there is very little historical documentation regarding how laypeople may have interacted with these large-scale symbols.[2] Medieval accounts of people standing or dancing on French church labyrinths do exist, but such texts foreground the clergy's use of the structures as they performed ball-tossing games and dances on the winding paths to celebrate Christ's victory over hell at Easter.[3] Reports indicate that laypeople on pilgrimage would sometimes sleep in the same area of the church in which labyrinths were located.[4]

However, many associations that we now have regarding labyrinths originate after Marguerite's lifetime, in the 1600s. From the seventeenth century onward, labyrinths became associated with walking within the French context because the laity were using them for that purpose.[5] In the late eighteenth century, the practice of labyrinth walking took on new dimensions, as texts from this time discuss laypeople treating church labyrinths as metaphorical pilgrimages, either advancing on their knees or pausing every so often on the path to kneel and pray. It is at this moment that the term *chemin de Jérusalem* (path to Jerusalem) appeared in conjunction with labyrinths in church settings, even if writers from the nineteenth century would go on to assert (without concrete evidence) that the concept of substitute pilgrimage, in which the faithful walked church labyrinths in lieu of the journey to Jerusalem, had existed since the Middle Ages.[6] Regardless of whether the historical record ever proves the idea that laypeople walked church labyrinths prior to the 1600s, we do know that in the medieval Christian tradition, labyrinths were multivalent visual symbols that reminded the faithful of core tenets of their beliefs and prompted them to shift their gaze from earthly burdens to spiritual contemplation.

Keeping this information in mind, we can turn to the two main types of labyrinth and the experiences they promote. In a unicursal labyrinth, which marked the queen of Navarre's lifetime, a person standing at the entrance will see a flattened and thus distorted series of curving lines leading in toward the center and then back out. If that same person were to either trace the labyrinth with the eye or enter it to walk its path, as is the modern-day practice, the experience would soon become dizzying and overwhelming. The eye cannot take in the many twists and turns at once, and the mind struggles to make sense of how the parts form a whole.[7]

For a walker, a physical sense of fatigue, instability, and unease may develop in an even more noteworthy way than for a viewer since the changing direction of the steps requires constant attention and creates a sense of disequilibrium caused by sharp turns to the right or the left.[8] Depending on the pace at which the walker proceeds, feelings of nausea could conceivably set in; these may also be possible for a viewer depending on the strength of his or her stomach. For walkers and viewers alike, the center of the unicursal walkway represents a moment of pause and clarity, but shortly thereafter, they must once again face the meandering path in order to proceed toward the structure's exit, as the example of the labyrinth at Chartres demonstrates. Although the experience of navigating the labyrinth by sight or by walking proves destabilizing, no choices must be made other than the choice to enter in the first place, as there is only one path, and no deviations are possible. This fact becomes evident when one views the entire structure from above. An aerial view takes the dizzying experience and transforms it into a moment of appreciation at the artistic complexity of the design, which predetermines the walker's course.[9]

While the unicursal labyrinth was the widespread form during Marguerite's day, with examples found in churches and in some cases in aristocratic gardens, after her death, during the late sixteenth century, a multicursal variant gained in popularity. This multipath pattern, which the Germans would term an *Irrgarten* or "error garden," was imported to France from Italian estates in which the nobility constructed high hedge mazes that concealed the walkers.[10] Error gardens, or puzzle mazes, offered amusement to the estate owner and perhaps to his or her guests, depending on their disposition. As the guests walked the Irrgarten's many conflicting and, in some cases, dead-end trails in search of the exit, the lord or lady of the estate could look on knowingly from an elevated vantage point, as he or she alone possessed knowledge of the correct path to take.[11] Walking the Irrgarten was an aristocratic pastime that, although lighthearted in some ways, also involved power dynamics, secret knowledge, and a disorienting experience in which darkness clouded sight.

This kind of labyrinth recalled elements of Greco-Roman mythology. In the legend of Theseus, King Minos's wife gives birth to a monster known as the Minotaur after her illicit encounter with a bull. The Minotaur demands a tribute of young people every year, killing and eating them. When the legend's hero, Theseus, arrives as tribute, the daughter of King Minos, Ariadne, falls in love with him. Ariadne offers Theseus a thread so that after he enters the labyrinth and slays the Minotaur, he can find his way back out of an otherwise inescapable structure.[12] The fact that this Cretan labyrinth was inextricable without outside help suggests that it contained multiple disorienting pathways, just as the Irrgarten did in early modern times.[13]

It is the Irrgarten that modern Anglophone readers most likely imagine when they encounter the word *labyrinth* and its adjectival forms, such as "labyrinthine" and "labyrinthian," even if many scholars writing in English employ the word *maze* for multicursal pathways.[14] It is important to note that in French, no lexical distinction exists between unicursal and multicursal pathways; the term *labyrinthe* applies to both. Given this book's focus on a French author, I will employ the term *labyrinth* throughout the analysis. The fact that this term can apply to both labyrinth formats is appropriate since, as we will see in later chapters, aspects of each model of labyrinth—unicursal and multicursal—are reflected in Marguerite's writings and life even if, as I will contend, the unicursal type proves more consequential for her.

Despite the parallels between the unicursal and multicursal formats, the latter presents numerous specificities. Although the walker or viewer must of course choose whether to enter the labyrinth, in a multicursal structure, there are numerous other choices that lie ahead. Multicursal labyrinths contain *bivia*, or diverging pathways in which the walker or viewer must choose which way to go. Some of these pathways lead to dead ends and will therefore cause those who engage the structure to retrace their steps.[15] One could become lost amid the many paths for long periods, tracing and retracing their steps to the point of exhaustion.[16] In the case of a multicursal hedge labyrinth, if the hedges are low enough, one could perhaps envision escaping the structure entirely by climbing over the side. Yet despite the existence of choices, which distinguishes the multicursal format from the unicursal one, many aspects of the labyrinth experience remain similar when engaging the two structures: disorientation, an inability to perceive the whole when within the structure itself, fatigue, the need for heightened attention and effort, and a potential for distressing physical and emotional symptoms. Here, too, however, a bird's-eye view reveals the intricate artwork that combines the various pathways into a coherent whole. Just as with the unicursal labyrinth, an aerial vantage point can replace distress with appreciation.[17] This overlap proves vital to understanding the labyrinth's symbolic meanings, a topic that the next section will examine.

II. The Labyrinth In Bono and In Malo

As Penelope Reed Doob shows, although the labyrinth as built structure existed in two different formats, the broader "idea of the labyrinth" remained singular in medieval and early modern Europe.[18] Because of the many similarities between the experiences that the two structures provide and also because of the predominance of the unicursal format for physical labyrinths in medieval and early modern Europe, the labyrinth was treated by medieval writers as a singular concept, with negative and positive connotations to which Doob refers with the Latin phrases *in malo* and *in bono*. The singular concept of the labyrinth stems from the fact that both labyrinth types emphasize the contrast of experience between process and product: "Both designs are thus *planned chaos*, examples of artistic elaboration that baffles or dazzles according to the beholder's perspective."[19] Although medieval authors were certainly aware of the Cretan labyrinth in the myth of Theseus and thus understood that a multicursal structure was possible, they defaulted to a unicursal understanding of the concept since that form figured in churches and on the estates of the wealthy during their historical moment.[20] In other words, the "idea of the labyrinth" during Marguerite de Navarre's time encapsulated both physical forms of labyrinth while ascribing one shared set of thematic meanings, some positive and some negative, some process-oriented and some product-oriented, to the labyrinth as a broader concept.

As the previous descriptions of encountering labyrinths might imply, the in bono interpretations of the labyrinth derive in part from the awe and appreciation one may feel when beholding an intricate work of art. In a church setting, the complex but unicursal pattern of the labyrinth reflects the intricacy of creation. The elaborate nature of creation glorifies the Creator by highlighting the intelligence and power of the divine. Another in bono interpretation of the labyrinth in an ecclesiastical context is Christ's harrowing of hell at Easter.[21] Just as in the Cretan myth, Theseus entered the seemingly inextricable labyrinth, slew the evil beast within, and found his way out in triumph, so Christ entered into hell and ransomed the just during the three days between his crucifixion and resurrection, according to medieval understandings of the Easter story.[22] The message is that Christ has made hell, or the labyrinth, extricable and that as such, the labyrinth now represents the one path toward salvation, with Christ as the guide to the Christian's eternal reward in heaven.[23] Ultimately, then, church labyrinths in bono represent reverence for God the Creator and gratitude for Christ the Redeemer.

However, since the concept of hell underlies in bono interpretations of the labyrinth, it should come as no surprise that in malo readings are also possible. Human life, marked by suffering and the potential for sin, may feel inextricable to some who observe or walk the labyrinth. Hell itself can be conceived of as an eternal prison, just as the Cretan labyrinth was built to contain the Minotaur. Those who entered the Cretan labyrinth as tribute would be killed and eaten, consumed by a bestial enemy. Similarly, the souls of the damned languish under the control of the devil for all of eternity. Among the damned, according to some medieval discourses, were heretics, who followed circular and untrue arguments in a downward spiral toward eternal torment.[24] Another in malo reading of the labyrinth foregrounds the burdens of pain and tribulation in a fallen world, reflected in the disorienting and potentially unpleasant experience of tracing or walking the labyrinth's erratic walkway. The Christian life becomes a life of endurance in the midst of trial; suffering awaits around every corner because the believer is living at odds with the fallen world.[25] Still, even in these in malo interpretations, hope remains present since however difficult the believer's experience may be, there is only one path of faith, with Christ being "the Way, the Truth, and the Life."[26] Success and eternal reward are assured; one need only persist on the singular path. The magnificent end result—wonder at how God creates order out of apparent chaos, good out of experiences that seem evil—reconciles the in malo and in bono readings, showcasing how labyrinths "create first confusion and then admiration."[27]

These in malo and in bono readings of the labyrinth converged in literary texts during the Middle Ages, impacting both content and form.[28] Doob analyzes numerous such texts, primarily from French and Italian sources, and thus from a combination of national contexts that provides important insights into the cultural background on labyrinths to which Marguerite de Navarre would have had access, given that she was born in the late 1400s and lived through a period of Italian-inspired innovation in French culture and intellectual life. As a highly educated woman who had received the same intellectual training as a king of France and who witnessed many shifting ideologies over the course of her lifetime, Marguerite would have been well positioned to grapple with the polysemous character of the labyrinth across genres and disciplines and in both overt formats and subtler allusions. As we will see, texts from the Middle Ages and from Marguerite's era sometimes mention labyrinths outright and sometimes imitate aspects of the labyrinth through their themes or structure.

III. Examples of the Idea of the Labyrinth in Literary and Religious Texts

Doob dissects the labyrinthine nature of texts by three Italian authors whose work Marguerite de Navarre would have known. First, although Boccaccio's *Decameron* is listed as a source of inspiration for the queen of Navarre's *Heptaméron*, despite the latter's divergences from many of the *Decameron*'s ideological and structural frameworks, it is his *Corbaccio* (ca. 1355–1365) that Doob considers, given its subtitle, *The Labyrinth of Love*.[29] The *Corbaccio*, whether one interprets it as a catalog of medieval misogyny or as a more personal commentary, presents love as an inextricable and hellish labyrinth from which men can only protect themselves by adopting an attitude of hatred toward women.[30] Here, the labyrinth functions as a prison, with the female object of desire acting as a devil figure who leads an unsuspecting man down the path of perdition.[31] One might even, as Doob suggests, read the image of the labyrinth as analogous to female genitals in Boccaccio's text, given that the rhetorician Boncompagno da Signa, whose metaphors feature in the *Corbaccio*, had termed the vagina a "labyrinth of shame."[32] Boccaccio thus adds a gendered dimension to in malo interpretations of the labyrinth, building on his interpretation of the myth of Theseus as a warning against lust, which he develops in his *Genealogy of the Gentile Gods*. Yet Doob also highlights Boccaccio's approval of labyrinthine complexity in poetic works, where the labyrinth would function in bono as authors showcased their artistic mastery to discerning readers, eager for a challenge.[33]

Like Boccaccio, Petrarch interweaves references to labyrinths in his writings. In sonnet 211 of his *Canzoniere*, the poetic voice calls love a labyrinth—just as the subtitle to Boccaccio's text does—and foregrounds "endless images of entrapment" as well as the idea that "love is blind, futile, filled with error, seemingly inextricable."[34] Furthermore, in his *Liber sine nomine*, Petrarch writes about the heresies and corruption that plagued the Avignon papacy, which he calls the "labyrinth of Avignon."[35] Doob therefore posits that for Petrarch, the labyrinth functions in malo, both in the context of love and in that of religious corruption.

Another example of a labyrinthine text is Dante's *Divine Comedy*. Even though the labyrinth is not explicit in the text, Doob nevertheless underscores its implicit labyrinthine themes, settings, and imagery. The text's opening lines describe how the protagonist wanders off the right way (or "diritta via") onto a dangerous path in the woods.[36] Later, he is struck with terror when, alongside his guide, Virgil, he encounters the Minotaur from the myth of Theseus:

> And at the chasm's jagged edge
> was sprawled the infamy of Crete,
> conceived in that false cow.[37]

In the journey that follows, Virgil leads the textual Dante from hell through purgatory and on to heaven as a means of righting his spiritual course. As he progresses through otherworldly spheres, the fates of individuals in hell and purgatory provide him with ample warnings about how to approach life in a wiser way than they did. This gesture of conversion is a key component of the text for Doob, who shows how erring down the wrong path and making the difficult journey of faith back to God reflects in malo components of the labyrinth, while the triumphant experience of heaven and divine glory harken back to in bono interpretations.[38]

Three other medieval texts that are the object of Doob's attention—two French, one English—merit further discussion here. *La Queste del Saint Graal* presents a labyrinthine narrative as the knights questing for the grail, whose stories unfold within a Christian moral framework, take different paths in pursuit of the same goal. Lancelot takes a wrong path, whereas Perceval walks a long and challenging road of spiritual purification, while Galahad embodies the unicursal way of Christ because he submits entirely to God's will and direction.[39] The reader joins the knights on their winding journeys and experiences secondhand a labyrinthine effect in the reading of the text, which Doob notes is "designed to afford transcendent enlightenment to readers who stay its course."[40] From her analysis of the knights' journeys, Doob develops multiple criteria for what constitutes a labyrinthine quest: "unusual circuitousness," "moral and physical *error*," "the labyrinth's characteristic duality," "contrasting points of view—process-induced ignorance versus transcendent understanding," "the physical unwinding of a path and intellectual unwinding of problematic meaning," and "the metaphorical meanings normally associated with the maze."[41] Even though Doob constructs these criteria in relation to quest narratives, they can provide useful barometers for evaluating the degree to which any text, regardless of genre, reflects the idea of the labyrinth.

Branching out from the French context into English-language literature, *The Assembly of Ladies*, penned anonymously in the mid-fifteenth century, depicts a group of aristocratic women walking the labyrinth as a pastime, but frustration and fatigue soon arise. The female protagonist receives guidance from the allegorical characters Perseverance and Diligence, who lead her on the way to Loyalty. By foregrounding in an overt manner the experience of the labyrinth, the text develops a commentary on the trials of earthly life and the need for endurance.[42] Finally, although Doob devotes less space to it than to other works, she states that she considers Chaucer's *Canterbury Tales* to be supremely labyrinthine in structure and content.[43] Chaucer's text, with its tales and conversations, recalls key features of both the *Decameron* and the *Heptaméron*, thus hinting at the labyrinthine nature of Marguerite's most famous work, which chapters 4–6 of the present study will analyze.

Given this book's focus on a sixteenth-century author whose education blended medieval and early modern influences, we might extend Doob's line of thinking to include texts by François Rabelais and John Calvin, two of the queen of Navarre's contemporaries. Like Marguerite, Rabelais and Calvin inherited a long medieval tradition of literature and theology that employed the labyrinth in malo or in bono. With respect to Rabelais, Marguerite knew him, protected and supported him, and was familiar with his work.[44] The adventures of Pantagruel and Gargantua offer a comedic reappraisal of the heroism and quest narratives that figure in much medieval literature. Through his characters' stories, Rabelais constructs well-known commentaries on humanism, education, and religion.

One portion of his multivolume work that proves particularly pertinent to the idea of the labyrinth is the *Tiers Livre* (1546), which suggests the dangers of obsessive and circular thinking. As Panurge consults many individuals in order to decide whether he should marry, the circuitousness of his mission, which cannot be completed without a final decision on his part, causes him great frustration. For example, Panurge's anxious discussion with a Pyrrhonian philosopher named Trouillogan, who refuses to answer plainly when Panurge asks whether he should marry, is elliptical in the extreme. When Panurge asks, "Me doibs-je marier?" ("Ought I to marry?"), he responds, "Il y a de l'apparence" ("There is some likelihood").[45] When Panurge continues by asking "Et si je ne me marie poinct?" ("And if I definitely don't get married?"), the philosopher replies, "Je n'y voy inconvénient aulcun" ("I can see no impropriety whatsoever in that").[46] The exchange continues in this manner over several pages, with Panurge returning from time to time to his initial question of whether he should marry. He receives no answer in the end and leaves the conversation highly vexed because he desires to have sure knowledge of the future that no human being can possess.

It is after this exchange that Pantagruel warns Panurge about the *lacs de perplexité* (snares of perplexity) into which he has descended through his tortured reasoning and circular discussions: "Vous, semblablement, efforçant issir hors les lacs de perplexité, plus que davant y demourez empestré" ("You, likewise, striving to free yourself from the snares of perplexity are more caught up in them than before").[47] The implication that Panurge is mired in a dangerous structure that threatens to pull him down to the point of inextricability recalls key elements of the labyrinth in malo. Panurge's own mind has the potential to become a hellish prison when he seeks knowledge he cannot obtain and when he relies on disorienting philosophical discourses. The meandering mind depicted in this passage recalls the warnings against heresy that figured in the list of the labyrinth's in malo connotations.

Since tensions between approved and innovative interpretations of scripture and religious practice undergirded the debates of the Reformation, it follows logically that Calvin would have much to say on the kinds of lacs de perplexité that Panurge encountered. We should note that, like Rabelais, Calvin was also in contact with Marguerite. However, the relationship between Calvin and Marguerite remained complicated. The queen of Navarre needed to pursue religious reform in a careful, non-schismatic manner because for centuries the Catholic Church had confirmed the power of monarchs. Breaking with the monarchy's top institutional ally would have likely seemed impossible from a political vantage point. Yet despite Marguerite's strong support for the activities of the évangéliques, Calvin accused her of hypocrisy, labeling her a "Nicodemite" and thereby drawing a comparison between her and the Pharisee who came to speak with

Jesus at night so as to avoid being criticized by his peers.[48] Even if Calvin and the queen of Navarre differed in their stances over whether reform should involve schism, both recognized the need for reform more generally and actively pursued that outcome.

Both also pondered the relationship between faith and intellectual endeavor, a subject that Calvin treated in connection with the idea of the labyrinth. In his *Institutes of the Christian Religion* (1536), Calvin writes at length about the limits of human cognition to argue that it is dangerous to seek definitive answers to religious questions that are too great for human beings to fully comprehend. In book 3, chapter 21, on the topic of predestination, Calvin explains, "The subject of predestination, which in itself is attended with considerable difficulty, is rendered very perplexed, and hence perilous by human curiosity, which cannot be restrained from wandering into forbidden paths."[49] One senses already the labyrinthine qualities of the human mind in Calvin's assertion, given the allusions to "forbidden paths" and moral error.

Calvin then makes an overt comparison between human curiosity and the labyrinth in malo, urging those who inquire about predestination to "remember that they are penetrating into the recesses of the divine wisdom, where he who rushes forward securely and confidently instead of satisfying his curiosity will enter an inextricable labyrinth."[50] In claiming, shortly after this assertion, that scripture is the only way out of this dangerous labyrinth, Calvin can be read as alluding to Christ as the Word made flesh, as well as to the concept of Christ-Theseus, who leads the way out of the labyrinth: "The moment we go beyond the bounds of the word we are out of the course, in darkness, and must every now and then stumble, go astray, and fall."[51] Using the idea of the labyrinth, Calvin argues for a humble reliance on scripture as the unicursal path to right understanding in matters of faith.[52] He therefore advocates a very different course than the one that Panurge took.

Whereas both Calvin and Rabelais warn of the dangers of labyrinthine curiosity as it functions in malo, texts with labyrinthine contents and structure can nevertheless function as praiseworthy works of art and as teaching tools that lead readers through a difficult process toward a larger perspective capable of appreciating the work's intricate design.[53] Texts whose aim was religious instruction needed to balance the desire to remain accessible to anyone and difficult enough to keep the attention of the learned, all while prompting readers toward a process of Christian conversion, which entails a literal changing of course. While such concerns were central to medieval preaching, one might also see traces of the balance between learning and intricacy in the dialogue genre in Marguerite's time.[54] Although a full accounting of Renaissance dialogues falls outside the scope of the present study, later chapters will examine the role of dialogue, with its accompanying ambiguities and instructional impulses, in the *Heptaméron*.

IV. Conclusion

As this overview has shown, the labyrinth functioned as a singular concept in religious and literary writings in medieval and early modern Europe. However, in this context, "singular" does not imply simplicity. On the contrary, the "idea of the labyrinth" combined numerous connotations, some positive and some negative. It likewise encapsulated multiple ideological traditions, including Greco-Roman mythology and Christian theology. The existence of unicursal labyrinths on aristocratic estates during Marguerite's time, including on properties owned by her mother and brother (as the introduction to this book explained) adds a further layer of meaning to the labyrinth as structure and symbol. Although these aristocratic labyrinths were most likely unicursal in the French context during Marguerite's lifetime and thus adopted the same format as the pavement labyrinths found in churches, artwork from the mid-sixteenth century suggests that romantic encounters may have occurred in these garden structures. Through the blending of worldly and spiritual themes, the unicursal labyrinth, whether in gardens or, more traditionally, in churches, recalls the complex interplay of sin and redemption inherent to Christian thought.

As a profoundly Christian writer who rubbed shoulders with the wealthy and powerful, Marguerite de Navarre experienced firsthand the tensions between earthly realities and spiritual ideals. Moreover, as a woman, Marguerite was poised to perceive abuses and contradictions in the power structures of her day, which lent her influence all while placing restrictions on her. As the next chapter will show, the queen of Navarre's life story blends together her experiences in the domains of politics, religion, and artistic endeavor, with the labyrinth's in bono and in malo symbolism underlying her analysis of and response to society's ills.

2

From the Labyrinth, a Vision

Competing Influences on Marguerite's Religious, Political, and Creative Endeavors

In a high tower, in the kingdom of France, a baby girl was born. It was 1492, a year made famous by Columbus's encounter with the so-called New World, but for the baby in the tower, a labyrinthine journey was just beginning to unfold. No prophetic declarations preceded the birth of Marguerite d'Angoulême, as they later would for her brother, François, whom Saint Francis of Paola predicted would one day sit upon the throne of France.[1] Indeed, Pierre Jourda underscores that Marguerite's mother felt far less joy at the birth of her daughter than she would later express in 1494 at the birth of her son, on whom her hopes for political influence rested.[2] No fanfare greeted Marguerite upon her arrival; her parents, Louise de Savoie and Charles d'Orléans, count of Angoulême, were modestly endowed members of the French aristocracy.[3] Moreover, Marguerite, as a girl in a country where women could not inherit the throne, likely seemed less well positioned to improve the family's fortunes than her brother later would. Yet despite the subdued atmosphere that marked Marguerite's first days, she would go on to become "the pearl of princesses," queen of Navarre, and an important figure in the early years of the Reformation. Her impact would encompass religion, politics, and literature, leaving a legacy that extends into the twenty-first century and transcends national borders. In Marguerite de Navarre's life, we see the story not of a fairy-tale princess but of a visionary queen.

The remainder of this chapter will tell that story, emphasizing the visionary and labyrinthine aspects of Marguerite's endeavors in the domains of politics, religion, and writing. A brief window into each of these aspects of Marguerite's life will prepare the chronological narrative that follows. Beginning, then, with Marguerite's political roles, we should note that she acquired the title of "queen" in 1527 through her second marriage to Henri d'Albret, king of the territory of Navarre on the Spanish border. As queen of Navarre, Marguerite had obligations to a second family and royal house, even if she loved her brother, François Ier, and rejoiced in his authority as king of France. After all, Marguerite's status as sister to the French king afforded her notable influence. She served, for example, on the king's secret council beginning in 1517, when her brother made her a ducal peer by giving her the usufruct of the duchy of Berry.[4] Diplomats quickly recognized her as a key player at court, one whose approval they should seek to obtain.[5]

Consequently, Marguerite fostered numerous clientage relationships, acting as a patron or a broker to provide favors or to seek them out on behalf of a client.[6] Her dealings involved such a noteworthy figure as King Henry VIII of England. Indeed, in response to hostilities among Henry VIII, Charles V, and François Ier, Marguerite pursued a peace agreement with the English, quite possibly without her brother's knowledge.[7] The queen of Navarre also used her familiarity with southwestern France to assist her brother in his military endeavors. In the 1540s, for instance, during a period of tensions with Spain, Marguerite surveilled Guyenne, building up fortifications and in at least one case, taking a prisoner.[8] The relationship between Marguerite's regional influence and her authority in the kingdom of France often proved harmonious.

At times, though, conflict emerged between her brother's objectives and her obligations to her husband's family. One important example was when François Ier arranged a marriage to which Marguerite's daughter, Jeanne, would not consent.[9] Local politics could never stand apart from the politics of the French kingdom. Still, at her own estates, the queen of Navarre enjoyed a greater measure of autonomy as well as an elevated political title. Despite her standing, she took a personable approach to her role. Jourda recounts, for instance, that in Nérac and Pau, she mingled freely with the inhabitants of the region, walking the streets en route to an artisan's shop or a church, or stopping by a farm for a bowl of milk.[10] One wonders whether any of these encounters shaped her representations of different social classes in the *Heptaméron*. What is certain is that in an aristocratic society that viewed women as matrimonial pawns, the queen of Navarre understood that social relationships and politics went hand in hand.

Political influence also converged with religious reform efforts in the queen of Navarre's life. In the early days of her brother's reign, she supported internal Church reform efforts in numerous ways. She founded and reformed convents, replacing unscrupulous or ineffective religious leaders with more trustworthy individuals and providing funds to repair buildings when needed.[11] She wrote to the pope to propose leadership changes; in 1517, for instance, she directed the reform of the convent at Almenesches, going so far as to build herself a small home on the premises to supervise progress.[12] Through her correspondence with Guillaume Briçonnet, the bishop of Meaux, she continued reforming individual orders while also developing a deep commitment to the larger concept of non-schismatic Church reform.

As Jonathan Reid has shown, Marguerite served as a central node in a network of internal Church reformers that scholars have called les évangéliques.[13] She used her standing at court to promote preachers sympathetic to the évangéliques' cause and facilitated the publication of their religious commentaries and translations of sacred texts into the vernacular.[14] Thanks to the Concordat of Bologna (1516), which granted the French king the authority to nominate religious officials, the queen of Navarre succeeded for some time in leveraging her relationship with her brother to ensure prominent posts for preachers who supported her religious agenda. When individuals she supported were targeted for their reform-oriented activities by the conservative theology faculty at the Sorbonne, she intervened to shield them. At Nérac, for instance, she harbored such figures as Clément Marot and Jacques Lefèvre d'Étaples.[15] She also protected individuals who became Protestant leaders such as John Calvin.[16] Whether overtly or through behind-the-scenes strategies, she protected such figures as Pierre Caroli and Gérard Roussel, defending the former before the Faculty of Theology and naming the latter bishop in a small town located within her territories.[17] We know additionally that her literary works also espoused religious reform, even as they reflected her political activities.[18]

Amid her many religious and political occupations, the queen of Navarre found time for reading and creative writing.[19] These efforts were supported by her library at Nérac, which held works from numerous literary traditions and authors, including texts from Arthurian legend, the writings of Boccaccio, and texts from the *querelle des femmes*, including *Le Roman de la rose* and selected works by Christine de Pisan.[20] She also spent time in Lyon, a hub of literary endeavor that attracted aspiring authors. Marguerite would go on to protect several of these writers, including Clément Marot, François Rabelais, Bonaventure des Périers, and Étienne Dolet.[21] Their works would inspire her own thinking on literature, Neoplatonist philosophy, and Christian faith.[22] For the queen of Navarre, creative, religious, and political pursuits proved inseparable.

As the introduction to the present study contends, such intersecting activities also revealed abusive power dynamics and the need to address institutional wrongs, two themes that appear in Marguerite de Navarre's writings as well as in her real-world endeavors. In her literary works, religious advocacy, and political interventions, Marguerite balanced a realistic view of human nature and the world with a belief that God's goodness and transformative power made societal improvements possible. Because she believed in the concept of the fallen world, Marguerite did not rush toward simplistic solutions to the abuses she observed. Her attitude toward corruption in the Church and aristocracy was neither defeatist nor naive. Instead, Marguerite chose a middle way, one that was difficult, realistic, and fruitful all at once: working through. In both her writings, which can be read as creative spaces in which to envision solutions to society's ills, and in her overt efforts to foster reform in the Church and aristocracy, a concern for justice emerges as an important motif in Marguerite's story.[23]

The ensuing pages offer an overview of Marguerite's life that draws on justice, reform, and the symbolism of the labyrinth. As a polyvalent symbol, the labyrinth encompasses the fallen world, as represented for instance by the courtly politics that Marguerite experienced, the guiding principle of faith that sustained the queen's religious reform efforts, and the notion of artistic complexity as found in her creative works. Although no single chapter could hope to encapsulate all of the queen's endeavors, this one will nevertheless highlight the labyrinthine and visionary components of her life and contributions. In so doing, the present chapter sets the scene for the explorations of Marguerite's political, religious, and creative influence that will unfold in the remainder of this study. Since politics, religion, and creativity overlapped in the queen of Navarre's life, the following analysis will proceed chronologically while blending all three influences against the backdrop of her tumultuous times.

I. Formative Years: From Birth to Her Brother's Coronation, 1492–1515

Interactions among religion, politics, and literature guided Marguerite's earliest education, which bore the mark of Louise's oversight. Louise's curriculum blended spiritual devotion with shrewd politicking and a love of reading. Her clear preference for François notwithstanding, she saw to it that Marguerite received the same education as a future king. The children's curriculum included literature, as reflected in Louise's personal motto "libris et liberis."[24] The family's significant library holdings included works by Dante and Aristotle, *Les Cent nouvelles nouvelles*, religious texts, writings on la querelle des femmes, and practical volumes on aristocratic pastimes such as falconry.[25] Texts by myriad authors and on widely varying topics would go on to influence Marguerite's thinking and writing later in life.

Louise likewise schooled Marguerite in a religious devotion that was more traditionally Catholic than the faith her daughter would later espouse. The religious lessons that Marguerite learned were perhaps more overt and concrete than the political ones. For instance, Louise purchased relics for her daughter and looked on as she diligently copied books of hours.[26] François Demoulin and François de Rochefort were responsible for teaching the children Latin and biblical history.[27] Moreover, Louise de Savoie's understanding of her family's place in history hinged on mystical visions and saints, as the aforementioned exchange with Saint Francis of Paola suggests. The major influences on Marguerite de Navarre's faith in her formative years, then, were rooted in traditional Catholic practices that had existed throughout the Middle Ages.

Her more informal education in politics also built on medieval precedents. Louise de Savoie drew on her own education, which she had received from Anne de Beaujeu, to teach Marguerite that women's political power depended in large part on their ability to appear deferential as they pursued their objectives.[28] Here, we see that tensions between appearance and reality, ideals and exigencies, made the court a place of intrigue and competing passions—themes that recall the labyrinth in malo, with its emphases on confusion, the fallen world, and difficult process. One might also envision here the diverging pathways of the multicursal labyrinth, which demanded choice and strategy of the walker or onlooker and which made no promise of success or extricability. Success or failure depended on individual will and skill of execution. These associations with the multicursal labyrinth and in malo readings reflect the fact that at court, honor and duplicity were both in play, as Castiglione, Machiavelli, and Marguerite's own *Heptaméron* illustrate.[29] When it came to female leadership, Louise, who would later become regent of France when her son went off to war, no doubt looked to the examples of previous female regents, most notably Anne de Beaujeu.[30] One might also recall the example of Blanche de Castille, whose strong maternal presence had bolstered her authority as regent some time prior, in the thirteenth century. Marguerite grew up observing the strategic behavior of shrewd women, and her life and writings suggest that she internalized what she witnessed and used it to navigate the labyrinthine environment of the court.

One aspect of courtly society, arranged marriage, caused adulthood to come relatively early for Marguerite by modern standards. In 1509, at the age of seventeen, she married Charles d'Alençon, a man whose military bent and lack of interest in intellectual matters made him a poor match for the new duchess. However, through this marriage, Marguerite developed a close relationship with her mother-in-law, Marguerite de Lorraine, a pious woman whose faith helped lay the groundwork for her daughter-in-law's endeavors on behalf of religious reform.[31] Isolated from her mother and brother, did Marguerite seek spiritual solace in the company of her mother-in-law? Might we glimpse here some indications that for the duchess, faith would provide a means of responding to the disingenuous atmosphere of the court in which she had been raised?

Six years later, in 1515, such questions would have become inescapable for Marguerite, as the prediction on which her family's fortunes depended came true. Although François had not originally been in direct line for the crown, when Louis XII failed to produce a male heir by any of his three successive wives—Jeanne de France, Anne de Bretagne, and Mary Tudor, respectively—François was crowned king.[32] This turn of events meant that his mother and sister were thrust irrevocably into the most politically charged environment in France. At her brother's coronation, Marguerite would have espied the famous unicursal labyrinth at Reims Cathedral. Amid the busyness of this important day, did she find time to contemplate the winding path and all it represented? Before her and her family lay sin, a fallen world, and courtly machinations, yet as the Church's confirmation of François as a "most Christian king" and the in bono symbolism of the cathedral's labyrinth suggested, in faith they might yet find salvation and a clearer vision for justice even amid the threats that society's wealthiest and most influential people could pose to them.

II. Burgeoning Political and Religious Roles, 1515–1524

Still, Marguerite and her family were members of this class themselves, and the Church was in many ways as political an institution as the monarchy. As such, the royal family was in no way immune to divided priorities or the privileging of political aims over eternal ones, even if Marguerite's heart began to seek after the latter. Before long, François had named his mother regent as he set out on his first great military conquest to recapture the duchy of Milan. Although Marguerite had responsibilities toward her husband and his family, after her brother's ascension to the throne, her primary obligation was toward the sovereign. She therefore traveled to be geographically closer to François during his military campaign. As François and his forces prepared to invade Italy, Marguerite accompanied her mother to Notre-Dame-des-Fontaines to pray.[33] At the battle of Marignano, in 1515, the French forces reconquered the city. François, along with his mother and sister, were overjoyed at this victory, which set an optimistic tone for the new king's reign. In thanksgiving, Louise de Savoie, François's wife, Queen Claude, and Marguerite undertook a pilgrimage to Saint-Maximin-la-Sainte-Baume.[34]

In the time of peace that followed, Marguerite presided over court functions, filling in for Queen Claude, who was both shy and encumbered by frequent pregnancies. From 1515 to 1518, it became clear to onlookers that Marguerite's power was among the most significant in the kingdom, as she held the role of François's trusted adviser and functioned as "queen in all but name."[35] Diplomats and Church officials demonstrated in their correspondence that they viewed the duchess of Alençon as a pivotal figure at court.[36] Moreover, during this time Marguerite began taking an active interest in Church reform, correcting immorality and derelict conditions at numerous religious establishments, including the convents at Hyères and Almenesches.[37] Even before Martin Luther's 95 *Theses* (1517) had kindled a full-fledged reform movement in France, the duchess of Alençon used her political authority as the king's sister to redress ecclesiastical abuses. The imbrication of religious and political influence hints at Marguerite's passion for justice and search for a vision that would enable the reform of institutions.

Her proximity to and implication in both government and the Church would only become more pointed in 1519 when François was passed over for the title of Holy Roman emperor, an honor for which European monarchs competed, since this individual was viewed as the secular counterpart to the pope. Seven electors who held prominent positions in the Church voted to determine to whom the title would go, but kings knew that their support could be bought with bribes. Although François had sent considerable sums of money to the electors and had also received word from the pope that he would support the French king's candidacy, in the end, his rival, Charles V, received the sought-after honor.[38] From that point onward, François and his nemesis harassed each other with warfare and subterfuge. Against such a backdrop, Marguerite faced the challenge of balancing her family's political interests with her spiritual inclinations and her wish to see the royal family furthering the cause of righteousness.

The duchess's desire to serve as an agent of reform features in, and derives in part from, her correspondence with Guillaume Briçonnet, the bishop of Meaux and an advocate of non-schismatic Church reform in France. From 1521 until 1524, Marguerite maintained a correspondence with him that combined her search for spiritual guidance with the bishop's hope of obtaining a powerful ally at court. Early in her exchange with Briçonnet, Marguerite asks for his prayers and spiritual insights, perhaps seeking in him some path toward peace and integrity, two aims that courtly politics tended to stymie. Surrounded by politicking, Marguerite desired for spirituality to play a greater role in her life. Like an onlooker contemplating a unicursal church labyrinth, Marguerite sought in her spiritual exploration to discover a way of responding to the fallen world in which she lived. In bono connotations of the idea of the labyrinth entered into dialogue with that goal during Marguerite's time, providing the assurance of eternal reward to the faithful who persevered through the challenges of earthly life. Moreover, thanks to Briçonnet's letters, the queen of Navarre would find in Christ a savior and hero guide who, like Theseus, triumphed over evil and knew the one path of salvation, the way out of the worldly labyrinth. In the development of her faith, Marguerite would nurture a passion and a vision for improving institutions.

However, her exchange with Briçonnet would not be entirely of her own definition, as she and the bishop initially had different understandings of their relationship. As Barbara Stephenson shows, Marguerite employed formulas in her first letters that indicated that she wanted Briçonnet to serve as her spiritual adviser. When she called herself Briçonnet's "daughter," however, he corrected her, saying that she ought to call herself his "mother" instead.[39] This reversal of terminology suggests that Briçonnet wanted to foster a different kind of interaction with Marguerite, one based on the model of a patron and a client.[40] Although he was more than willing to expound on scripture and teach Marguerite spiritual lessons through his use of metaphor and Augustinian exegesis, what Briçonnet truly hoped to obtain from the duchess was her support for nonschismatic Church reform. Like so many others in the religious and political arenas, he recognized that Marguerite's support could very well win the king and thus the full power of the monarchy to his cause.

The duchess of Alençon did, in turn, advocate successfully for Church reform at court, striving to make spirituality a more central concern for her peers. Although Briçonnet had begun to implement a program of nonschismatic reform in 1518, Marguerite's influence proved crucial to ensuring the growth of the movement. Beginning in 1521, Marguerite actively sought the group's success, promoting their publications, including a French translation of the Bible as well as a preaching handbook in the vernacular.[41] Moreover, Marguerite invited Michel d'Arande, an influential member of the group, to preach at court in 1523 and 1524 during Advent and Lent. Her support also made possible Roussel's lessons for the laity, on the Psalms and on Paul's letter to the Romans.[42] When the group's preachers and writers inevitably attracted the ire of conservative officials at the Sorbonne, Marguerite persuaded her brother to extend his protection to them, as in the case of Louis de Berquin, who had been found in possession of Luther's works, which he had been working to translate.[43] In the face of such impactful efforts, one might expect that Briçonnet would have thanked and praised his patron.

On the contrary, he criticized her and said she should be doing even more. He hoped to see the court ablaze with enthusiasm for Church purity.[44] For him, the monarchy's support would guarantee the success of his efforts to reform the Church from within. For Marguerite, however, reforming the Church entailed the formidable task of converting the aristocracy away from its worldly concerns and toward a more sincere faith. Given Marguerite's love for her mother and brother, who remained invested primarily in bids for power and territory, one senses in Marguerite's collaboration with Briçonnet a desire to see François become, in a more genuine way, a "most Christian king," one whose reign fostered justice in institutions and in society.[45] Until the king and his mother were as personally committed to the cause of the évangéliques as was Marguerite, royal support for the movement was not yet assured.

Although superficially supportive of Briçonnet and his entourage, François remained preoccupied with political objectives, and this division caused Marguerite to walk a delicate line. When François returned to Italy, determined to claim territories he felt were rightfully his, Louise de Savoie became regent for the second time and from 1525 to 1526 used her newfound authority to oppose her daughter's support for more progressive religious practices. The conservative religious authorities had persuaded her to take repressive action, claiming that the French king's military setbacks were a sign of God's anger toward those who supported Church reform.[46] Louise's pushback, coupled with the king's absence, impeded Marguerite from making the quick strides toward non-schismatic reform that Briçonnet would have liked to see. Their correspondence came to a halt in 1524, slightly before the persecution of the évangéliques intensified.

Whatever the precise reason for the end to their correspondence, in 1525, Marguerite would yet again find herself torn between her spiritual goals and her political duties, her in bono aims and in malo realities, when François's defeat at the battle of Pavia led to his captivity. Along with this crushing news came yet another misfortune, as Marguerite's husband, Charles d'Alençon, died shortly after returning home from the battle. Although the historical record does not offer evidence of great passion between the spouses, Marguerite nevertheless grieved her husband's passing even as she worried ceaselessly about François, the captive king.[47] To face such troubled times, she would have to rely on her own internalized faith, her political training, and her deep loyalty toward her brother, as she was about to embark on the most important diplomatic mission of her life: negotiating the terms of his release.

III. Diplomacy and Religious Conflict, 1525–1539

Setting out for Spain over choppy seas and then riding ten to twelve leagues per day on horseback, Marguerite traveled to Madrid, a harrowing journey that foreshadowed the events that were to come.[48] Upon her arrival, Charles V greeted her and accompanied her to the cell where François was being held. The latter was gravely ill, plagued by an abscess in his nose and an unrelenting high fever that would eventually cause him to lose consciousness.[49] Negotiations no longer occupied Marguerite's mind; her sole concern became nursing her brother back to health. At first it appeared that her efforts would fail, but after having an altar brought to the cell and sharing communion with her brother, the abscess broke, as did his fever, and he began to recover.[50] One wonders if Marguerite saw in this recovery a miraculous sign that François might yet turn his attention more fully to God. For the moment, with her brother's life no longer in immediate danger, she turned to the task at hand.

Negotiations began cordially, and the duchess had high hopes that she would be able to reach an agreement with the emperor, perhaps with some help from his sister, Eleanor. Marguerite saw her as a potential bride for her brother, who had lost his wife, Claude, as well as his daughter, Charlotte, in 1524. Although Eleanor remained obedient to Charles V, she betrayed romantic interest in François, a fact that made Marguerite optimistic. Unfortunately, this seemingly auspicious beginning turned into a protracted series of discussions that cast courtly politics as a labyrinthine prison with such in malo associations as sin, confusion, diverging paths, and intrigue. The duchess laid out possible terms for François's release, including France's acceptance of the emperor's dominion over Milan and multiple other territories, as well as Eleanor's marriage to François, the restoration of the properties and rights of the duke of Bourbon, who had defected to Charles V from the French side, and 350,000 crowns in ransom money.[51] Her opponents refused her terms, insisting that France cede Burgundy to the emperor, an outcome the French Parliament was unlikely to approve, given the considerable size of the region.[52] Frustrated, Marguerite hoped to appeal to Eleanor for help, but Charles sent the latter away in order to impede that outcome.

All the while, Marguerite wrote to the king to keep him informed of the proceedings. She told him that by announcing her intent to leave and end negotiations, she would force her adversaries to enter into a more serious dialogue with her.[53] In the end, however, she was unable to make them budge. She had put her considerable political experience to work and had persevered valiantly in support of her brother, but she could not force Charles's hand; she thus departed for France.[54] In 1526, François and Charles finally signed an agreement: the Treaty of Madrid. The agreement stipulated that France would cede Burgundy (an obligation on which François would later renege) and that the king's two sons would remain in Spain as hostages. The treaty secured the French king's release and return to court, but his sons would suffer several years of captivity.[55] It was not until 1529, with the Peace of the Ladies, that the dauphins would return to France, along with Eleanor, whom François would finally wed.[56]

In the intervening years, from 1526 to 1530, Marguerite found respite from international politics and heartily approved of her brother's decision to reverse the persecutions that Louise de Savoie had authorized against the évangéliques in his absence. During this period, Marguerite enjoyed heightened favor from her brother, who would never forget the way she nursed him back to health from his near-fatal illness. Her bond with François enhanced her ability to support the évangéliques, whom the Faculty of Theology had targeted by prohibiting the publication and possession of religious books and by becoming more aggressive in their accusations of heresy.[57] Many of the reform-oriented figures whom Marguerite had supported, such as Roussel, Guillaume Farel, and Lefèvre d'Étaples, had fled France during the king's absence to seek safe haven in Switzerland or Strasbourg.[58] The end of Louise's regency meant that Roussel and Lefèvre d'Étaples were safe to return to France.[59] Moreover, François demonstrated support for the évangéliques' commitment to exegesis by making Hebrew and Greek two of the key subject matters of the Collège de France, which he would found in 1530.[60]

One can only imagine that Marguerite would have derived renewed hope from her brother's support, especially after her encounter with Charles V, whose dissimulations she had considered extreme. Her experiences in Spain no doubt rendered the gap between human sin and spiritual ideals, in malo and in bono influences, even more obvious to her than they would have been previously.[61] Given her continued push for religious reform, it would appear that to her, the way out of the labyrinth of the fallen world remained the one path of faith, by which Christ would lead the aristocrats to salvation.

Marguerite had additional reasons for encouragement as she pursued her vision for religious reform, since in 1527 she married the dashing Henri d'Albret, king of the disputed territory of Navarre, which lay at the border between France and Spain. Given François's perpetual struggle against Charles V, this territory was of interest as a space in which to surveil and defend against his adversary's activities via reports from his sister and her new husband. The following year, Marguerite enjoyed yet more happiness upon the birth of her first child, Jeanne d'Albret; however, Marguerite's second child, Jean, died in 1530 before reaching his first birthday.[62] Even if the queen of Navarre regretted the fact that only one of her children lived to adulthood, Jeanne would become an important figure in her own right, converting to Protestantism and giving birth to a king of France, the future Henri IV.

The late 1520s had, overall, proved a prosperous time in Marguerite's life,[63] but when it came to her creative endeavors and closest relationships, tensions would soon begin to mount. In 1531, the queen of Navarre published a devotional poem titled *Le Miroir de l'âme pécheresse* in which she meditated on the sinful soul's relationship to Christ, drawing on biblical allusions and speaking from a feminine vantage point. Marguerite's first published literary work appeared only a year after her brother had founded the Collège de France, an important intellectual venue that still exists today. The time was ripe for Marguerite's intellectual endeavors, but her family's needs never ceased to intervene. In 1531, Marguerite tended to her mother as the latter attempted to pass a kidney stone; unfortunately, Louise de Savoie did not survive this ordeal.[64] Within only two years of Louise's death, the religious and political landscape of France would change drastically. In 1533, Marguerite printed a second edition of her *Miroir*, this time with her name attached and with references to Marot's French translation of the Psalms.[65] The Sorbonne theology faculty moved to condemn the work because it included scriptural passages in the vernacular, a fact that, in their eyes, implied allegiance to Luther. The queen of Navarre was beginning to make a name for herself as an author, but with her newfound status came increased opposition from the religious authorities. It took her brother's protection to silence the religious authorities, who backtracked, claiming that their only concern had been that the *Miroir* lacked the necessary authorization for publication.[66]

Both the *Miroir* and Marguerite's *Dialogue en forme de vision nocturne*, a text that appeared the same year and that featured a conversation between the author and her deceased niece, Charlotte, bring the painful realities of human life into conversation with spiritual truth. These writings, among others, offered a space in which to envision ways to make the temporal more spiritual and more whole, both for herself and for her readers. Through her writings, the queen of Navarre continued to push for religious reform from within the aristocracy and to find creative vision to sustain her in that process. In this sense, her texts balance sad realities with spiritual joys, in malo and in bono themes, multicursal and unicursal designs, all while inviting the reader to contemplate this complexity and find in Christ the one way out.

Unfortunately for Marguerite, her brother's wholehearted support for her spiritual strivings would wane beginning in 1534 with the Affaire des placards in which Antoine Marcourt and other provocateurs posted virulent critiques of the mass in several French cities, with one flyer ending up on the king's bedchamber door.[67] Sensing a threat to his authority, François responded with swift reprisals, lending his support to efforts by Parliament and the Sorbonne to arrest, try, and in some cases, execute reform-oriented individuals in France.[68] Marguerite herself retreated to Pau and afterward to Nérac.[69] Then, in 1535, François signed the Edict of Coucy, enabling reformers who were imprisoned or in exile to return to France if they renounced their unorthodox views within six months.[70] Although Marguerite would continue her whole life to work toward reform efforts, both in her real-world activities and in her writing, her brother would never again openly support her religious engagement in the same way he had previously done.

IV. Marguerite's Final Years, 1540–1549

For her part, although Marguerite loved her brother dearly, she found herself divided between her obligations to the crown and her obligations to her husband's family. These tensions came to the fore in 1540 when François signed a marriage contract between Marguerite's daughter, Jeanne, and Guillaume de Clèves.[71] Jeanne was horrified by the match and refused to consent to it. For a full year, her parents attempted to forestall the undesired union but to no avail. In 1541, Jeanne was forcibly carried down the aisle.[72] As a last attempt to help her daughter, Marguerite managed to persuade the duke that Jeanne was too young to consummate the marriage, an agreement that would lay the groundwork for an annulment at a later date.[73]

After the strain of the late 1530s and early 1540s, Marguerite finally had what she thought was good news when in 1542, at age fifty, she believed herself to be pregnant. More than likely, she had a molar pregnancy, as she became very ill as time went on and had to take to her bed.[74] For modern-day readers, the queen of Navarre's bed rest holds particular significance, since it was during this time that she turned once more to literary projects. Chief among them was her collection of nouvelles and dialogues, which would come to be known as the *Heptaméron*.[75] The text would be published under its current title in 1559, ten years after the queen's death, but Marguerite worked on the manuscript versions of her stories in the company of her retinue during long trips;[76] her project was therefore no secret during her lifetime, and she even exchanged anecdotes en route with her friends, an experience that Jourda believes provided material for her nouvelles.[77] Although the tales claim Boccaccio's *Decameron* as their source of inspiration, they contain far more pointed societal critiques and religious endorsements than their Italian predecessor, hinting at the queen's interest in reform efforts and her vision for fostering a more just society. The stories also demonstrate the queen's hard-won political and spiritual insights, which recall the labyrinth through their foregrounding of the fallen world, human sinfulness, and salvation in Christ. She continued to work on these stories for the rest of her life, completing seventy-two tales by the time of her death.

If Marguerite attempted through her tales to avoid overtly religious genres that could cause problems for her brother, the development of the Protestant Reformation within France's borders nevertheless kept François occupied. Although he had decided in 1543 to pardon the Protestant rebels at La Rochelle,[78] in 1544 he signed the Treaty of Crépy with the much-despised Charles V, officially uniting the two monarchs in a pro-Catholic stance.[79] This public endorsement of the Catholic Church preceded the slaughter of 3,000 reformers at Mérindol the following year.[80] It was also in 1545 that the French king's health declined yet again, this time due not only to an abscess but also to syphilis.[81] Two years later, after a period of faltering health, François passed away.

Marguerite, herself weak and in seclusion at a convent in Tusson, had been unable to visit him earlier in his illness. The nuns had kept the news of his final decline and death from her,[82] although her tortured dreams of an ailing François had warned her of what was to come.[83] In her profound grief over losing her most cherished friend, the brother whom Louise de Savoie had represented as the family's raison d'être, Marguerite remained among the nuns at Tusson for four months.[84] When she had recovered enough to resume some semblance of living, she took to her pen, pouring her energy into several important works, all of which reflect the spiritual

longings and earthly ills that Marguerite had her whole life tried to reconcile through Church reform and the conversion of her aristocratic peers.
Such works include *La Navire*, in which she dialogues with her deceased
brother, *Les Dernières poésies*, *La Comédie sur le trépas du roy*, *Les Chan-
sons spirituelles*, *Les Marguerites de la Marguerite des princesses*, *Les Pris-
ons*, *La Comédie de Mont-de-Marsan*, and of course, her *Heptaméron*.[85]

Following her brother's death in 1547, Marguerite suffered many causes
for strain in addition to her grief. The new king, Henri II, had never been
overly fond of his aunt, and Marguerite worried he might discontinue the
pension that François had left her. She also recognized that with new leadership came new alliances that inevitably relegated the old vanguard to the
sidelines. Thanks to the intervention of Anne de Montmorency,[86] Henri did
confirm the queen of Navarre's pension, but her influence waned notice-
ably, such that diplomats now considered her the eleventh most important
member of the royal family.[87] Moreover, Henri had arranged a marriage
between Jeanne d'Albret and Antoine de Bourbon, a match that pleased
both Jeanne and the king but which Marguerite and her husband opposed.[88]
Their opposition proved ineffective, and the marriage took place in 1548.[89]
Cauterets, which features in the *Heptaméron*'s prologue, became Marguerite's refuge in 1549 when her health began once more to decline as a result
of these stresses.[90] The queen of Navarre came in time to rejoice in her
daughter's happiness.[91] In her final year of life, after a visit with Jeanne and
her husband, Marguerite retired to her residence at Odos. There, she lin-
gered outdoors late at night to watch a passing comet that was considered
a spiritual omen. Gazing at this heavenly sign seemed a fitting activity for a
visionary queen who, in all her earthly activities, had sought to bridge the
gap between the human and the divine. While outside, she developed
chills, and her doctors ushered her back into the warmth. Her symptoms
progressed quickly, most likely as a result of pleurisy, and on December 21,
1549, she passed away, having died in her faith, saying "Jesus" three times
before breathing her last.[92]

V. Conclusion

Thanks to her reform efforts and her literary texts, the queen of Navarre's
legacy lives on. In the short term, Marguerite's support for Church reform,
even of the non-schismatic variety, eventually permitted large-scale religious change in the form of Protestantism. Even though it may not
have been the outcome for which Marguerite had hoped, given her desire
to maintain unity in addition to the long-standing alliance between the

Catholic Church and the monarchy, the Protestant movement nonetheless responded to her concerns about clerical abuse and her desire to see sacred texts distributed in the vernacular. Indeed, Marguerite's daughter, Jeanne, went on to become one of the leading figures of the Protestant Reformation in France. Although aristocrats could never fully divorce their lives from politics, spiritual zeal did bring about significant changes in religious practice throughout Europe, in part because of Marguerite's early efforts.

Marguerite's writings are also still read and studied today, with her *Heptaméron* garnering ongoing interest through its interrogation of social mores, its timeless human conundrums, and its spiritual questions. Although other works by Marguerite address similar themes, the *Heptaméron* strikes a chord that resonates especially well with modern readers. Through its focus on institutional abuses, its display of human sin in many scandalous forms, its foregrounding of romantic relationships, and its search for spiritual meaning in a broken world, this text speaks across the centuries to readers in our own times, who have witnessed large-scale injustices and tragedies of their own. The idea of the labyrinth reflects the complexities of the present day as well as of the queen of Navarre's era, featuring numerous connotations that come to the foreground or retreat to the background depending on how one reads and why. Marguerite de Navarre parsed situations and texts according to her experience in political contexts, her religious belief and advocacy for reform, and her participation in literary circles. Hermeneutics and the challenges it posed united all three domains of her life. The next chapter therefore explores the act of reading: what it meant for the queen of Navarre and her contemporaries, what it means for reception theorists today, and how these approaches can inform our understanding of the written word across time.

3

"We Walk by Faith, Not by Sight"

Exegesis, Pilgrimage, and Labyrinthine Connections
in the Reformation

In 1521, Guillaume Briçonnet, the bishop of Meaux, wrote to Marguerite de Navarre as part of a lengthy exchange that would endure until 1524. In this correspondence, Briçonnet considered with Marguerite the topics of faith and hermeneutics, two subjects that also informed the thought of the évangéliques. In his letter dated August 1521, early in his correspondence with Marguerite, Briçonnet compared the God of the scriptures to a path, one that offers wisdom and guidance in the midst of life's uncertainties. He wrote that he prayed his correspondent would be blessed by the "excessive and invincible" love of God, which would "blind you and illuminate you, so that you are in seeing blind and in blindness seeing, and thus arrive at the Way without path."[1] The references to sight and paths in Briçonnet's letter call to mind the symbolism of the labyrinth and the disorienting experience it induces in those who walk or contemplate it. Still, Briçonnet asserted that divine love acts as the believer's eyes, keeping the Christian on the path of Christ.

This treatment of paths and sight recurs nearly ten years later in the first complete translation of the Bible into French, produced by yet another évangélique, Jacques Lefèvre d'Étaples. In that translation, 2 Corinthians 5:6–7 combines allusions to sight and paths with the topic of pilgrimage: "We are therefore always confident, knowing that when we are in the body, we are pilgrims of the Lord, since we journey by faith, not by sight."[2] These exegetical writings by Lefèvre d'Étaples and Briçonnet not only suggest interrelations among the concepts of sight, paths, and pilgrimage but also reflect the Augustinian influence on the hermeneutics that the évangéliques practiced. Indeed, according to an Augustinian model of exegesis, Christians need to look past surface appearances in scripture and the natural world, reading them through faith, such that divine love and charity emerge.[3]

Marguerite demonstrated her appreciation for this Augustinian mode of hermeneutics, which informed Briçonnet's letters to her, by advocating publicly on the évangéliques' behalf. Although critics sometimes consider her influence to have waned in this regard after the Affaire des placards in 1534, scholarship also shows that in later years, the queen channeled her evangelical sentiment into her literary texts, including the *Heptaméron* (1559).[4] Indeed, Robert Cottrell shows that even at the end of her life and literary career in the 1540s, when she was working on the *Heptaméron,* Marguerite continued to cite Briçonnet's letters: "More than twenty years later, ill, despondent, and knowing that she would soon die, she alluded over and over to ideas and actual phrases in the letters she had received years before. Either she had kept the letters and reread them toward the end of her life or—and this is even more remarkable—she had read them so thoroughly in the 1520s that she was able in the late 1540s to cite them from memory."[5] In either case, this "champion of the evangelical cause," as Jonathan Reid terms her, continued to produce texts containing concepts that she had first learned from Briçonnet.[6]

As Briçonnet's allusions to sight and the path of God suggest, the idea of the labyrinth, with its dual connotations in bono and in malo and its simultaneous status as process and product, reflects themes in the debates about exegesis that occurred in Marguerite's era. If believers read according to an Augustinian model of exegesis, they will ultimately interpret all signs, whether written or visual, in bono, including those signs that might at first glance appear to function in malo. Due to the labyrinth's meandering path, the walker's or onlooker's "vision ahead and behind is severely constricted and fragmented," leading to disorientation.[7] This aspect of the labyrinth operates in malo and "represent[s] the entanglements of this deceitful world, fatal unless God is one's guide."[8] At the same time, the labyrinth recalls God's sovereignty and complex design of the universe, just as the labyrinth is itself an intricate and aesthetic structure.[9] In keeping to one interpretive path in which everything signifies divine love and charity, exegetes in an Augustinian vein relate process to product, holding onto faith in the goodness of God and the victory of order over chaos. Despite sudden twists and turns, the unicursal labyrinth, found in church settings, offers only one path to the walker or viewer, and its complex design recalls for the faithful the notion of divine artistry. Attaining the spiritual prize of a transcendent perspective that encompasses the coherent whole is what urges the labyrinth walker, as well as the Augustinian exegete, forward on the arduous path.

This pursuit of a spiritual goal even when faced with a difficult trajectory recalls the practice of pilgrimage as well as the larger metaphor of the

Christian life as a challenging journey through the fallen world and back toward God, as Lefèvre d'Étaple's translation of 2 Corinthians 5:6–7 suggests. During Marguerite's life, pilgrimage persisted as a religious practice; Marguerite herself undertook several pilgrimages, as a later section in this chapter will discuss. When completing pilgrimages to certain cathedrals that housed relics, pilgrims might espy unicursal labyrinths that were built into the church floors. Although there is no historical record during the queen of Navarre's lifetime of the faithful treating church labyrinths as substitute pilgrimages—that is to say, as replacements for literal journeys to holy sites—the labyrinth's connotations of "difficult process" and "perseverance" would likely have resonated with anyone arriving at a cathedral after a long and tiring voyage. The labyrinth's symbolism of complex artistry and finalized product might also have inspired joy in pilgrims who had at last reached their destination.

The unicursal labyrinth within a church setting served a spiritual purpose, but it also recalled the larger idea of the labyrinth as a symbol encompassing process and product as well as in malo and in bono features. Church labyrinths intensified those aspects of the idea of the labyrinth that most clearly describe the life of faith, which pilgrimage, in many ways, represented on a metaphorical level. The journey through life requires interpretation in much the same way as the reading of a text, according to Augustinian exegesis. As such, the topics of pilgrimage and exegesis converge when viewed through the symbolism of the labyrinth.

Exegesis and pilgrimage also come together in the writings of numerous authors of the Reformation, as well as in texts by foundational writers of the early church, who offered insights into the subjects that Reformation-era thinkers were debating. This chapter will therefore show how the idea of the labyrinth, with its in bono and in malo duality and its rendering of both process and product, helps frame discussions of pilgrimage and exegesis in Marguerite's era.[10] Because the unicursal pathway was the type of labyrinth located in churches, allusions to labyrinths as built structures in this chapter refer to the unicursal type; however, the larger concept of the labyrinth, with its many symbolic meanings, remains of primary importance.

The chapter first considers how the topics of exegesis and pilgrimage, as well as labyrinthine allusions, develop in Marguerite's correspondence with Briçonnet compared to the writings of Augustine and Gregory of Nyssa (ca. 335–395). The next section discusses exegesis and its relationship to pilgrimage and the idea of the labyrinth in writings by Marguerite's contemporaries, including Martin Luther, John Calvin, and Erasmus. This analysis precedes an investigation into Marguerite's own treatment of exegesis and pilgrimage in her *Heptaméron*'s prologue and how it reflects Augustinian hermeneutics, a non-schismatic approach to reform, and the idea of the labyrinth, which can be said to symbolize key aspects of her approach to reading both sacred texts and human society. Finally, the chapter closes by comparing notions of hermeneutics in Marguerite's era to reception theories in the present day.

I. Marguerite's Hermeneutic Development

Two labyrinthine themes—difficult realities and spiritual yearnings—underlie Marguerite de Navarre's first letter to Briçonnet in June 1521. In their critical edition of the correspondence between Marguerite and the bishop of Meaux, Christine Martineau, Henry Heller, and Michel Veissière explain what prompted the queen to initiate contact at this particular moment. In 1521, Marguerite's less-than-compatible husband, Charles d'Alençon, was preparing to leave for Champagne to fight on behalf of François Ier. Marguerite found herself removed from her family and still adjusting to the ways in which her brother's reign had changed her political and social identity.[11] She cited several of these factors when she wrote to Briçonnet, asking him for "secours spirituel" (spiritual aid).[12] Not only did she request that he pray for "Monsieur d'Alençon qui, par le commandement du Roy, s'en va son lieutenant general en son armée" (Monsieur d'Alençon who, on the king's command, leaves to serve as lieutenant general in his army), but she also expressed fear and loneliness: "Car il me fault mesler de beaucoup de choses qui me doivent bien donner crainte. Et encores demain s'en va ma tante de Nemours en Savoye" (For I have to be involved in many things that give me cause for fear. And what's more, tomorrow my aunt de Nemours leaves for Savoie).[13] Briçonnet responded by offering over the next several years a series of lessons that employed metaphors and biblical allusions to address his interlocutor's evolving needs, guiding her down a singular but winding path of faith.

By mid-June 1521, Marguerite conveyed mounting encouragement as well as enthusiasm for the spiritual education that Briçonnet was providing. She opened her letter by praising God for her increased longing to find the path of salvation, a phrasing that recalls the labyrinth as well as the assertion in John 14:6 that Christ is the Way, the Truth, and the Life: "Monsieur de Meaulx, je loue de toute ma puissance le seul bien necessaire, qui, par sa bonté, permect à celle qui se peult dire moings que rien, tant de grace que d'avoir eu, par vostre lettre . . . occasion de desirer commancer d'entendre le chemin de salut" (Monsieur de Meaulx, I praise with all my power the one necessity, who by His goodness, permits her who can call herself less than nothing, so much grace as to have had, by your letter . . . occasion to desire to begin to understand the path of salvation).[14] She then went on to say that Briçonnet's letters had inspired in her a desire to love God more sincerely: "Et, puis qu'il luy plaist avoir ouvert l'œil (puisque par nature aveugle) et par vostre bon moyen l'avoir tourné du cousté de la lumière, je vous prie . . . rompre la trop grande ignorance de mon entendement, affin que le pauvre cœur verglacé et mort en froit puisse sentir quelque estincelle de l'amour" (And as it pleased Him to have opened my eye (since it is by nature blind) and by your good endeavor to have turned it toward the light, I ask you please . . . to break the exceedingly great ignorance of my understanding so that my poor heart, frozen and dead in the cold, may feel some spark of love).[15] In making references to sight, blindness, love, and the path of salvation, Marguerite incorporates into her vocabulary the same figures of speech that Briçonnet employs, which draw on Christian themes.

It is important to note, however, that these same allusions also reflect the in malo and in bono components of the labyrinth. After all, the labyrinth functions on one level as a confusing process, disorienting the observer or walker through its fragmentation of sight. Only later does it grant an appreciative, transcendent vantage point to the one who perseveres. From a Christian perspective, perseverance represents the unfolding of a spiritual process with a known and positive outcome. The assurance of salvation functions as a mark of divine love offered by Christ, the harrower of hell and the guide of the labyrinth. It is a prize for which Marguerite appears willing to pursue the challenging process of learning Augustinian hermeneutics.

In his letter dated July 10, 1521, Briçonnet suggested this stance on interpretation by analyzing several concepts that echo the experience of the labyrinth. In his commentary on the themes of sight, faith, and paths, he asserted that only God can grant Marguerite love for Him and an eagerness for spiritual understanding, since all creatures, in their natural state, are blind, and depend on God to transform their "tenebres" (shadows) into "lumiere" (light).[16] Briçonnet asserted that in this regard, he was no exception: "Parquoy, Madame, moult vous esgarez ailleurs sercher chemin que en luy, qui est la voye, qui à vraie et vivifiante amour maine et attire" (That is why, madam, you wander too far afield by seeking a path elsewhere than in Him, who is the path that leads and attracts you to true and life-giving love).[17] Through his letters, Briçonnet urged Marguerite to view God as the only path worth following and to avoid the temptation to fix her attentions too closely on him as a mentor figure.

In addition, he emphasized that God alone can open Marguerite's eyes and call her, through love, to the path of enlightenment, where she would pass from blindness to sight: "Car, comme il est voie, aussy est il vie, verité et amour, qui est pour satisfaire à voz humbles et gratieuses lettres, par lesquelles, Madame, pour neant desirez estre addressée, par cecité et par glassons eschauffée à l'amour du seul necessaire" (For just as He is path, He is also life, truth, and love that can respond fully to your humble and gracious letters, by which, madam, you express your desire to be addressed as nothing, from blindness and ice warmed up to the love of the one necessity).[18] Briçonnet thus teaches Marguerite that God Himself is the path of salvation, the "chemin sans chemin" (Way without path). He suggests that God will lead Marguerite from earthly concerns toward a spiritual way of living in which divine truth provides a hope that can supersede life's hurts and conundrums. Much as in the labyrinth, the earthly and the spiritual coincide to reveal both in malo and in bono interpretations and to facilitate positive transformations that take the individual from process to product.

By combining references to sight, blindness, and God as path, Briçonnet builds on two topics with labyrinthine connotations that were pertinent to both schismatic and non-schismatic reformers: exegesis and pilgrimage. In regard to exegesis, Cottrell explains that for Briçonnet, and for Augustine before him, "things become words that the Christian must read in such a way that he will arrive at an interpretation pointing to the law of love."[19] Briçonnet foregrounds the concept of *figura*, "or signs whose referent is always God," to "[provide] Marguerite with a way of reading, i.e., a way of seeing, that is applicable not only to Scripture but to that larger text which is the natural world created by God."[20] In this interpretive model, reading aright entails seeing aright. Because both material and spiritual interpretations of human experience are possible, the believer must choose which way to read, and this choice entails an act of faith. When interpreting the complexities of scripture and the visible world, the observer faces a kind of labyrinth. A unicursal pathway might, for the onlooker, constitute either a stone structure or a symbol with a higher meaning. If individuals decide to read symbolically, then they must still propose an interpretation: one that foregrounds sin, redemption, or the intersection of the two. As chapter 4 will discuss in greater detail, Augustine chose in *The City of God* (426) to acknowledge literal meaning while also seeking out its far-reaching spiritual implications, and his disciples, Marguerite and Briçonnet, do likewise in their approach to interpreting the written word and the world.[21]

In addition to providing an exegetical approach that would inspire both Briçonnet and Marguerite, Augustine furnished writings on pilgrimage that would later influence reform-oriented individuals who were reevaluating the utility of this practice, especially when it came to the importance placed on ritual versus hermeneutics. Early in the history of Christianity, Augustine had argued against pilgrimage, "since the holy could not be localized in any given place."[22] Moreover, in *De doctrina Christiana* (397–426), Augustine combined allusions to several Pauline verses to cast all Christians as pilgrims: "So, in this mortal life we are like travellers away from our Lord: if we wish to return to the homeland, where we can be happy, we must use this world, not enjoy it."[23] In the view of Augustine and before him, Paul, a Christian's spiritual development already constitutes a metaphorical pilgrimage. In the world, Christians are like pilgrims following the path of salvation toward the City of God, and as Augustine's parsing of Paul's writings implies, the interpretation of scripture figures into that process. The life of faith, as Augustine shows in his model of hermeneutics, requires the believer to read signs, whether written or tangible, through the lens of belief. Consequently, for Augustine, exegesis and the Christian life entailed process and outcome, as well as in malo and in bono themes, while ultimately privileging the latter in each pairing over the former. Given this metaphorical approach, as well as the fact that in Paul's perspective the holy does not reside any more in one place than in another, Augustine opposed literal pilgrimage, and reformers of schismatic and non-schismatic stripes would later reflect his views to varying degrees.

However, Augustine was not the only Christian authority whose writings shaped Reformation-era attitudes toward pilgrimage and exegesis. Like Augustine, Gregory of Nyssa referenced Paul to argue that pilgrimage constitutes a metaphor for the Christian's passage from physical reality to spiritual truths: "For the changing of one's place does not bring about any greater nearness to God. . . . Therefore, beloved, counsel the brothers to quit the body to be with the Lord (2 Corinthians 5:8), rather than quit Cappadocia to be in Palestine."[24] As Wes Williams explains, Gregory of Nyssa wrote "at a time when the call to *peregrinatio* in Paul's letter [2 Corinthians] was being interpreted as a call to travel, and supporting the new institution of pilgrimage."[25] Writing against this interpretation, Gregory of Nyssa took up a "resolutely figural reading of Paul" to frame pilgrimage "not as a literal journey, but as the construction of an inner self worthy of Christ's habitation."[26] The idea of self-construction adds another layer to Augustine's treatment of pilgrimage and textual interpretation because it takes two large-scale themes—the Christian life and the study of scripture—and personalizes them to the individual. Self-construction requires transformation; individuals must be self-aware enough to recognize their attachment to material existence before they can undergo a process of spiritual growth and refinement.

Figural readings of scripture, such as the one that Gregory of Nyssa proposed, can aid in that transformation, taking individuals from process to product, earthly difficulty to spiritual reward, sign to interpretation. All of these procedures are likewise associated with the idea of the labyrinth, which invites onlookers and walkers on a metaphorical journey toward God and away from the world, which the nave—the site of labyrinths in church settings—represented.[27] In this way, the idea of the labyrinth symbolizes the transformative process for which Gregory of Nyssa advocated; however, since self-construction could be undertaken through exegesis, he contended that Christians would do better to internalize their faith rather than externalize it by traveling to see relics.

II. Luther, Calvin, and Erasmus

Unlike Gregory of Nyssa and Augustine and unlike those with non-schismatic religious views, Protestants such as Martin Luther criticized pilgrims' motives in a sharper manner, critiquing them for their boredom, desire for excitement, and lack of commitment to family and local parishes. His "Address to the Christian Nobility of the German Nation, concerning the Reform of the Christian Estate," published in 1520, reveals that pilgrimage occupied his thoughts from the early days of the Reformation. Luther asserts that while there is nothing inherently evil about going on a pilgrimage, most pilgrims choose to leave home for reasons that he deems inappropriate, such as vain curiosity or a belief that traveling to a holy site will atone for their sins: "He thinks, poor foolish man, to atone for this disobedience and contempt of God's commandments by his self-willed pilgrimage, while he is in the truth misled by idle curiosity or the wiles of the devil."[28] Here, Luther echoes Augustine's assertion that no one physical location is holier than another and suggests that it is believers' relationship to the place in which they find themselves that matters.

Luther appears to be advocating a stronger tie between believers and their local churches and communities and suggesting that the spiritual potential in such contexts is greater than in a trip to see holy sites. He expounds further on this idea by arguing that in staying where they are, the faithful are better equipped to serve God: "[Pilgrimage] is but a little good work, often a bad, misleading work, for God has not commanded it.

But He has commanded that each man should care for his wife and children and whatever concerns the married state, and should, besides, serve and help his neighbour."[29] What matters most in this passage is the idea of an active faith rooted in community. Building up the Kingdom of God where one finds oneself is more important in Luther's eyes than spiritual sensation seeking in a faraway place.

In making this assertion, Luther is advocating self-examination in a slightly different way than Gregory of Nyssa. Instead of focusing on the individual's transformative process, Luther points out the divergence between what people do and what they ought to do. Luther suggests that people ought to fulfill their responsibilities toward others, but instead they chase after vain and idle pursuits, and to justify this choice, they frame it as piousness. Luther is, in fact, pointing his readers toward the spiritual and away from the material, but his approach is sterner and less individually tailored than that of Gregory of Nyssa. However, he does make reference to the scriptures—specifically, the Ten Commandments—to support his point of view, and in so doing, he gives priority to the interpretation of sacred texts and not to ritual.

Luther condemns those who lead the people astray by encouraging them to engage in ritualistic behaviors instead of exegesis and self-examination. He uses particularly strong language to denounce the leaders of country churches who encourage pilgrimage by claiming that miracles have happened on-site: "They think that it is a godly, holy thing, and do not see that the devil does this to strengthen covetousness, to teach false beliefs, to weaken parish churches, to increase drunkenness and debauchery, to waste money and labour, and simply to lead the poor people by the nose."[30] It would seem that for Luther, dishonest church leaders tempt the undiscerning into spiritual error, just as heretics wound their way further and further down into the labyrinth of perdition until they could no longer escape.[31] In malo connotations of the labyrinth can be read as figuring corruption in the institutional Church and the seriousness of its consequences for everyday people in Luther's time. Whether Luther associates pilgrimage with sexual promiscuity, as in the above citation, or simply the curiosity of the eyes, the general theme of lust recalls the idea of the labyrinth in malo, which functions as a prison and a trap.[32]

In the Francophone context, John Calvin likewise warned against pilgrimage in his *Traité des reliques* (1543).[33] Like Luther, Calvin criticizes pilgrims for their desire to see relics.[34] He uses pointed language with the aim of inspiring his readers to abandon their fascination with material things, citing Augustine to establish his critique: "Saint Augustin, au livre qu'il a intitulé *Du labeur des Moines*, se complaignant d'aucuns porteurs de rogatons, qui déjà de son temps exerçaient foire vilaine et déshonnête portant çà et là des reliques de martyrs, ajoute, 'voire si ce sont reliques de martyrs'" ("Saint Augustine complains, in his work entitled 'The Labor of Monks,' that certain people were, even in his time, exercising a dishonest trade, hawking about relics of martyrs, and he adds the following significant words '*should they really be relics of martyrs*'").[35] In addition to putting Augustine's authority behind the critique of pilgrimage and relics that he will elaborate, Calvin suggests that a great many relics of his own time are likely inauthentic: "Puisque l'origine de cet abus est si ancienne, il ne faut douter qu'il n'ait été bien multiplié cependant par si long temps" ("Since the origin of this abuse is so ancient, there can be no doubt that it has greatly increased during a long interval of years").[36] By referencing a text from the first centuries of Christian practice and bringing it into conversation with his own historical moment, Calvin simultaneously lends weight to his viewpoint and justifies his focus on pilgrimage as a topic of debate.

Citing Augustine is an effective strategy in part because the former's status as a church father meant that Christians of many persuasions esteemed him and his writings. Indeed, although Calvin was an overtly Protestant reformer, he expressed admiration for Augustine just as Marguerite de Navarre and Briçonnet, two non-schismatic reformers, did in their model of exegesis. Moreover, by drawing comparisons between Augustine's time and his own, Calvin is able to throw into sharp relief what he considers to be the degradation of the sixteenth-century Church. After all, Augustine lived and wrote at a time when the Church was relatively young. If pilgrimage was already a corrupting influence in that time—one that depended on the deception of the eyes and the minds of believers—how could it possibly be a constructive practice to Calvin and his contemporaries?

Yet again, one notes here an emphasis on the need to move past an attachment to worldly sights and focus instead on the inner life of faith. Otherwise, one may become enmired in a labyrinth of pointless, heretical thinking and practices, as Calvin contends through his treatment of the labyrinth's symbolism in his *Institutes of the Christian Religion*, discussed in chapter 1.[37] In the *Institutes*, Calvin uses the idea of the labyrinth in malo to highlight the need to practice biblical exegesis while not seeking to resolve questions that the Bible does not directly address. Instead of becoming intrigued by curiosities, such as obscure theological questions or supposed relics, Calvin recommends that believers focus on what scripture says regarding God, salvation, and the life of faith and accept that anything it does not say is not intended for human beings to know with certainty.[38] In

Calvin's view, adopting this mentality toward pilgrimage and exegesis will help the faithful progress in their metaphorical journey away from material existence and toward God.[39]

Non-schismatic reformers likewise questioned the legitimacy of pilgrimage as a literal journey; however, as their aim was to reform the Church from within, they did not necessarily adopt as clear-cut a stance as Calvin or Luther did. An example of a non-schismatic line of thought, in which the development of genuine faith proves of greater concern than debates about travel, is Erasmus's *Enchiridion* (1503). In that text, Erasmus writes to a courtier to provide him with a handbook for Christian living.[40] After imparting some general reflections on the nature of living as a Christian in the world, he elaborates a series of more specific rules. Under the heading of rule five, in which he analyzes pilgrimage and exegesis, Erasmus states that "perfect piety is the attempt to progress always from visible things, which are usually imperfect or indifferent, to invisible."[41] As an illustration, he examines popular fascination with relics and pilgrimages: "With great veneration you revere the ashes of Paul, which I do not condemn, if your religion is consistent with your devotion. If you venerate mute and dead ashes and ignore his living image still speaking and breathing, as it were, in his writings, is not your religion utterly absurd?"[42] Erasmus argues that in fixating on material objects and undervaluing scripture, Christians may fail to move away from the body. They may also fail to interpret surface appearances through a spiritual lens, which proves problematic, because as Erasmus asserts, "since we are but pilgrims in the visible world, we should never make it our fixed abode, but should relate by a fitting comparison everything that occurs to the senses either to the angelic world or, in more practical terms, to morals and to that part of man that corresponds to the angelic."[43] The problem, then, is not so much the reality of travel itself in Erasmus's thought but rather one's approach to Christian faith. Regardless of whether one chooses to travel, Erasmus recommends that believers focus on exegesis and self-examination, turning away from visual stimuli and toward an inner life of faith.[44]

This inward movement of faith is central to the Reformation, and it is a trend that Erasmus shares in common with Protestant reformers like Luther and Calvin, even if Erasmus does not forbid pilgrimage, provided that pilgrims are truly developing their inner faith in the process. It would seem that for Erasmus, then, a literal journey of faith can complement a metaphorical one. Much like in Augustine's hermeneutics or in the idea of the labyrinth, process and product, sign and interpretation coexist, even if it is ultimately most important that the end goal of spiritual transformation and right reading be achieved. The idea of the labyrinth can function in bono since its spiritual significance extends beyond the literal, just as relics need not constitute a mere sight for pilgrims to behold. In this line of thought, both labyrinths and relics retain the ability to foster in the faithful a more transcendent perspective, if approached with the proper hermeneutical attitude.

III. Marguerite de Navarre's Pilgrimages and the Heptaméron's Prologue

For the French évangélique Marguerite de Navarre, this moderate approach also prevails. As the introduction to this study mentioned, Marguerite's library contained a variety of items that demonstrated her love of biblical analysis alongside her interest in more traditional Catholic rituals. For instance, in addition to a multivolume Bible, Marguerite possessed in her library incense and relics, which she employed as part of her spiritual life. She may not have approved of all aspects of the Catholic Church in her lifetime, but neither did she break with the Church nor renounce all of its traditions.

We see this nuanced attitude in Marguerite's own relationship to pilgrimage. Indeed, the queen of Navarre went on several pilgrimages in her lifetime. Early in her brother's reign in 1515, when he invaded Italy in what would prove a successful attempt to capture Milan, Marguerite accompanied her mother, Louise de Savoie, and her sister-in-law, Queen Claude, on a pilgrimage to the South of France, where they could be closer to François's location: "[Marguerite] undertook the traditional pilgrimage from Amboise, locus of the court for the duration of Louise's regency, to Notre-Dame-des-Fontaines to pray for victory and the speedy return of her loved ones."[45] Shortly before reuniting with François in 1516, the three women also "fulfilled a vow by making a pilgrimage to Saint-Maximin-la-Sainte-Baume, supposedly the site of Mary Magdalene's grave."[46] Later on, in 1528, after having experienced a very difficult labor before the birth of her daughter, Jeanne, Marguerite likewise fulfilled a promise to journey to Notre Dame de Cléry in the Loire Valley.[47] These personal experiences of pilgrimage suggest that a sense of sacred space mattered to Marguerite. Indeed, there were long-standing ties between Marguerite's family members and Notre Dame de Sarrance, an abbey and pilgrimage site that features in her Heptaméron. In the fifteenth century, at the end of which Marguerite was still a child, the then-king of Navarre built a residence next to Notre Dame de Sarrance so that he would have somewhere to stay when he came to the site on pilgrimage. The French artistocracy, more generally, was also familiar with the site, as Louis XI of France likewise completed a pilgrimage to Notre Dame de Sarrance in the 1400s. Finally, the house of Albret, whose name Marguerite's daughter, Jeanne, was to bear in recognition of her father's lineage, was closely connected to the abbey.[48]

We see, then, that Marguerite, as a non-schismatic reformer, went on pilgrimage and maintained ties to pilgrimage sites despite the fact that she could not have been unfamiliar with more overtly Protestant viewpoints on the matter. Moreover, critics show that given the presence of Lutheran ideas in some of Marguerite's works as well as her correspondence with individuals in Luther's circle, she most likely obtained and read Luther's works in translation.[49] Marguerite was aware of Protestant ideology and was even in contact with some of its key disseminators, yet she chose not to renounce pilgrimage as a practice. One could perhaps argue that the pilgrimages she undertook in 1515 and 1516 reflect her mother's religious practices more than her own, given that Louise de Savoie, whose spirituality was more orthodoxly Catholic than Marguerite's, was regent at the time, and Marguerite could not have simply rejected the directives of France's ruler.[50] One might also suppose that Louise's more conservative religious practices may have influenced Marguerite's interest in non-schismatic, as opposed to schismatic, reform, given that her mother had directed her early spiritual education.[51] Still, Marguerite chose to embark on a pilgrimage in 1528 after the safe delivery of her daughter, a point when Louise was not actively serving as regent and when the Reformation had already been underway for over a decade. It is thus noteworthy that Marguerite did not abandon the practice of pilgrimage, even if she championed the non-schismatic reformers and worked to wipe out corruption in the abbeys and convents she visited.

In addition to indications in her lived spirituality, we find evidence of her moderate views on pilgrimage in her *Heptaméron*, whose prologue recounts how a group of French aristocrats become accidental pilgrims. The members of the group include Oisille, Hircan, Parlamente, Longarine, Dagoucin, Saffredent, Nomerfide, Emarsuitte, Guebron, and Simontault, to use the spellings in the Cazauran-Lefèvre edition.[52] When flooding strikes, the company flees the thermal springs at Cauterets. The oldest noblewoman, Oisille, seeks shelter at the aforementioned abbey of Notre Dame de Sarrance, located on the route to Santiago.[53] The others face many dangers before arriving at the abbey of Saint Savin, where they encounter a monk who is making a pilgrimage to Sarrance. The monk informs them that he encountered their friend Simontault on the road and gave him directions to Sarrance, where Oisille had taken up refuge.

Upon learning this news, the aristocrats trade their secular aim of obtaining spa treatments for a laborious pilgrimage to Sarrance. The prologue's narrator details the difficult route "par les montaignes" ("over the mountains") and specifies that the road was so challenging that they had to go on foot as opposed to on horseback; the company finally arrived "en grande sueur et travail" ("exhausted and bathed in sweat").[54] The company's entry into the abbey occurs after the dangerous experience of navigating their way through the woods, where bears, robbers, and swollen streams that washed away horses and people underscored the perils of the fallen world and the need for safe passage, two themes associated with the idea of the labyrinth. Upon their arrival at Sarrance, they have thus completed not only an unexpected pilgrimage but also a meandering trajectory, much as pilgrims to such sites as Chartres would have passed by the unicursal pavement as they advanced into the sanctuary. The environment of the abbey, coupled with their prior wandering and disorientation, evokes the idea of the labyrinth. Here, as in Erasmus's text, we see both process and end result, the in malo dangers of the perilous forest and the in bono assurance of faith and security as the travelers realize that somehow, their journey has brought them all to the same place: a spiritual refuge. As part II of the present study will show, the *Heptaméron* can be said to unfold in a labyrinthine manner, and what the company may consider a passage from an earthly environment to a religious one is actually just the beginning of a lengthy and transformative process.

To pass the time as they wait for a bridge to be built that can connect their spiritual and courtly environments—a project that summarizes the *Heptaméron*'s ideological goals—the pilgrims study scripture in the morning and share true stories in the afternoon, thus engaging in the exegesis of both Word and world. When one compares the events of the *Heptaméron*'s prologue to the combined venture of exegesis and storytelling in which the aristocrats participate, one sees that both literal and figurative perspectives on pilgrimage can hold value, even if the latter is more essential. The prologue, for instance, suggests that there is meaning in traveling to a sacred space since the rainstorm (which the text implies is God's handiwork) forces the company out of a hedonistic environment and into a space of spiritual reflection.[55] However, the company does not marvel at the statue of Mary, which according to legend, appeared on the hilltop years before. On the contrary, Oisille dismisses this story as superstition.[56] Oisille's skepticism toward the legend of the statue is significant, considering that it was a major draw for pilgrims, who had been coming to Sarrance to venerate Mary for centuries.[57] Moreover, the text suggests that the worth of the place does not derive from the presence of monks, since at Sarrance, they demonstrate low interest in spiritual matters, and Oisille takes on the leadership role in Bible study. Thus, one sees that the space itself does not inspire instant piety in the company. Only Oisille is content to propose daylong scripture lessons as their occupation; the others clamor for a worldlier and more amusing pastime, hence the decision to tell true stories.[58]

It would appear, then, that the primary value of this pilgrimage site is not its statue, its clergy, or its location on the road to Santiago, but rather its ability to isolate the company from the rest of courtly society, break their normal routines, and encourage them to redirect their thoughts toward spiritual topics. By making exiles of the company, Sarrance provides a space in which reflection and metaphorical pilgrimage can occur. As a type of interior journey, this exegetical pilgrimage based on faith rather than sight harkens back to Paul's assertion in 2 Corinthians 5:6–7 that Christians must walk through life by faith in God's providence, taking each new step without knowing what will come next. This stance is the same one that the unicursal labyrinth promotes in those who walk or contemplate it, suggesting that there is only one path through life, designed by God, but in human experience, that path may appear undulating or induce confusion if interpreted through sight alone. As in Augustinian hermeneutics, in bono readings proceed from faith rather than the literal faculty of sight.

Like those who walk the labyrinth or those who embark on a metaphorical pilgrimage through scripture, Marguerite's storytellers must parse their peers' stories step by step, comparing the information they receive to their previous experiences and knowledge of the Bible to formulate an interpretation.[59] On a second level, the *Heptaméron* projects its readers into a similar position as that of the storytellers since they must proceed in the faith that from this assemblage of tales, colored by diverse ideologies, some larger in bono meaning will emerge. After all, the *Heptaméron* bears the mark of the évangéliques, for whom God remained a guarantor of meaning and truth.[60] In examining the tales, which the prologue frames as recounting true events, the *Heptaméron* invites readers to see the world as a text.

The idea of the world as a readable source of knowledge recalls Augustine's teachings on visible phenomena pointing, as corollaries to scripture, toward the love of God. One might thus infer that for Marguerite as an évangélique, reading the world and reading sacred texts could be seen as related endeavors. The human experience is, in a Christian perspective, inherently labyrinthine in that it occurs in the fallen world, with all its in malo connotations. Nevertheless, there is hope for those who learn to balance earthly realities with spiritual ideals and move beyond acknowledging problems to envisioning solutions rooted in faith. In this interpretive approach, the process of seeing what is but also envisioning transformation through divine love and charity prepares believers to face the labyrinth of life and of institutional reform. Hermeneutics and the relationship between written and visual texts and their interpreters undergird the concern for reform that we see in Marguerite's life and writings.

Still, the notion of interpretation is historically relative and shaped by a given culture's understanding of words, the world, and the place of humankind in the universe. The notions of reading that marked the Reformation, whether through the influence of Augustine or through more pragmatic initiatives, such as the translation and distribution of scripture into the vernacular, do not always overlap with understandings of the text-reader relationship today. At the same time, neither do modern-day reception theories totally exclude key aspects of interpretation that existed in Marguerite's time and that guided her thinking as she read and as she composed texts of her own. In order to better comprehend not only how the queen of Navarre's writings reflect debates about Reformation-era hermeneutics but also how they can intersect with our efforts to interpret her literary output, it will prove useful to interrogate our own models of the interpretive process. The next section undertakes that work, making cross-temporal comparisons to contextualize the analysis of interpretation in the *Heptaméron* that will constitute the primary concern in part II of this book.

IV. Connections to Modern-Day Reception Theories

In the wake of structuralism and, later, of deconstruction, notions of the text-reader exchange have shifted considerably. Post-Derrida, reception theorists such as Stanley Fish have argued that the text is what the reader decides it is. To demonstrate this idea, Fish recounts how he once left notes from a previous class on the board and told his students that the words they saw formed a poem.[61] He explains that students believed his assertion and proceeded to interpret the supposed poem's meanings. In response to the students' musings, Fish argues for the "transferring of responsibility from the text to its readers" because "it is the structure of the reader's experience rather than any structures available on the page that should be the object of description."[62] One might wonder whether, left to their own devices, students would have considered the notes a poem. Nevertheless, reader response theory lends credence to the view that readers retain the power to analyze texts according to their own experiences and opinions.

These trends suggest a desire to assert the individual's influence over interpretation, not only of the text, but of the world, as well. On the one hand, such a stance empowers readers, enabling them to identify political causes and find connections between them and the texts they read. This tendency has inaugurated many important fields of study in relation to literary criticism, such as women's, gender, and sexuality studies, critical race studies, disability studies, and queer theory, to name only a few disciplines. The resulting work has helped foster interdisciplinarity and a keener sense of social justice within academia over time, two extremely valuable and positive developments. On the other hand, a reader-first approach, if practiced in an extreme way, could imply to readers, and especially to students, that texts have no power to alter the way they think or to inspire transformation, since readers can choose to interpret texts as affirming only that which they currently believe or understand. This hermeneutic approach could risk hindering the exploration of many diverging viewpoints and the development of nuanced, critical thinking, two goals that inform university-level education. In the twenty-first century, when the echo chamber effect has garnered considerable attention on social media, especially amid contentious election cycles, it seems wise to consider what models of reading might empower readers while also enabling them to grow and to develop flexibility in their thought processes.

Two reception theorists, Umberto Eco and Yves Citton, respond to this concern by adopting a middle way, much as Marguerite did in her approach to non-schismatic reform. Instead of espousing models of reception based solely on structuralism or deconstruction, Eco and Citton consider the interactions between texts and readers and how each may impact the other. Eco, for instance, considers historical modes of reading from the Middle Ages through the early modern period. Whereas in the Middle Ages, texts required readers to understand established meanings for symbols, especially in religious contexts, as the early modern era progressed, more encyclopedic views of knowledge called for different reading practices.[63] According to Eco, a form of reading based on the trope of the multicursal labyrinth, or Irrgarten, emerged alongside encyclopedic writing.[64] Instead of seeing a symbol and knowing immediately what it meant, readers after Marguerite's time faced, with increasing regularity according to Eco, a series of options and had to make choices about which "paths" to follow. This type of reading was much messier and offered the reader more liberty to explore.

However, in Eco's view, even in this freer version of the text-reader interaction, which prefigures our twenty-first-century notions of interpretation, the reader is not all-powerful over the text. Instead, Eco contends that the text's literal components, such as plot, act as guardrails that discourage readers from negating the text's literal information. Readings that ignore this foundational information will therefore constitute "impertinent" readings.[65] They represent the "use" of a text for purely solipsistic purposes, whereas the "interpretation" of a text requires readers to engage sincerely with its literal components. Still, readers who account for the text's literal information may still arrive at different interpretations. Eco is not, therefore, suggesting that a text can have only one possible reading but rather that some modes of reading represent more genuine engagement than others. We see, then, that for Eco there are limits both historically and in the present day to the power of text and reader, respectively. Although the text may push back against impertinent readings, it cannot, in Eco's view, actively support any one reading that accounts for the text's literal content as more appropriate than another.

This is because in the theoretical model of reading that Eco develops, what is at stake in the act of interpretation is not a flesh-and-blood reader or author but rather a model reader and a model author, two theoretical concepts that represent textual roles or functions.[66] The model author is not the person who wrote the text. Rather, it is what Eco calls a "textual strategy," a lingering trace of tone, ideology, or sociohistorical influence that hovers over the text's literal content.[67] Similarly, the model reader is the interpretive role that the text envisions for itself, a kind of imaginary audience that would be capable of engaging with the text in an idealized way, activating every code that the text presents and drawing on all necessary context rooted in culture, belief systems, and history.[68] Both the model reader and the model author, then, are abstract notions that underlie an interpretive exchange in which all roles contribute to the creation of meaning.

Nevertheless, as Citton asserts, flesh-and-blood readers are the ones who actually interpret texts in the real world, and their experiences should likewise inform our understanding of the reading process, especially if we seek to comprehend how interpretation can help change sociopolitical realities. Indeed, Citton foregrounds a concern for social justice in his account of the text-reader exchange through what he terms "actualizing readings," or interpretations in which readers project a certain amount of their own experience onto the text.[69] Although Eco expresses wariness toward this gesture, Citton views it as an unavoidable aspect of the reading process, especially when readers confront texts that hail from other times and places. For Citton, readers attempt to bridge the gap between their own experiences and those of the text by finding points of overlap. This gesture does not necessarily represent the mere "use" of a text according to Citton, however, since the text's difference—meaning its historical or cultural or ideological alterity—can prompt readers to consider new ideas and to understand that their current reality is relative, existing in a specific place and at a particular point in time. By demonstrating through its difference that nothing about the reader's society need be as it currently is, texts from other time periods can help flesh-and-blood readers uncover their own assumptions and envision new personal and social possibilities.

V. Conclusion

Part II will engage with Citton and Eco in greater detail by considering how Marguerite de Navarre's *Heptaméron* encourages a model of reading that reflects some of their ideas while challenging others. The queen's text can be read as participating in a larger project of reforming institutions and destructive societal norms, thus reinforcing the social justice angle that Citton privileges in his writing. Furthermore, the *Heptaméron* suggests through its literal content that it envisions a certain brand of model reader and also adopts an unexpected approach to the notion of the model author. However, unlike in Citton's and Eco's accounts of reading, the *Heptaméron* promotes a form of interpretation that acknowledges the labyrinthine nature of human experience, both in general and in Marguerite's challenging times, more specifically. The in malo themes of the fallen world, the difficulties of human life, and the challenging process of envisioning paths to reform converge with in bono meanings, such as admiration of the divine, persistent faith, and assurance of God's sovereignty, all of which inform the text's treatment of justice amid the realities of corrupt institutions.

As part II will show, the queen of Navarre's most famous text bases its understanding of the text-reader interaction on the assertion that scripture is "living and active" (Hebrews 4:12) and can shape the reader's thought life and behavior. Like scripture, the queen's text seeks to alter the thinking and comportment of those who encounter it, as part of the larger goal of fostering faith, justice, and reform. This process of transformation functions like the metaphorical pilgrimage of the Christian who journeys through life, the exegete who studies the Bible, or the individual who engages the labyrinth. However, I contend that to further the goal of transformation, the *Heptaméron* employs genres and the structure of the frame, rather than the stories' literal contents alone, as Eco would suggest.

In the évangéliques' view, the hope for a more just future is found in the grace of God and in the study of scripture through Augustinian hermeneutics. Indeed, the stories and debates that the *Heptaméron*'s readers encounter can be viewed as aiming not only to teach people how to distinguish between acceptable and unacceptable behaviors but also as training them to recognize the consequences of interpretation. By demonstrating how to combine a realistic outlook on the present with faith in positive change, the *Heptaméron* comes to incarnate what Nicolas Le Cadet has termed fictional evangelism.[70] The text suggests that exegesis has the potential to prompt individuals to work for justice in the world. As chapter 4 will argue, the text conveys this idea through scenes of wrongdoing that confront readers with the question of how to interpret what they behold—whether by sight alone or by the combination of sight and faith.[71] By depicting the fallen world and implicating readers in the sins they observe, the *Heptaméron* demonstrates the need to envision a path toward reform.

Part II

The *Heptaméron* as Textual Labyrinth

4

Into the Labyrinth

Mirroring Sin, Prompting Reform

The present chapter inaugurates part II of *The Visionary Queen* by building on the preceding analysis of Marguerite de Navarre's visionary endeavors, which intersect with the idea of the labyrinth and Reformation-era debates on pilgrimage and exegesis. Specifically, part II illuminates how the aforementioned topics converge in the *Heptaméron* (1559), the queen of Navarre's most famous work and a text that represents the culmination of her political, religious, and creative efforts throughout her life. As the previous chapters contended, it is in the *Heptaméron* that the three main factors of Marguerite's multifaceted identity work together to reveal most clearly her commitment to institutional reform. As a visionary, the queen of Navarre not only recognized the realities of the fallen world, which the faculty of sight made plain to her through scenes of suffering and injustice, but also sought to bring about a better future, drawing on the hopeful, if not utopian, vision that her faith provided. To show how the *Heptaméron* combines literal sight with a faith-based vision for justice and reform, part II will continue to engage with the idea of the labyrinth, arguing that the *Heptaméron* is a labyrinthine text in its thematic content and structure, as well as in the ways in which it invites the model reader to respond to the tales and debates.

Chapter 4 begins to work toward that goal by interrogating the *Heptaméron*'s depiction of sin and the fallen world. The present chapter thus focuses on the recognition of problems in the institutions of Marguerite's day and also in broader society. This groundwork is important because it helps to characterize trends in the text regarding the forms that corruption takes and why. Understanding the problems themselves proves crucial to any effort at problem-solving and must therefore precede discussions of reform efforts and strategies for promoting justice. Because chapter 4 examines the specific patterns of corrupt behavior within the Church, the aristocracy, and wider society, it examines the idea of the labyrinth in malo.

Rather than focusing on one particular format of labyrinth—whether unicursal or multicursal—the analysis in this chapter considers how the *Heptaméron*'s depiction of corruption implies in malo themes, such as sin, the fallen world, and earthly trials. While Marguerite's magnum opus depicts all of these in malo elements, it also develops a pro-woman critique of one in malo reading that is present in both the original myth of Theseus and in Giovanni Boccaccio's *Corbaccio*.[1] Rather than associating the labyrinth with a corrupting female sexuality, such as Pasiphae's lust for a bull, which led to the birth of the Minotaur, or the grotesque depiction of the widow's sexuality in Boccaccio's text, which cures the protagonist of his previous desire, the *Heptaméron* effects a reversal; it depicts female sexuality as the target of male institutional representatives, who threaten the social order as a result of *their* sexual wrongdoing.

Indeed, the queen of Navarre's text showcases how men in positions of power within the Church and aristocracy have a disproportionately negative impact on the institutions they represent and on wider society due, in large part, to their targeting of women's sexuality.[2] The present chapter contends that through repeated scenes of sexual abuse and injustice toward women, the *Heptaméron* not only asserts women's dignity and humanity but also frames institutional corruption and respect for women as matters of consequence for society as a whole. After all, the social order in Marguerite's era depended on women's sexuality in an obvious way. Their arranged marriages and offspring guaranteed political lineages, and their social and familial roles overlapped with Church sacraments, such as marriage and baptism. The *Heptaméron* thus suggests, in a subversive fashion, that male leaders ought to be as alarmed at sexual threats against women as women are, refrain from such behavior themselves, and seek to correct institutional ills. Women would clearly benefit significantly from such changes. In some cases, men could also benefit, as when both parties in a relationship would consent to consummation if social or religious dictates allowed. Ideology and more concrete forms of abuse coincide within the queen of Navarre's patriarchal society. The text can therefore be read as adopting a subversive approach to implicating male leaders, in addition to the Church and aristocracy more generally, in a vision for reform.

In directing the labyrinth's in malo themes toward institutional representatives, the *Heptaméron* functions as a mirror and therefore calls to mind the miroir, a literary genre that had existed throughout the Middle Ages and that Marguerite herself practiced in her *Miroir de l'âme pécheresse* (1531, 1533).[3] The mirror genre aimed to provide moral insights to readers by reflecting back to them some aspect of their own experience.[4] As Robert Cottrell asserts, the miroir has two primary sets of functions: to "reflect man's image back to him, revealing a creature that is base and sinful" and to "disclose the image of man as God would have him be, pure of heart and filled with charity."[5] Nancy Frelick adds that the mirror, as a more general symbol in the medieval and early modern world, was "associated with both self-improvement (moral edification or spiritual purification) and vanity (excessive pride and preoccupation with the self or worldly goods)."[6] In revealing both what is and what could or should be, the *Heptaméron* as miroir functions on the same symbolic plane as the labyrinth; but rather than simply gesturing toward problems that, in a Christian worldview, are common to all humanity, the queen's text seeks to make the contrast between worldly realities and spiritual ideals more personal and convicting for the reader.[7] In personalizing abundant and recurring scenes of injustice, Marguerite's text implicates readers in what they are witnessing, prompting them to consider whether what they behold may resemble aspects of their own behavior, or whether they may be guilty of a complacent attitude toward wrongdoing when they could in fact take a more active stance.

All of these mechanisms take on added significance when one considers that the prologue to the *Heptaméron* frames the stories the narrators tell as true tales. The stories' truthfulness can be interpreted in numerous ways.[8] For instance, one might interpret the phrase "true stories" to mean that the tales are based on true events or that they tell the truth of Marguerite's society and of human existence in a fallen world. The fact that the tales are called nouvelles, a phrase that means "news" in addition to short narratives, further underscores the prologue's claims to truth telling.[9] Still, the nouvelles are couched within a larger, literary frame of intricate design that gestures toward the queen of Navarre's extensive experience as a writer in many genres. Indeed, her corpus spans devotional poetry, dialogues, and plays in addition to the tales and debates in the *Heptaméron*. Although the *Heptaméron*'s prologue underscores the importance of truthfulness as an ideological value, this moral orientation need not be read as negating the literary quality of the text. It is helpful to consider on this point that for Marguerite, the gospel, or "good news,"[10] was true regardless of the style in which certain texts of the Bible were written. The gospel of John, for instance, which takes a more mystical and metaphorical tack than the synoptic gospels, would not have been deemed less truthful by Marguerite and her entourage because of its style or tone. One might argue that truthfulness is ultimately measured, in this context, by the underlying message and by the value placed on that true message rather than on elaborate or extensive description.[11] Eschewing wordiness can be considered a stylistic choice, one that opposes the *Heptaméron*'s values to those of Boccaccio's *Decameron*, as chapter 6 will contend. For now, suffice it to say that the claim of truthfulness functions ideologically and morally in the *Heptaméron* and that such functions factor into the queen of Navarre's artistic skill and strategic use of genre in the text.

Indeed, the *Heptaméron*'s emphasis on truthfulness supports the larger goal of reform by demonstrating the in malo realities of Marguerite's society across a large corpus of tales; as such, the methodology in this chapter combines the traditional approach of analyzing individual tales with a broader examination of statistical trends across the seventy-two stories. Like a labyrinth, the *Heptaméron* features many twists and variations; these could become overwhelming and contribute to an in malo sense of difficult process and trial if viewed at the level of individual stories, just as a person walking a labyrinth for the first time might experience, upon entering, a sense of disorientation and instability. However, it is noteworthy that these stories are subsumed within an overarching frame that holds them all together within a single artistic work. It is therefore important to adopt an analytical approach that accounts not only for the parts but also for the whole. When dealing with a lengthy and complex work with many components, such as the *Heptaméron*, one could easily miss larger tendencies in the work if one focuses only on individual stories. Analyses of individual tales can yield rich and valuable insights; however, they do not represent the full picture. In the *Heptaméron*, as in the labyrinth, both part and whole, process and product contribute to the overall effect of the work, as chapters 4 and 5 will likewise show.

Using this combined approach, chapter 4 begins by examining the miroir genre as practiced by Marguerite and by other writers whose work in that genre resonates with her own. This commentary prepares an analysis of how the miroir functions in conjunction with the labyrinth's in malo themes in the *Heptaméron* as part of a larger project to implicate the model reader in sights of injustice committed against women by individuals who represent institutions and their ideologies. The following section employs concepts from reception theories to consider how the text mirrors the sin of sexual misconduct in the aristocracy. Another section dealing with sexual wrongdoing in the Church then follows. Finally, the chapter concludes by considering how wrongful behaviors by male figures in these two institutions create toxic norms and ideologies that inform wider trends in the populace, across social classes.

I. Marguerite's Use of the Miroir Genre

As chapter 2 explained, one of Marguerite de Navarre's more famous works, apart from the *Heptaméron*, is her *Miroir de l'âme pécheresse*, for which the Sorbonne theology faculty attempted to censure her in 1533. The reason for the text's fame was the controversy it stirred up in conservative religious circles; it offended the theology faculty by referencing Clément Marot's French translation of the Psalms, a move toward the vernacular that the Sorbonne felt implied agreement with Martin Luther.[12] Although the text received an incendiary reaction, its engagement with an established literary genre, the miroir, did not necessarily garner the same level of attention. Yet, Marguerite's use of the miroir in this text proves important to our understanding of how her literary endeavor intersects with her faith and her experience of institutional politics. Although a full accounting of the text lies outside the scope of part II, which focuses on the *Heptaméron*, this section will show how the labyrinth's in malo themes inform Marguerite's *Miroir de l'âme pécheresse*. It will also provide commentary on the queen's sources of inspiration. The analysis will preview how these same labyrinthine themes take on a mirroring function in the *Heptaméron*.

At the outset to the *Miroir*, the narrator, or "the sinful soul," begins by citing Psalm 51, asking God to create in her a pure heart and thereby implying her need for God to rescue her from sin.[13] A striking component of Marguerite's *Miroir* is the way it employs themes commonly associated with in malo readings of the labyrinth to describe the inextricability of sin and the need for divine intervention in order to rescue humanity. Indeed, the text opens with a depiction of a hellish prison from which the narrator cannot escape, much as the original labyrinth in the story of Theseus served as a prison to house the Minotaur and much as the labyrinth in malo can represent imprisonment, sin, and even damnation:

> Où est l'enfer remply entierement
> De tout malheur, travail, peine, et torment?
> Où est le puitz de malediction
> Dont sans fin sort desesperation?

> (Where is that hell fraught with misery,
> suffering, pain, and torment?
> Where the pit of maledictions
> out of which emerges endless despair?)[14]

The sinful soul asks such questions because she feels she deserves condemnation and because the reality of her sin already torments her, creating for her a self-perpetuating prison from which she cannot escape. As a result of her distress, her existence is characterized by suffering, an in malo reading of the labyrinth, with its connotations of sinfulness and difficult process in a fallen world. She goes on to assert that her sins are so bountiful that she cannot begin to count them all and that even attempting to do so blurs her vision, casting her into further obscurity:

> Mes pechez . . . sont en si grand nombre
> Qu'infinitude rend si obscure l'ombre
> Que les compter ne bien veoir je ne puys
> Car trop avant avecques eulx je suis
>
> (So great in number are they [my sins]
> that the vastness blurs my vision
> so that I cannot see well enough to count them.
> I am overwhelmed)[15]

The blurring of the narrator's vision, combined with her allusions to shadows, infinitude, and her feeling of being overwhelmed, recall the experience of walking or tracing the labyrinth. In malo readings of the idea of the labyrinth find resonances here, but neither a unicursal nor a multicursal design type prevails. Instead, the narrator's diction can be read as blending aspects of each labyrinth type, with obscurity referring primarily to the multicursal model, which was known in Marguerite's time through the legend of Theseus, and the blurring of vision, which one might more readily associate with the twisting path of the unicursal labyrinth.

These in malo themes take on a gendered orientation as the text unfolds, moving from an initial expression of despair at the narrator's sin and inability to extricate herself from it to a metaphorical accounting of women's familial roles—such as sister, daughter, mother, and wife—and how these help the narrator understand her relationship to Christ.[16] The text draws on numerous biblical allusions to develop these familial analogies.[17] For the role of sister, the *Miroir* recounts the sin of Moses's sister Miriam, who was struck with leprosy for contesting the authority that God had granted Moses over the community.[18] It was Moses's prayer on her behalf that restored her to health.[19] To develop how motherhood relates to sin and grace, the narrator discusses how Solomon discovered the true mother of a baby when two women each claimed it was theirs. He suggested that the baby be cut in half so that each woman could have a portion. The baby's real mother was the one who was willing to let him go rather than see him killed.[20] The narrator likewise references the story of the prophet Hosea, who took back his wife after she had become a prostitute, to reflect how the married state in this story figures both sin and redemption.[21] To depict the vantage point of a daughter, the narrator reenvisions the story of the prodigal son.[22] By foregrounding the different relationships that women have to others in her society, the queen of Navarre adds a feminine vantage point to the Pauline and Augustinian discourses of the évangéliques.[23]

This gesture has surprising and subversive consequences when one considers the yoking of a corrupt female sexuality to the labyrinth in malo in the legend of Theseus. At first glance, the feminine and the labyrinth in malo appear to overlap in Marguerite's *Miroir*, but ultimately, the text can be said to rework an association that was established since the time of the Cretan myth and in the writings of Boccaccio. The text initially provides a measure of familiarity to male readers in their thinking about femininity and the in malo labyrinth, only to challenge that comfort by projecting them into a feminized position: that of the female narrator, or sinful soul. The female narrator makes her perspective the entry point into the text and into a larger, labyrinthine discussion of sin and grace that in the queen of Navarre's faith extended to all of humanity, both women and men. Instead of taking the masculine position as the norm, Marguerite's text requires that all readers see themselves and their sin reflected in the words of a female narrator. This feminization of the Christian vantage point has precedents in the book of Revelation, which calls the entire community of believers, both men and women, the "bride of Christ."[24] Here, the feminine functions according to a universalizing principle.[25] As such, sinfulness is not associated only or even especially with the feminine; instead, the feminine comes to represent the human condition, more generally, thus emphasizing women's complex humanity.

It is only Christ-Theseus, the harrower of hell, who can deliver the sinful soul of humanity from her prison.[26] Yet, the soul must still acquiesce to this guidance: "it cannot be saved by itself, nor yet without itself."[27] Cottrell adds that the ideal of what the soul becomes in Christ coexists with the reality of the soul's sinfulness without a savior and asserts that this combination is part of what makes Marguerite's miroir innovative.[28] It is worth noting that this same combination of elements—in malo and in bono—underlies the idea of the labyrinth. This overlap is especially appropriate when one considers, as Cottrell does, the interrelations among circularity, scripture, and Christ: "The notion that a circle can signify Christ is closely related to the idea of *orbs doctrinae Christianae*, or the belief that Scripture itself describes a circle and provides an exegesis of itself."[29] Circularity, in this sense, undergirds Augustinian exegesis, but it also alludes to the form of a physical mirror as well as to the traditionally circular shape of the unicursal labyrinth, yet another positive rethinking of connections between the labyrinth and the feminine.

The innovations that the queen of Navarre brings to the miroir genre build on a tradition of religious and political influences that subtend this literary form. In a religious vein, one might cite as a source of inspiration the *Miroir des âmes simples* by Marguerite Porete (1250–1310), a beguine nun who ran afoul of the Church authorities for her mystical exploration of divine love. Since the beguines did not take binding religious vows and could choose whether to embrace an active or contemplative life, they were not traditional nuns.[30] One senses this untraditional orientation in Porete's work. The deeply personal account of Christian spirituality that Porete provides foregrounds the progressive annihilation of the soul in the love of God, an aim that her text presents as more valuable than the Church's sacraments and authority. For this reason, the Church labeled the book heretical and burned its author alive.[31] Although Marguerite de Navarre fared far better against the ecclesiastical authorities when they objected to her *Miroir de l'âme pécheresse*, her text's personal form of devotion recalls Porete's earlier writings.

Given the queen of Navarre's position at the intersection of Church and state, it is important to note that the mirror genre encompassed politics as well as religion. A subset of the genre, called the mirror for princes, also marked the medieval and early modern literary landscape.[32] Just as the more religious mirror texts sought to instruct readers by implicating them in the text's contents, mirrors for princes provided guidance to leaders about how to govern. Within the context of Western Europe, the mirror for princes genre outlined appropriate forms of secular authority and their relation to Christian morality. Chapter 5 will examine a famous example that was contemporaneous to Marguerite: Erasmus's *The Education of a Christian Prince* (1516). However, given the queen's association with the évangéliques and her adoption of their Augustinian exegesis, which chapter 3 discussed, it is significant that Augustine's *The City of God* (426) also falls into the mirror for princes genre. Augustine's text develops the allegory of the city to comment on the differences between worldly mentalities and Christian ones, especially when it comes to governance and human society.[33] Although this text is important in part because it demonstrates the process of Augustinian exegesis, which acknowledges the confluence of literal and figurative readings of scripture,[34] it also interrogates how Christians ought to live in secular society and how the city of the world, which in its temporal focus encompasses the state, might be brought closer to the City of God.[35] Within Augustine's framework, the City of God denotes Jerusalem on a literal level, but on a figurative level, it evokes God's Kingdom. This symbolism reflects common associations between the labyrinth and major cities discussed in the Old Testament, most notably Jerusalem and Jericho;[36] however, it also recalls the concept of the "New Jerusalem" in the Book of Revelation. In Revelation we read that God's Kingdom, or the New Jerusalem, will be fully realized upon Christ's return[37] but that it began with the birth of Christian community and continues on through Christian outreach until the End Times. Meditating on such concepts, Augustine wrote shortly after the sack of Rome in the year 410 to address the crisis of governance that arose in his era. He suggested that since Rome was not, in fact, the "eternal city," a better city—God's city—should replace it in the minds of his contemporaries, and both leaders and members of Christian community should work toward that outcome.[38] As they do so, they resemble pilgrims en route to a holy city, foreigners in a fallen world.[39] Their experience of redemption and awareness of sin likewise call to mind the duality of the labyrinth. Yet as we will see, the *Heptaméron* can be said to take Augustine's treatment of the City of God and the city of the world in a new direction by adding a gendered component to discussions of religion, politics, and reform.

II. Reading Sights of Sin: Reception and the Mirror's Reflection

To show how the *Heptaméron*'s project of reform begins with sights of corruption that entail both old and new connections between the labyrinth *in malo* and discourses of gender, the ensuing analysis employs concepts from reception theorists Umberto Eco and Yves Citton, who discuss modern-day approaches to reading, in conjunction with the Augustinian exegesis that Marguerite practiced. Specifically, Eco's concept of the "model reader" will prove central. As chapter 3 discussed, the "model reader" is an interpretive position possessing the cultural and historical background to perform "the entire range of the interpretive actions the reader is encouraged or allowed to perform by the text."[40] This distinction permits nuanced interactions between twenty-first-century readers and early modern texts because, as Citton suggests, readers tend to project aspects of their experience onto earlier texts, but the historical and cultural differences that these texts reveal can also inspire readers to see the world in new ways and even espouse activist causes.[41]

The *Heptaméron* can be said to pursue that goal by attempting to transform individuals who can then work to reform society and its institutions.

The frame provides the ideological anchoring that the model reader needs to contemplate the in malo labyrinthine components of the text, and in so doing, it provides hints as to the model reader's identity. Specifically, the frame suggests that the model reader is familiar with sixteenth-century institutions and cultural norms, has a personal need for reforming, is aware of the tensions between spiritual ideals and worldly realities, and possesses the ability to effect change in Marguerite's society. That description could apply to members of either of the day's leading institutions: the aristocracy or the Church. This idea bears out in the audiences that the text depicts. First, there are the nobles, who actually tell the tales and who are completing a project set forth by François Ier and his companions. Their position in the text's foreground suggests that they are the primary intended audience. Second, there are the monks of Notre Dame de Sarrance, who sit behind the hedge and listen. They inhabit the background, and as such, they constitute a secondary audience.[42]

Through this process of bifurcation, the *Heptaméron* implies that due to the imbrication of Church and state in early modern France, it is interested in reaching members of both institutions, even if Marguerite, as an aristocrat, attempted to harness her influence on behalf of the évangéliques and thereby promote reform.[43] The *Heptaméron*'s model reader can thus be said to fill the role of an institutional representative, since he or she belongs to an institution and can be interpreted as reflecting its priorities. Even though aspects of the text suggest a single model reader—one with the potential to reshape institutions—members of the Church and aristocracy alike can fulfill that role. Since men and women both comprise the institutions that the *Heptaméron* critiques, both can function as model readers, but the instances of corruption that the text seeks to correct through its mirroring are perpetuated by men against women. This means that while women can derive a sense of defiant self-worth and dignity in response to wrongful behavior toward female characters in the stories, the text lays particular blame at the feet of male leaders and seeks to prompt them toward self-examination and change.

Analysis of statistical trends across the *Heptaméron*'s seventy-two tales provides useful insights into this phenomenon and will prepare more in-depth examinations of how the text mirrors the need for reform to clergy and aristocrats through its in malo allusions. All of the *Heptaméron*'s tales deal in some manner with human sin and the reality of the fallen world. Some do so by depicting egregious forms of wrongdoing, such as rape or murder, whereas others foreground infidelity and trickery. Regardless of the storyteller's attitude to the tale he or she tells, the contents reflect the realities of human society and its institutions in the queen of Navarre's day. As in Marguerite's life, religion, politics, and social class often overlap in the stories. This means that in some instances, a perpetrator of sexual wrongdoing who hails from the Church or the aristocracy may assail or otherwise harm a noblewoman, and in others he may attack a bourgeoise, a nun, or a woman of modest means. It is therefore possible to organize certain tales in multiple ways according to the types of characters involved. For instance, the first tale in the collection involves a proctor, a bishop, a lieutenant's son, and a noblewoman, demonstrating the confluence of different life stations and ideological influences in Marguerite's tales. Deciding how to categorize wrongdoing in each story thus involves a measure of interpretation, and several different organizational models could prove valid.

However, this chapter is focused primarily on how the *Heptaméron* depicts the inappropriate behavior of male institutional representatives toward women and thereby gestures toward the need for reform. Consequently, the following overview is organized according to the institution or, failing that, the social class of the perpetrator(s) or in some cases, the source of a toxic ideology. Attempts to categorize the tales recognize their plasticity while also seeking out connections to the institutions of Marguerite's day and the ideologies they perpetuate. After all, the patriarchal order and its efforts to control women's sexuality ultimately structure the queen's stories, either by depicting male perpetrators who plot sexual assault or by refusing women's sexual agency and fulfillment through aristocratic social mores and Church practices.

To begin, it is significant to note that of the seventy-two tales, all but four deal with women's sexuality or sexual roles in some way.[44] Although it would be impractical to describe every tale individually, this section provides an analysis of trends to facilitate examinations of individual tales and their interrelations. For their reference, readers will find lists in this paragraph's endnotes of all the tales that fall under the headings of the aristocracy, the Church, or wider society. Looking at the sixty-eight stories that depict scenarios involving female sexuality, one finds that the majority of them—thirty-seven, when one takes institutions as the primary organizing principle—portray injustice perpetuated either by noblemen or patriarchal aristocratic mores.[45] Several of these tales involve inappropriate sexual behavior not only between aristocrats but also by noblemen toward characters from other social classes. Of the remaining thirty-one tales, seventeen highlight sexual wrongdoing perpetrated by male clergy.[46] Some of these nouvelles involve nuns, while others involve noblewomen or women of modest means. The last fourteen tales focus on characters from the bourgeoisie or from working milieus as well as those who provide services to the aristocracy, and the ways in which women's sexuality is targeted in those contexts.[47] Although as previously stated, there is some overlap between these main categories, they will nevertheless help provide a basic organizational schema to an analysis of how the *Heptaméron*'s stories reflect back to institutional leaders both the fallen world and the need for reform, two themes associated with the idea of the labyrinth and the *miroir* genre, as practiced by Marguerite.

III. Mirroring Sin in the Aristocracy

Turning first to the tales that foreground the aristocracy, we see that the *Heptaméron* implicates the nobility in its depictions of sin and sexual wrongdoing and thereby prepares to contradict the associations between the labyrinth *in malo* and female sexuality that this learned class of people might possess. In tales with aristocratic perpetrators, one finds stories of attempted or completed rape. In tale 4, for instance, the princess of Flanders fights off a nobleman who breaks into her bedroom at night. In the famous tale 10, Floride discovers the perfidy of Amadour, a charming knight who eventually tries to assault her. Lord Bonnivet demonstrates similar violence when, in story 14, he rapes a Milanese woman who once refused his advances, taking her lover's place at a late-night tryst. Story 62 also recounts how a nobleman rapes a woman who had rejected him, sneaking into her bedroom while she is sleeping. In addition to stories of sexual violence, aristocratic characters face injustice in the form of ideological interdiction. Story 40, for example, recounts how a young aristocratic couple live happily for several years after their clandestine marriage until the wife's brother discovers the pair together and takes vengeance by killing the husband, whom he deemed an insufficient match due to his lesser rank.[48] Although the couple had gotten married, they had done so without their families' approval and had thus flaunted aristocratic social mores.

The issue of arranged marriage underlies much suffering in the *Heptaméron*, highlighting the ways in which patriarchal imperatives can function in tandem with an unjust and fallen world to create situations from which women cannot easily extricate themselves. In many tales, the power that relatives wield over marital prospects causes grave injustice, either by establishing unsuitable matches which then lead to infidelity or by denying couples the ability to marry when they would otherwise choose to do so.[49] A well-known example in the latter class is story 21, in which Rolandine cannot openly marry the man she loves but instead finds herself locked in a remote castle, during which time her beloved betrays her.[50] Tale 19 also features a lovestruck pair who cannot marry. In the end, both the story's heroine, Pauline, and her suitor enter religious orders because the only solution to their anguish is to sublimate their love in the worship of God. Story 50 tells how a suitor undergoes bloodletting to treat his lovesickness before finally receiving his beloved's consent, but weakened by loss of blood, he dies not long after consummation.[51] In story 43, a noblewoman who desires to be known as chaste develops feelings for a man at court and carries on a secret affair with him on the condition that she will conceal her identity and he can never seek to know it. Their sexual encounters, though physically gratifying, are nevertheless alienating since the woman can only access her lover in a distant way, forgoing relational intimacy and risking her social standing.

While all of these tales highlight human sin and suffering, two components of the labyrinth in malo, they also identify women's sexuality as a prize for noblemen, a bargaining chip for aristocratic families, and a barrier for women themselves. The complex rendering of women's sexuality in the tales formulates an implicit challenge to the connections between the labyrinth and female depravity in mythology. In the *Heptaméron*, the stability of the social order depends on women and their sexuality, and yet the wrongful behavior of noblemen combines with self-sabotaging social mores to threaten female sexuality and promote corruption.

A closer analysis of tales 62, 19, and 43, in particular, will reveal how patriarchal social mores in the aristocracy harm women by rendering their sexuality off-limits, not only to men but to women themselves. This gesture prompts abusive, covetous behavior in male predators, who seek to obtain what appears unattainable. In so doing, they engage in duplicitous practices that recall the labyrinth in malo, much as Pasiphae constructed a false cow in which to accost the bull, and much as Daedalus constructed the labyrinth to conceal Pasiphae's shameful progeny. Story 62 provides insights into such forms of deceit. Moreover, tales 19 and 43 serve as examples of a larger trend in the *Heptaméron*, which is that women must either accept a lack of sexual fulfillment, even going so far as to remove themselves from aristocratic society, or blatantly transgress their class's expectations of them in order for their needs to be met.

Beginning with tale 62, we see how alienating women from their own sexuality represents an attempt to maintain patriarchal dominance, in this case through the conflict between the aristocratic mores of female chastity and masculine combativeness. In the story, a young wife rebuffs a courtier who solicits her for adulterous sex over the course of several years. Despite his persistent harassment, she rejects his advances to demonstrate her virtue. In response, the perpetrator concocts a plan to attack his victim while she is sleeping.[52] He sneaks into the woman's bedroom without bothering to remove his spurs, a detail that suggests his violent intent, his militaristic viewpoint, and his intention to make a quick getaway.[53] Because his fear at being discovered blends with his adherence to a conquest-based masculinity, he uses scare tactics in an attempt to force compliance. His efforts succeed; the young woman freezes in shock when she detects the presence of an unauthorized male. Whereas noblewomen in other tales sometimes fend attackers off physically, such as in tale 4, or call for help, as in tale 10, the woman in story 62 attempts to reason with the would-be rapist in the hope that he will desist.[54] When her attacker threatens to tell everyone about her lost chastity if she resists, she decides that it is better to forfeit her chastity in secret than resist, fail, and suffer social ridicule when her failure becomes known.

Ironically, the damoiselle's wish to avoid public humiliation ends up causing her disgrace since she later recounts what happened, framing it as an anonymous tale during a storytelling session at court. On one level, telling her story would seem to offer an opportunity for self-assertion, but unfortunately, when she slips up and uses the first person, thereby identifying herself with the events she is recounting, her listeners suspect that she must have actually consented to the man's behavior because she had not hesitated to talk about it.[55] We see that the text depicts aristocratic society as considering female sexuality to be exploitable and shame inducing, thereby encouraging women to internalize misogynistic discourses, live in fear, and alienate themselves from their bodies and their agency rather than risk ostracization.

Tale 19 presents another example of a woman who has to accept alienation from her sexual agency in order to comply with aristocratic dictates. In the story, a young noblewoman named Pauline falls in love with a nobleman. Neither she nor the nobleman possesses considerable wealth by aristocratic standards, and her family members point out that the match would prove financially unwise. Rather than make her wishes known, Pauline abides by the notion that aristocratic women should obey their families' directives regarding the marriage market. Still, she knows in her heart what her preference is and thus reveals that she does in fact possess personal and sexual agency. What we see in Pauline is not the absence of will but the suppression of it. After a time of military service, her suitor returns and asks her family for her hand in marriage. They refuse, again citing financial motivations, and to further discourage his pursuit, they forbid him from seeing Pauline again, allowing him only one last conversation.[56] Discouraged, he informs Pauline that he intends to enter religious orders because he cannot marry her. Even when the gentleman shares the depth of his sorrow at being unable to marry her, Pauline does not permit herself to speak openly with him because she does not believe she can express her love for him; in fact, the text indicates that she faints with grief because she was "honteuse" ("overcome with shame") at having revealed strong emotions along with a will that society tells her she should not possess.[57] In the end, she finds a creative, but chaste, means of subverting patriarchal limitations; after dissimulating her intentions for many months, she takes the veil so as to at least remain in the company of her beloved, even if they cannot marry.

From this choice comes the *Heptaméron*'s well-known discussion of *parfaicte amitié* or "perfect friendship." In the debate the story generates, Parlamente—an outspoken female storyteller—explains that she thinks the couple illustrates the notion of parfaicte amitié since they base their love on virtue.[58] As Émile Telle notes, the emphasis on virtue as the source of love rather than beauty combines with the tale's religious backdrop to "translate" Neoplatonic love into a Christian moral context.[59] This context permits Pauline to convey her love for the gentleman, but she cannot consummate her desire for him.[60] Even in the solution she finds, she remains alienated from her body within a patriarchal order that views women as prizes, nuns, procreators, or lust personified.

That last representation features in story 43, which describes the deeds of a noblewoman named Camille who develops a reputation for austerity. Whereas other married women accept the advances of *serviteurs*, Camille expresses disdain for such practices. In reality, however, she harbors a secret attraction toward a nobleman and works out an arrangement in which he may sleep with her as long as he never seeks to discover her identity.[61] Eventually, Camille's lover breaks his promise by marking her shoulder with a piece of chalk so that he can identify her after their rendezvous.[62] In uncovering Camille's identity, the nobleman obtains a position of power over her; he possesses the ability to conceal their affair or reveal it. When he approaches Camille to tell her he has discovered her secret, she denies everything: "Avez vous jamais ouy dire, que j'aye eu amy ne serviteur?" ("Have you ever heard of my having a lover, of my having any man devote himself to my service?").[63] Because of the nobleman's persistence, Camille decides to report him to her mistress, who banishes him from the grounds. In the end, Camille's behavior harms both her and her lover; she loses him, and he endures humiliation.

The *devisants'* analysis of Camille's story shows that the tensions between the two characters arise from the importance afforded to social standards for gendered behavior. Camille insists on her supposed chastity because she wants others to see her as conforming to societal expectations. She cares more about social prestige than about fidelity, as Guebron asserts at the debate's outset.[64] Of course, the difficulty is that Camille could never have been assured of sexual fulfillment in her society. Arranged marriages operated politically, and although families technically sought the consent of both parties, women were expected to obey their relatives' will when it came to the choice of a partner. This limitation explains why many of Camille's female friends have serviteurs. Her struggle is not with unbridled lust, but rather with an overall lack of sexual fulfillment and the absence of a socially sanctioned means of resolving her dilemma. She engages in deception not because she wants to be duplicitous or because her desire necessarily exceeds that of other women but because she acknowledges both her desire and the power that aristocratic ideologies have over her social standing.[65] In the end, she chooses sexual agency over alienation from the body, but unfortunately, this is not a choice that her society permits her to make in good conscience. Consequently, she cannot, in the eyes of her peers, be both a good woman and a sexually fulfilled one, unless she had been so lucky as to marry a man she found attractive and well suited.

The cases of Camille, Pauline, and the unnamed woman in tale 62 provide detailed reflections of aristocratic realities that, when coupled with statistical trends in the text, reveal both the importance of female sexuality to the social order and the threats against it.[66] Unlike in the tale of Theseus, these threats do not come from women themselves but rather from male-run institutions and the ideas they disseminate. Patriarchal ideology, as funneled through the aristocracy, seeks to fit women into roles that separate them from sexual desire and fulfillment, even within the Church-sanctioned confines of marriage. Whether as nuns, rape survivors, or wives and mothers, the text implies that female characters are expected to perpetuate the patriarchal structures in which they live. Married female characters certainly engage in sexual activity, but the concepts of duty and obedience mean that marriage does not necessarily entail fulfillment or agency. The irony is that women's role in sixteenth-century French society depended on reproduction, yet even their ability to fulfill the role that patriarchy imposed on them was threatened by patriarchal ideologies and codes of behavior.

Here, the *Heptaméron* holds up a mirror to the nobility to show them the conundrum they have created, one that foregrounds sin, fallenness, and suffering. Although Marguerite de Navarre, as an aristocratic author and a devout Christian, would not likely have suggested any ideological shifts that would have overthrown her own social class or the institution of marriage, her text's emphasis on female sexuality as a target for various forms of abuse suggests the need for reflection and reform. The stories make evident that women suffer from the current arrangement, but they also demonstrate to noblemen that even they, as the dominant members of patriarchy, fail to benefit as much as they might hope. From infidelities to thwarted marriages to destructive behaviors, the aristocracy's attempts to deny and control female sexuality end up hurting everyone in one way or another. Consequently, the text implies that noblemen ought not only to see themselves in the stories' male characters but ought also to care on a personal level about these issues, which harm women most but which harm men as well in a secondary way. The text also suggests that the nobility as a whole should consider whether they are contributing to the city of the world, analogous to the fallen world, or to the City of God, in which leaders attempt to bring the fallen world into closer alignment with God's plans for redemption. In so doing, they can take meaningful steps toward the City of God as metaphorical pilgrims of the Lord, a journey that the labyrinth embodies.

IV. Mirroring Sin in the Church

Another influential group in Marguerite's time that could promote the City of God and that supposedly existed for that purpose was the clergy. The *Heptaméron* treats the clergy as a significant yet secondary audience, an unsurprising gesture given that Marguerite, as an aristocrat, helped advance the cause of the évangéliques. Much as in the case of tales about the aristocracy, stories about wrongdoing by the clergy depict many forms of abuse that attack female sexuality and that call into question the traditional in malo associations between women and the labyrinth. Some tales involve overt sexual violence whereas others entail exploitation, coercion, or the direction of Church practices and ideologies toward nefarious aims.

As previously mentioned, seventeen of the sixty-eight tales that highlight threats to female sexuality show the Church abusing women in some way. In tale 5, for instance, a pair of friars threaten to rape a ferrywoman if she refuses to sleep with them. Thankfully, the woman has a support system and manages to trick the friars into waiting behind while she gets help, but the clergy's wrongdoing toward the poor reveals particular hypocrisy, given that this is a group that the scriptures instruct them to assist. Women of all social classes and life situations keep a wary eye on the clergy in the *Heptaméron*'s tales. In story 41, for instance, a priest attempts to sexually abuse a young noblewoman during confession, claiming that he will not absolve her unless she does as he says. The young woman's mother intervenes and ensures justice. In story 11, we see an allegorical rendering of sexual violence and the corrupting influence of the clergy when Mme de Roncex emerges from a filthy monastery privy with excrement all over her dress and backside.[67] Women of middling means also feature in tales of clerical malfeasance. In story 23, a clergyman rapes a woman by impersonating her husband. She commits suicide when she discovers what has transpired, accidentally kicking and killing her baby in the process. Another Church official tries to kidnap a woman in tale 31 and take her back to the monastery, where he and his peers have locked away a whole slew of sexual abuse victims.[68] Not even family or fellow religious are safe from the clergy's behavior. Tale 33 recounts how a clergyman impregnates his own sister and then tells her to claim that she is a second iteration of the Virgin Mary. Moreover, in tales 22 and 72, churchmen attempt to coerce and assault nuns. Whether women are married or unmarried, secular or religious, related or unrelated, wealthy or poor, the clergy target their sexuality for abusive purposes.

The dynamics underlying this mistreatment differ in many ways from those that motivate wrongdoing in the aristocracy. Given that in the Catholic tradition, religious officials cannot marry, sexual relationships of any kind should, in theory, be out of the question for them. In interpreting Paul's statements concerning marriage or singleness at a time in which the early Christians thought Jesus's return was imminent,[69] the Church associated religious devotion with celibacy. Marriage, while not a sin, was considered inferior to a life subsumed in the love and the work of the Lord. Of course, Marguerite's *Heptaméron* has been read as revalorizing marriage, even if, unlike Luther, she never stated outright the idea that clergy ought to marry.[70] Instead, her *Heptaméron* examines the problem that the Church has created in presenting some people as more spiritual and less human than others. Since in Marguerite's *Comédie de Mont-de-Marsan* we learn that for the évangéliques, human experience is both physical and spiritual, the denying of one half of human reality facilitates sin and disorderly conduct.[71]

As the *Heptaméron* itself asserts, "le peché forge l'occasion" ("sin manufactures the occasion") and not the other way around.[72] This means that the clergy's assertion of celibacy and their partial removal from secular life do not erase their potential for sin. Perhaps that is a reason why in the tale 37 debate, Oisille praises the married state, despite the many heartaches it can bring, especially in a society in which marital contracts were often more political than personal.[73] None of this is to say that Marguerite sought to completely overhaul the Church hierarchy. In her real-life reform efforts, her approach was to replace clergy who behaved poorly with those whom the évangéliques had vetted for their character. Much as in the case of the aristocracy, the *Heptaméron* does not advocate tabula rasa but rather reform and improvement. Holding up a mirror so that Church officials may contemplate their misdeeds more readily and understand the ways in which they are failing their mission constitutes the first step in that process. Through its mirror effect, the *Heptaméron* suggests that the clergy are no less human than secular individuals and that they, too, are on a pilgrimage to the City of God, passing through a land of worldly mentalities and temptations. To arrive at their destination unscathed and to bring the institution they serve closer to the City of God, they will need to acknowledge their full humanity and accept that the in malo connotations of the labyrinth, as well as the need for redemption, apply as much to them as to their parishioners. A closer look at stories 5, 41, and 22 will illuminate these tendencies while also demonstrating that the *Heptaméron* can be said to communicate a threat to clergy who refuse to examine and correct their ways.

In tale 5, two Franciscan friars ask a ferrywoman to transport them across the river. When the boat takes off, they begin to press her for sex, threatening to throw her into the water if she resists. She shrewdly tells the friars that she will gladly sleep with them one at a time, each on a separate island. Once they set foot on their respective islands, she returns to town, gathers her husband and male legal authorities, and brings them back to punish the friars. The threat of punishment by laypeople proves extremely intimidating for them, so much so that they tremble to the point of feeling "demy morts" ("half dead").[74] The ferrywoman's story suggests a number of ideas about ecclesiastical corruption and Church reform. First, we see that secular authorities are needed to counterbalance the Church's power. In the absence of obstacles to corruption, the friars pursue evil aims, hence the importance of a strong and effective judicial system. Moreover, tale 5 suggests that secular Christians should support and protect one another and that men can serve as allies to women in this process. The legal authorities are men, as is the ferrywoman's husband, and it is this group that succeeds in punishing the friars.[75] Interestingly, lay Christians, when unified in purpose, achieve far greater justice and righteousness in the tale than the clergy. Here, we find a nod to Marguerite's advocacy on behalf of the évangéliques. Finally and building on that last point, it is a woman who acts as the catalyst for justice by resisting and exposing the friars' misdeeds.[76]

As a working woman, the story's heroine would have been considered an easy target by men of all social classes during her era, yet the story says that with God's assistance, she obtains the victory, and justice is won.

Tale 41 lends further support to the notion that God favors those who act rightly and will intervene on behalf of women who resist clerical abuse. In the story, a priest tells a girl that he cannot absolve the sins she enumerated during confession unless she agrees to wear the cord from his habit against her naked body. When the girl suspects he intends to violate her, she flees. When she tells her mother what happened, the latter deduces the priest's intent and develops a plan for punishing him. In the meantime, she exhibits her capacity to restore ecclesiastical order by finding an upright clergyman to hear her daughter's confession. The mother proves her capacity to direct her daughter's spiritual life, since "where the corrupt patriarchal institution excludes the young woman from communion and community, a maternal intervention reconciles her daughter with God, with the church, 'la mere saincte Eglise,' and with the community of women who 'receurent toutes ensemble.'"[77] As a countess, the heroine in tale 41 also possesses the authority to chastise wayward religious officials. In an ironic reversal, she forces the priest to do penance for the penalty he had attempted to impose on the girl, such that the scandal he tried to perpetrate rebounds on him. Eventually, he confesses to his attempted crime "à force de verges" ("under the hail of blows").[78] Mary McKinley rightly points out in her reading of this tale that the term *verge* means "penis" in addition to "rod."[79] The same organ with which he intended to assault the young woman, and the same symbol of patriarchal power, becomes the cause and symbolic instrument of his humiliation. Moreover, the mother underscores her influence by sending him back to his superior "pieds et mains liez" ("bound hand and foot") and urges the latter to exercise greater care in selecting preachers.[80]

Unlike in story 5, the mother and her daughter do not have recourse to male allies in the wider community, likely because their aristocratic rank affords them greater authority on their own than the ferrywoman enjoyed. Yet like the ferrywoman, the daughter and her mother suggest that sincere Christians should assist each other in combatting ecclesiastical corruption and that even those whom society views as less powerful, such as women, can prevail through God's support of their cause. Tale 41 implies, then, that the patriarchal institution of the Church ought to support, and not threaten, the wider community of believers. In an era of schism, the idea that unity and purity should be the aims of both the congregation and the officials who lead it echoes Marguerite's own commitment to Church reform.

A final tale of clerical corruption shows the urgency of the reform efforts for which Marguerite advocated, as it demonstrates that the Church risks undermining its own practices, hierarchical systems, and even authority when it threatens women. The clergyman in nouvelle 22 attacks a nun, not a layperson, and he does so within the confines of a convent. Even an exclusively female community cannot escape abuse by male religious officials. The tale reinforces the idea that clergy should examine their motives intensely, lest they fall into sin, since the would-be rapist in the story begins his career as a respected Church official, known as "le pere de vraye religion" ("the father of true monasticism").[81] With time, he becomes proud and falls into a life of indulgence, seeking out naive nuns to seduce.[82]

Unfortunately for him, he underestimates one nun in particular, Marie Héroët, who ends up exposing his predatory pastime. Before Marie achieves the victory, however, she must contend with a man bent on rape. The prior imitates the noblemen in the *Heptaméron*'s many tales of aristocratic abuse toward women, approaching Marie with the language of courtly love. He delivers "plusieurs propos de la grande amitié qu'il luy portoit" ("a few words about his great love for her") as a prelude to what he hopes will be a seduction scene.[83] He then follows his words with actions that reveal his true motivation: "luy voulut mettre la main au tetin" ("[He] tried to put his hand on her breasts").[84] By rendering the attacker's actions more anatomically explicit than they are in many tales, story 22 depicts the clergyman as especially vicious due to his moral hypocrisy. Marie fights him off before fainting when he scratches her. Before he can rape her, the abbess returns, and when Marie regains consciousness, the prior claims that his extreme love forced him to behave the way he did. After numerous vindictive acts on the prior's part as well as courageous speeches by the embattled nun, Marie obtains justice and vindication when her brother informs her mother of what has been happening.[85] As a result, the king acts as an agent of justice, punishing the errant prior and promoting Sister Marie to the rank of abbess.[86] The tale thus implies that those who put their trust in God, like Marie, will emerge victorious. It also suggests that the clergy have nefarious reasons for self-isolating since if they did not do so, laypeople would witness their hypocrisy. As the female storyteller Nomerfide puts it, "moins on les voit, moins on les cognoist" ("the less you see of them, the less you know about them").[87] Highlighting the divergence between spiritual ideals and worldly realities in the clergy's behavior toward women, the *Heptaméron* invites Church officials to perceive their sin in the textual mirror.

Although in the tales mentioned here, the clergymen do not succeed in their ill-meaning pursuits, in other tales, they do, and as a result, a male model reader who hails from the Church has the opportunity to see in himself the potential for serious harm. The text prompts model readers to respond by more earnestly promoting the City of God and becoming metaphorical pilgrims who walk through the fallen world with care, much as the in malo symbolism of the labyrinth, a fixture in many cathedrals, would have reminded them to do. This is a purpose they can share in common with the aristocracy, which accepts the Church's religious teachings. As in Marguerite's life, we see the inevitable overlap of politics and religion and the translation of that dynamic into creative endeavor.

V. Mirroring Sin in Wider Society

In its mirroring of the labyrinth in malo, the *Heptaméron* portrays the aristocracy as its primary intended audience and the Church as its secondary audience, but it also includes stories that uncover threats to female sexuality in other social classes. Some of the tales considered in previous sections began to gesture toward this fact; tale 5, for instance, featured a working woman. However, this section will deal specifically with perpetrators who hail from the bourgeoisie or working class.

Of the sixty-eight tales that portray physical or ideological threats to women's sexuality, fourteen involve characters from outside the Church and aristocracy. In tale 2, for instance, a mule driver's wife engages in physical combat with her attacker until he stabs and rapes her. Tale 8 explains how a man named Bornet, who takes an interest in his chambermaid, attempts to sleep with her. His wife tricks him by taking the maid's place, but unfortunately, Bornet promises the maid to his friend as well, and his wife winds up sleeping with this other man without even realizing it. Tale 45 likewise entails sexual deception, as a tapestry maker tells his wife he is going to beat his maid but then rapes her instead; the wife pays no attention to the maid when she cries, as she thinks the girl is being punished for her poor service. In story 36, the president of Grenoble harbors resentment toward his wife for an affair she once had. Pretending to forgive her, he lulls her into a false sense of security and then feeds her a poisonous salad that kills her. Gruget's tale 44 recounts the story of two young bourgeois. The man and woman desire to marry but must wait for a time, and so the man presses the woman for sex. She does not explicitly consent, but the man imposes himself on her anyway when they enter a garden where they are well concealed, much as they would be in a garden labyrinth, although the tale does not specify that detail.[88] The presence of sexual wrongdoing toward women in every class of society highlights the wide-ranging nature of this injustice and the need to redress it.

Given that the most literate people in Marguerite's time were not those of lesser means but rather the aristocrats and the clergy, we can surmise that the text's primary and secondary audiences would have been in a more likely position to receive these tales than the members of the depicted classes. This detail is important because it suggests that the text invites the clergy and aristocracy to consider themselves implicated in the malfeasance they perceive among bourgeois and working people. Although they do not self-identify with these social groups, their role as leaders can nevertheless prompt them to consider the impact of the institutions they comprise and the norms those institutions promote. Together, the Church and the aristocracy guide the whole of Marguerite's society, and although sin and the fallen world are universally human problems in a Christian worldview, they also thrive most when those in positions of authority misuse their power. The *Heptaméron* convicts leaders of the same sins as those to whom they might like to consider themselves superior. Moreover, the text implies that rather than take pride in their station, aristocrats and Church officials should feel shame and responsibility for the impact their failures might be said to have on wider society.

We see the negative influence of the aristocracy and the Church on other classes especially clearly in stories 2 and 45. In tale 2, religious and political ideologies converge to glorify aristocratic concepts of gendered behavior, framing chastity as saintly and masculine conquest as inevitable. When, in tale 2, the mule driver's wife awakes because she detects her attacker's presence in her bedroom, she realizes that she cannot embody the feminine "virtues" of silence and obedience and maintain her chastity—the chief feminine virtue of her day—at the same time. She therefore fights back verbally and physically. In disobeying the assailant, she feels she is proving her obedience to God, whom she calls "sa force, sa vertu, sa patience et chasteté" ("my strength, my virtue, my suffering and my chastity").[89] One sees from this phrasing that the protagonist conflates chastity, an aristocratic mandate for women, with religious devotion, an unsurprising transposition given that the Church imposed celibacy on its officials. By story's end, the heroine has sacrificed her life in the defense of her chastity since the attacker stabs her in order to immobilize and rape her. As she lies dying, she addresses a prayer to God that reveals that she views her actions as self-sacrificial because she believes that preserving her chastity at all costs honors God. She prays that God would accept her blood, which she believes she is shedding "en la reverence de celuy de son fils" ("in veneration of the blood of His Son").[90] As if this prayer did not sufficiently reveal the mixing of ideologies, the townswomen gather to pay the woman homage after her death, calling her a martyr of chastity.[91] This is an interesting reaction given that the martyrs whom the Church honored were those who died rather than abdicate their faith, not those who proved faithful to societal standards.

The fact that neither the story's protagonist nor the women who admire her can tell the difference between the sacred and the political implies that ecclesiastical and aristocratic discourses have become muddled as they have filtered down to the less wealthy classes. As a result, individuals like the mule driver's wife are replacing genuine religious devotion with man-made rules, a tendency for which the Catholic Church came under fire during the Protestant Reformation. This is likely because religious and social dictates overlapped for the aristocracy as well. Indeed, as Elizabeth Chesney Zegura notes, no debate follows tale 2, and the frame narrator presents the listening noblewomen as admiring the story's protagonist.[92] If, in the queen of Navarre's eyes, the aristocracy ought to reform the Church and the two institutions ought to better society, they are clearly failing in that mission due in part to their unclear values. The mirror of the *Heptaméron* seeks to make this problem known to them.

Story 45 likewise demonstrates that the influence of patriarchy filters down in a toxic way to the lower classes through the norms that the aristocracy and the Church endorse. In the tale, a tapestry maker devises a plan to rape his chambermaid, using a Church feast day and a local cultural practice as a joint excuse. He takes as his context the Feast of the Holy Innocents, which the Catholic Church still marks on December 28. The feast day commemorates how Herod, having learned of the birth of Jesus, attempted to secure his death by ordering the massacre of young children. Nicole Cazauran explains that in Normandy, this occasion blended with the Feast of Fools, meaning that trickery became a common practice. More specifically, workers would wake early in the day and chastise those who slept in by surprising them in their beds and whipping them for their supposed laziness.[93] The corrupt husband in the tale claims that he finds the chambermaid lazy and so proposes to his wife that he should beat her on the feast day. His wife, whom the tale presents as gullible, accepts the plan.[94] The tapestry maker prepares sticks as if he is going to beat the maid, but he rapes her instead. When the maid complains to her mistress, the latter replies that she had sanctioned what her husband had done, so the maid did not dare to raise the matter again, even when the errant husband accosted her repeatedly. Not only does he force adulterous and nonconsensual sex on the chambermaid, but he then takes her outside in the snow, such that the neighbor witnesses his infidelity firsthand. To create a cover story, the tapestry maker takes his wife out in the snow afterward, such that when the neighbor confronts her, she replies that it was she, and not the maid, whom the neighbor had witnessed.

As with the other tales in the collection, story 45 foregrounds themes that recall the labyrinth in malo, all while suggesting the need to rethink associations between those themes and female sexuality. On a literal level, this story depicts marital infidelity, rape, and indecent public exposure while also demonstrating how this behavior harms women. On a metaphorical level, however, the tale represents the profound state of corruption into which wider society has fallen, surpassing the concept of the fallen world to encompass political and religious discourses of Marguerite's day. We see that the text creates a sense of horror and disgust via the perspective of the neighbor, who witnesses the husband's public sexual encounters and who is "si courroucée, qu'elle se delibera de le dire à sa bonne commere" ("so angry that she made up her mind to tell her good neighbour all about it").[95] In addition to depravity, the tapestry maker betrays certain attitudes toward power. First, although he lacks the prestige and authority that noblemen and clergy possess, he rages against his lesser status through an excessive display of dominance when he rapes (and pretends to beat) the chambermaid. This attitude suggests that he believes having authority entails intimidating others into compliance and getting away with one's misdeeds. Unfortunately, given the plethora of stories about churchmen and aristocrats who attack women's sexuality, the tapestry maker's beliefs about power do, in fact, reflect the abuses that institutions in his time perpetuate.

Moreover, much as in story 2, we see that the protagonist confuses religion and sociopolitical norms. At its core, the practice of whipping those who fail to rise early suggests that certain people exist solely to work—that is, to fulfill a societal function that benefits those who are wealthier than they are—and that if they fail to do so diligently enough, they deserve violent retribution. Such people are reduced to their services, their humanity erased. Ironically, in asserting his dominance over his household, the tapestry maker participates in a practice that confirms his own socioeconomic subjugation. In so doing, he fails to consider the religious origins of the feast day on which he proposes to beat his chambermaid. The Feast of the Holy Innocents is a day intended to mourn the loss of innocent life and to remember the injustice done by a violent man with a selfish, dehumanizing agenda. If the tapestry maker truly understood what the Feast of the Holy Innocents represented, he should have at least recognized the incongruity of this day with his actions, even if he chose to pursue them anyway. Yet the tale gives us no evidence that he is even aware of the feast day's religious meaning; he seems to equate it only with the practice of whipping.

Consequently, it seems clear that the Church has failed this man in terms of education and oversight. Had the tapestry maker been under the care of one of Marguerite's évangéliques, he would have received religious instruction through preaching in addition to keeping such practices as confession, which aim to foster accountability and self-examination. Ultimately, then, the Church's lack of guidance pairs with the abuse of women by both clergy and noblemen to provide a negative example of power that men of lesser means may end up emulating. The *Heptaméron* mirrors this pattern of imitation to institutional representatives in order to suggest that whether aristocrats or Church officials recognize it or not, the norms that they create may have far-reaching consequences that promote the city of the world as opposed to the City of God.

VI. Conclusion

Through their contrasting of spiritual and worldly mentalities and their depiction of widespread abuse toward women, the *Heptaméron*'s tales can be said to rethink the theme of female sexuality and the connotations of the labyrinth in malo to suggest the need for institutional reform. The model reader, as an aristocrat or Church official, has the opportunity, in encountering the mirror of Marguerite's text, to practice self-examination. The *Heptaméron* implies that a process of personal transformation will constitute an important step toward unity of vision and successful collaboration on large-scale reform. After all, as Augustine asserts in *The City of God*, "in the family of the just man who lives by faith and is as yet a pilgrim journeying on to the celestial city, even those who rule serve those whom they seem to command; for they rule not from a love of power, but from a sense of the duty they owe to others—not because they are proud of authority, but because they love mercy."[96] Such a statement provides both a goal and a challenge to the leaders in Marguerite's society.

The question remains as to how institutional representatives should pursue such reforms once aware of the need for change. The next chapter addresses that topic by analyzing the disparate solutions that the devisants propose as responses to wrongdoing in the tales. As we shall see, some responses prove more effective than others but may not yield consistent results across tales. Still others raise moral dilemmas or align with political ideologies rather than spiritual ones. In examining appropriate or inappropriate ways of responding to injustice, Marguerite's storytellers engage in the complicated process of envisioning change and thus echo the queen's own creative process as a visionary. As chapter 5 will show, the problem-solving aspect of the *Heptaméron* harkens back not only to the in malo theme of difficult process associated with the idea of the labyrinth but also to the multicursal labyrinth type, specifically, whose diverging avenues generate confusion and create longing for the one correct path. Since this yearning for the one way out ultimately calls to mind the unicursal labyrinth, we can expect in due course for order to emerge out of the apparent chaos of the devisants' proposals, even if their conflicting opinions offer a realistic perspective on the fight for justice in a complicated world.

5

Down Tortuous Paths

Exploring Approaches to Justice and Reform

_____

As chapter 4 showed, the *Heptaméron* depicts sin and the fallen world, two themes associated with the idea of the labyrinth in malo. In treating these themes, the *Heptaméron* can be read as participating in the miroir genre, implicating the model reader, a representative of the Church or aristocracy, in tales of institutional ills that target women. Once the model reader has encountered myriad tales that suggest the need for reform, the next step, which chapter 5 analyzes, is to consider different approaches to achieving justice and defending women's sexuality. As the *Heptaméron* portrays the process of envisioning responses to wrongdoing, the text reflects further facets of the labyrinth's complexity. Like a multicursal labyrinth, the *Heptaméron* proposes many stories that function as paths down which the model reader walks, seeking out the correct pathway that will solve the puzzle of reform. The model reader cannot know when embarking down the path of a given tale whether the response to injustice that is depicted in the story will yield results, nor whether it will conform to the Christian morality and worldview espoused by the évangéliques. Indeed, as the tales accumulate, it becomes clear that numerous possibilities exist and that not all are effective or morally sound from a Christian perspective.

This finding proves problematic for the model reader, whom the text charges with pursuing institutional reform. The process in which the model reader participates becomes messy and disorienting, even fatiguing; some paths may lead nowhere fruitful, and the walker may end up retracing certain trajectories several times in the search for the right direction. Like a person who walks a multicursal labyrinth, such as the one in the legend of Theseus, the model reader faces the distinct possibility of becoming overwhelmed by the conflicting approaches that the characters take in response to injustice in the stories. As Penelope Reed Doob explains, this notion of "difficult process," associated with the idea of the labyrinth, has particular applications to teaching and learning. Indeed, "metaphorical labyrinths involving the idea of difficult process appear frequently and explicitly in the context of mental activities, particularly the processes of teaching, learning, and understanding."[1] The model reader, who is receiving a form of education via the *Heptaméron*'s labyrinthine treatment of justice and reform, faces the difficult task of sifting through what may, at times, feel like too many data points.[2] Yet this feeling of disorientation and challenge serves a transformative purpose because it can, as in the case of the multicursal labyrinth, increase an individual's longing for the one right path.

The present chapter therefore examines the model reader's experience of walking down the numerous paths of the *Heptaméron*'s tales and how that experience constitutes a form of education. Because this education occurs within the framework of Christian faith, as the morning Bible study sessions in the *Heptaméron*'s frame demonstrate, the model reader's destabilizing instructional process gestures not toward meaninglessness but rather toward the limits of human cognition; within the context of Marguerite's faith, confusion encourages humility and reminds Christians that they cannot choose wisely apart from God, whose sovereignty guarantees truth and meaning.[3] Although Christians may not perceive that meaning fully or clearly while sojourning on the earth, Augustine suggests that believers can nevertheless read earthly phenomena through the eyes of faith and engage actively in the work of redeeming the city of the world, or the state, and thus fostering the City of God.

The text suggests that pursuing the work of God's city does not come with easy answers. Ultimately, the abundance of tales, reactions to injustice, and results of those reactions prove too much to process on a tale-by-tale basis. Consequently, it is useful for us, as flesh-and-blood readers in the twenty-first century, to balance readings of the *Heptaméron*'s individual tales and debates with an analysis of larger statistical trends within the work when it comes to different responses to wrongdoing and what outcomes they yield across the seventy-two stories. This two-pronged approach is well suited to the *Heptaméron*'s labyrinthine nature, which combines diverging paths within a larger design that, when viewed from above with the help of statistical information, forms an artistically intricate design. Chapter 5 is thus about the educational process that aims to guide the model reader from a focus on parts, or individual tales, toward an appreciation for the larger, complex structure of the text as a whole.

Given the *Heptaméron*'s emphasis on the role of textual interpretation in educating a model reader, who is an institutional representative, the text shares themes in common not only with Augustine's *The City of God*, as discussed in chapter 4, but also with Erasmus's *The Education of a Christian Prince* (1516) and Juan Luis Vives's *On Assistance to the Poor* (1526). Both Vives and Erasmus lived in Marguerite's era and wrote on topics germane to her life and literary endeavor, including the roles of the aristocracy and the Church in ensuring justice in society. As a female author in a patriarchal society, however, Marguerite de Navarre offers a gendered perspective on topics treated by her male contemporaries. Her *Heptaméron* suggests that because male leaders in the aristocracy and the Church have brought about the corruption that now needs resolving, they cannot be trusted to pursue reform on their own. Just as the targeting of women's sexuality by corrupt institutional representatives threatens the social order, the social order can only be saved through the active participation of women in reform efforts.

Here, we find certain resonances with modern-day standpoint feminist theories, which assert that women's diverse experiences and struggles against injustice generate standpoints from which to rethink power structures in patriarchal society.[4] Today's standpoint feminisms have benefited from studies on the confluence of race, gender, and social class and therefore recognize the importance of intersecting factors of identity.[5] They also consider relational exchanges since in some interactions a woman may have greater privilege, while in others her privilege may lessen. Marguerite's simultaneous empowerment and disempowerment as a royal and a woman recalls this idea while also suggesting her ability to perceive society from the vantage points of the powerful and the oppressed simultaneously, as Elizabeth Chesney Zegura contends.[6]

The *Heptaméron*'s tales reorient discussions of reform toward women's concerns, a gesture that proves pedagogically important, since the stories function as examples for the model reader to evaluate as part of a learning process. In the tales, we see two main ways in which women prove central to envisioning paths toward reform. First, Marguerite's text proposes a gendered criterion for evaluating avenues to reform in the stories. Whereas Erasmus and Vives suggest that any path toward reform must promote the good of the people, rather than the self-interest of leaders, and that such a path must also demonstrate a Christian mentality, the queen of Navarre's *Heptaméron* suggests that if efforts to redress wrongdoing are to succeed, they must protect women and their sexuality. Defending women and defending the public good go hand in hand. Second, gender shapes the format of each text. Vives and Erasmus wrote overt treatises on the intersection of governance and Christian faith. Marguerite, on the other hand, was keenly aware of the threat of censure after her controversial *Miroir de l'âme pécheresse* (1531, 1533). She could not have written openly on such a polemical topic as institutional corruption and the need for reform. Instead of telling, her *Heptaméron* opts to show, using the tales as educational examples for the model reader to examine.

In order to show how the *Heptaméron*'s stories encourage the model reader to attempt to learn about reform through examples, the remainder of this chapter focuses on trends within the tales themselves and how those trends create an interpretive process for the model reader that resembles the multicursal labyrinth. Whereas chapter 6 will interrogate how the devisants' discussions factor into the model reader's instructional transformation, the present chapter focuses on the contents of the tales when it comes to responses to injustice since the tales themselves constitute the examples and thus the primary pedagogical substance that the model reader encounters. The model reader, let us recall, is not analogous to any specific storyteller in the *Heptaméron*'s frame; instead, the model reader is an interpretative role that the text envisions, one that in the case of the *Heptaméron* takes on the generic identity of an institutional representative. It is therefore important to consider the education that the information in the tales presents to the model reader on the topic of reform—a topic that dovetails especially well with the previously mentioned texts by Erasmus and Vives—before analyzing the function of the devisants' conversations about the various stories in chapter 6.

The first section below places the tales' status as instructional examples into a larger historical and literary context that includes Erasmus and Vives, who wrote on related subjects. The second section examines statistical trends in how the seventy-two tales depict reactions to injustice and which categories of response appear the most or least frequently. These statistical observations are complemented by analyses of tales that represent different response types. At chapter's end, we see the outcome of the model reader's education and how it prompts the model reader to take additional steps to move from process to product, a metamorphosis that the idea of the labyrinth encapsulates.

I. Marguerite de Navarre, Erasmus, and Vives on Institutional Reform

The mindset that the *Heptaméron* aims to develop in the model reader entails reconciling earthly realities and Christian principles, two topics that feature prominently in the work of Erasmus and Vives. These two male authors lived and wrote at the same moment as Marguerite de Navarre.

Erasmus actually penned a letter to Marguerite, though she did not respond. Some historians have speculated that her silence may have been due at least partially to the fact that Erasmus was under the protection of Charles V, François Ier's captor and archnemesis.[7] Vives wrote on Christian education and virtues for women, two topics of interest for Marguerite. In Vives's writings on the poor and Erasmus's discussion of royal education, we see princes and the monarchy, more generally, working for the common good, a phenomenon that Marguerite sought to encourage at court. Erasmus's use of the mirror for princes genre to prompt ongoing self-examination in leaders and Vives's assertion that the state ought to succor the poor and the oppressed pair well with the queen of Navarre's visionary project. After all, in both her writings and her real-world engagement, Marguerite strove to convert the aristocracy to the faith of the évangéliques so as to purify the Church and help both leading institutions in sixteenth-century France live up to their Christian callings.

In order to situate Marguerite de Navarre's contributions to the conversation on Church and state that these two male authors overtly pursue, it will prove useful to examine their writings in greater detail. Taken together, *The Education of a Christian Prince* and *On Assistance to the Poor* analyze the intersection of religion and governance, the same position from which Marguerite wrote and engaged in reform efforts. The two texts also complement each other in that the former focuses on the perspective of the monarch whereas the latter seeks to reach the monarch by depicting the suffering of the poor and examining the reasons for their poverty. Much as in the *Heptaméron*, different vantage points combine to create a more complete picture of early modern society.

Educating the heir to the throne is the primary concern of Erasmus's text, as its title suggests. Published a year before the onset of the Protestant Reformation, *The Education of a Christian Prince* predates the notion of schism and reflects Erasmus's status as a "secular" priest. Indeed, Erasmus had entered the priesthood but later received a perpetual dispensation from the pope that enabled him to travel and write outside of monastic life. In his writings, Erasmus combined his experience of learning and religion with everyday life. In this respect, he had much in common with Marguerite de Navarre. He likewise shared with Marguerite a commitment to internal Church reform. Even as the Protestant Reformation developed, neither Erasmus nor the queen of Navarre broke with Rome. Instead, both advocated spiritual education for rulers.

To further that objective, Erasmus adopted an approach based on positive and negative examples. Much like the *Heptaméron*, *The Education of a*

Christian Prince draws on the exemplum tradition, which had originated in the Church as a didactic tool for preaching.[8] The point of the exemplum was to prompt reflection in the listener or reader, who sought to evaluate the behaviors in question and decide whether to emulate them. As part of this pedagogical agenda, Erasmus furnished examples of rulers from antiquity and Christian history in the hope of teaching his reader to distinguish between "princes" and "tyrants": "A prince is chiefly concerned with the needs of his subjects, even while engaged in his personal business. On the other hand, if a tyrant does ever do well by his subjects, he turns this very fact to his private benefit all the same."[9] He then urged his readers, and especially his dedicatee, the future Charles V, to consider the weight of responsibility on the Christian monarch in his time. He argued that the then-modern Christian prince should surpass pagan predecessors in morality and efficacy.[10] He also contended that the prince should hold himself to a higher standard than the one that prevailed in the courts of Europe, influenced by Machiavelli and his commentaries on ruthless politicking.[11] For Erasmus, the only acceptable way for a prince to govern would be to emulate Christ in putting the public welfare ahead of his own self-interest.[12] He warned against extravagant expenditures, including for warfare, saying that he would "exhort the princes who bear the name of Christian to set aside all trumped-up claims and spurious pretexts and apply themselves seriously and whole-heartedly to making an end of this long-standing and terrible mania among Christians for war."[13] He likewise disapproved of alliances that the prince might be tempted to make out of a desire for riches, power, or territory rather than out of loyalty toward the people.

Interestingly, some of the critiques that Erasmus makes of European leaders as a whole could apply to François Ier in particular. The French king required large sums of money to pursue his failing Italian Wars against Charles V. By the early 1520s, the French royal treasury was virtually bankrupt, and François resorted to such drastic measures as melting down Church treasures to fund his political objectives.[14] Despite these expenditures, the king's warfare ultimately resulted in his capture at Pavia in 1525 and the long imprisonment of his sons in enemy territory. François was also known as a flashy individual. At tournaments, he strutted his physique before women he found attractive. One notable example was when, prior to becoming king, he showed off his physical prowess at a tournament in an attempt to impress Mary Tudor, the wife of Louis XII, who was at that time king of France.[15] Moreover, he came close to emptying the royal coffers on over-the-top decorations and entertainment for the Field of the Cloth of Gold. For this event, he invited Henry VIII of England and his entourage to France with a view to establishing a political alliance against Charles V.[16] He prepared "a village of golden tents" for the French, set up opposite the English, who had brought with them an imposing, prefabricated building.[17] He likewise funded feasts, dances, tournaments, and gifts.[18] These, too, would prove to be futile expenses, as Henry VIII went on to support Charles V instead.[19] Later in life, he formed an alliance with the Turks.[20] Erasmus had argued that the Turks, whose military presence had spread as far as Vienna, constituted a common threat to European welfare.[21] Although in the early years of his reign, François did offer support to the évangéliques at his sister's request, his overall orientation was less devout than Marguerite's and fell short of Erasmus's precepts for a spiritual prince who puts faith and the public before his own self-interest.

The queen of Navarre knew full well that if members of the French aristocracy were to exercise power from a mindset of service, they needed to draw nearer to God and guard against the temptations of the world. The *Heptaméron* prompts institutional representatives to undergo this process via the exempla that it offers for the model reader's contemplation. Yet unlike in Erasmus's text, the *Heptaméron* declines to identify in a clear-cut manner which examples are praiseworthy or shameful. The model reader must determine that information, drawing on the cues that the text offers.[22] Possible cues include motifs in the nouvelles, especially surrounding questions of injustice and the ways in which it impacts women. Another crucial factor, given the author's background, is the primacy of faith and the question of whether a given behavior proves consistent with Christian morality or merely with social norms. The *Heptaméron* thus functions as a pedagogical text, implicating the model reader in the learning process, instead of lecturing directly, as Erasmus's text does. It also recenters the idea of just rule around institutions' obligations toward women, and women's ability to reform institutions.

Women constituted one of the underprivileged groups of Marguerite's time, but another such group was the poor. Vives wrote to move the hearts of monarchs in favor of assisting the growing number of destitute individuals who were flocking to urban centers, either to beg or to look for work. Published one year after François's defeat and capture at Pavia during his costly Italian Wars, *On Assistance to the Poor* describes the plight of the impoverished and argues that the state should take responsibility for them. Vives situated his argument within the context of the city in part because he grew up in Valencia and witnessed there the effectiveness of secular programs to assist the poor, as opposed to ecclesiastical outreach, which was then considered the norm in Europe.[23] However, the foregrounding of the city in Vives's text can be read another way as well. Just as Augustine contrasted the City of God with the city of the world, pinpointing the divergence between the fallen world and the unfolding of redemption, Vives used the literal city as a starting point for a larger commentary on the roles of Church and state and how they ought to change to promote the public good.[24]

Rather than leaving the care of the poor to the Church, whose efforts do not suffice to meet the great surge in need, Vives contended that the state should direct poor relief efforts and that the Church's outreach should function as a supplement to state-run programs.[25] This reversal in power dynamics recalls Marguerite's own engagement with institutional reform. Like Vives, she demonstrated through her attempts to foster religious reform at court, as well as her oversight of individual religious orders, that she believed the monarchy ought to monitor the Church and act as the ultimate arbiter of justice in the land. In order for this change to prove viable, however, rulers needed to undergo a conversion of heart, shifting their focus away from their own worldly gains to the welfare of their people. Vives shamed leaders for not caring adequately for the people, who looked to them as father figures: "Just as it is disgraceful for the head of a household to allow any member to suffer the lack of food or the embarrassment of wandering in rags, so it follows that, in a wealthy city, its magistrates would not permit its citizens—even a few—to be pressed down by undue hunger and misery."[26] His diction recalls the Christian analogy of God as Father to the faithful. Given that the Church confirmed the king's authority, anointing him as a kind of temporal priest, Vives's metaphor underscores the severity of the state's failure toward the poor, presenting it as tantamount to a failed ministry. The exhortation to a life of charity in Vives's text suggests that although the state should direct poor relief efforts, it should do so informed by faith. In that regard, Vives echoed both Erasmus and Marguerite, implying that while one institution should take the lead in creating a more just society, Christian faith should nevertheless reign supreme over both institutions, such that spirituality motivates temporal endeavors.

Vives built on that idea by developing a specific plan of action for assisting the poor. First, he maintained that government officials needed to consider the different categories of people within the larger heading of "the poor." He reminded rulers that people might find themselves in difficult financial straits for many reasons and might also respond to their poverty in diverging ways. All such factors should be considered in distributing aid. One crucial step, he argued, would be for the government to take a census of the impoverished, noting their names, residences, and life situations.[27]

This would enable them to determine which individuals living at the hospitals—facilities not just for the sick but also for the indigent—were well enough to work. Those with robust physical and mental health would be required to work for a living.[28] Consequently, hospitals would no longer be overrun and would have funds left over.[29] For those well enough to support themselves, Vives advocated state-run vocational assistance in which those who did not yet possess a trade would receive training, and those who did possess a trade would be placed in a job that employed similar skill sets.[30] Working people whose income fell short of their family's needs would become eligible for supplemental funds from the state.[31] Those who fell into poverty through a sudden misfortune, such as a house fire, would likewise have access to emergency funds.[32] All of these programs could be funded, he argued, not only through the reduction of hospital expenses but also through the elimination of unnecessary state expenditures, such as ceremonies, feasts, and gifts for foreign dignitaries.[33]

Moreover, Vives asserted that the children of the poor, both boys and girls, should have access to state-funded schools that would prepare them to live virtuously and sustain themselves financially in their adulthood.[34] As in *The Education of a Christian Woman* (1524), which chapter 6 will examine in greater detail in conjunction with the *Heptaméron*'s female educator, Oisille, Vives saw education as pivotal to ensuring successful living. In this stance, he reflected the sentiments of both Erasmus and Marguerite de Navarre. Finally, Vives affirmed that if leaders adopted his proposals and put them into practice, both the state and society as a whole would see significant benefits. Not only would criminal activity and begging decrease, but women would no longer practice prostitution to provide for themselves and their families, and poverty would no longer carry over from parents to children. Most importantly, rulers and the governed would live, if not perfectly, then more peaceably and sincerely as Christians, remembering the City of God.[35]

The *Heptaméron* shares with Vives a commitment to justice, institutional reform, education, and the betterment of society. A notable difference between the two texts, however, is that although the poor do feature in the queen's nouvelles, which depict all social classes, the group that the *Heptaméron* foregrounds as requiring justice is women. Vives's care for women and their sexuality finds parallels with the recurring depictions of sexual abuse toward women in Marguerite's text. Still, the *Heptaméron* goes one step further in revealing that women at all levels of society, rather than a single socioeconomic class, are the group that most require institutional reform and that the security of society as a whole depends on institutions promoting their safety and well-being.

Addressing this large-scale problem, rooted in ideology and not only in practical circumstances, proves more ambiguous in the *Heptaméron* than in Vives's text. While Vives developed a set of concrete agenda points, his argument drew on the long tradition of the miroir genre, aimed at educating princes, and the idea of poor relief, which was deeply ingrained in Christian thought. Princes of Vives's day may have been failing their mission in his eyes, but they were also familiar with the discourses that Vives was propagating and that ultimately derived from the scriptures. Marguerite de Navarre's text pursues a trickier aim. The institutions of Church and state had tended to relegate women to the sidelines, especially in France where Salic law forbade women from inheriting the throne. Catholic hierarchy also placed men above women in authority and influence. Because neither institution of the day considered women's rights of particular importance, the queen of Navarre could not adopt Vives's strategy of drawing on well-established ideas and then using them to promote specific reforms; doing so would not likely have garnered sufficient support. Moreover, the queen of Navarre could not risk such a polemical act as to state reform-oriented ideas outright, especially not as sister to the monarch. Instead, her *Heptaméron* seeks to change the hearts of male institutional representatives so that they come to realize that women's rights deserve their support.

II. Responses to Wrongdoing in the Heptaméron: *Statistical Trends and Individual Tales*

The change of heart that the *Heptaméron* seeks to create in the model reader, and especially in male aristocrats and Church officials, entails a greater concern for women; but for all institutional representatives, whether male or female, the text also promotes a Christian vision for societal improvement and the humility to realize the limits of human cognition. These themes reflect aspects of the labyrinth's symbolism, with its emphases on not only sin and fallenness but also redemption. Such trends become clearer when statistical information and individual tales contextualize each other. Looking at the seventy-two tales, we see that the characters demonstrate numerous reactions to injustice, so many that the model reader may become disoriented if reading each tale as an individual unit, just as a person walking a multicursal labyrinth wanders down one path and then another, losing a sure sense of direction. As stated in chapter 4, any effort to organize the *Heptaméron*'s tales involves a measure of interpretation. Different readers may, for instance, generate different labels for characters' responses to injustice and view some as more prominent in one story than in another. Nevertheless, an overview of trends will provide a framework for examining the text's stance toward institutional reform.

For example, some characters employ trickery or deceit to punish ill-meaning individuals or assert agency in the midst of unjust constraints. Others show mercy toward those who have wronged them or simply retreat from their presence. Still others exhibit passive acceptance of the wrong. In some cases, a verbal reproach follows wrongdoing, whereas in others, physical retribution dissuades offenders from repeating their errant behaviors. Certain tales depict justice through official channels, such as appeals to the monarchy or to the Church hierarchy, as well as other nonviolent forms of justice. A handful of tales highlight the realistic nature of the nouvelle genre by showing that in some instances, circumstances prevent an organized response to injustice. Finally, a great many stories combine two or more responses to injustice in a prominent way, either successively as the plot unfolds or all at once at the story's conclusion.

In order to determine which tales belong in each category of response, one must first establish what counts as injustice and who, in a given tale, may be considered to respond to it. After all, the queen's nouvelles reflect many intersecting influences and factors of identity, including gender, religion, and social class. Whereas chapter 4 considers how institutions and their norms perpetuate harm against women in all classes of society, chapter 5 focuses instead on how individuals respond to unjust situations that patriarchal institutions and their ideologies establish. The types of responses provide the schema for statistical analysis, rather than the class origins of the character who responds to wrongdoing.

Moreover, injustice is defined not in terms of interpersonal relationships alone but rather in terms of the larger power structures that dictate the treatment of women and the ways in which men and women interact with each other. Just as in Augustinian exegesis each entity represents not only itself but also a higher spiritual meaning, the exempla in the *Heptaméron* can be read as contributing to the development of a vision for institutional reform and societal improvement. As such, the personal points toward the political. This means that in a story of infidelity, the errant spouse not only figures human sin but also the injustice of arranged marriage and of a concept of the marital state that downplays the importance of sexual compatibility.[36] The fault lies not merely with the unfaithful husband or wife but also with the erring institutions and mores that prompted him or her to sin. Ultimately, the categorization of reactions to injustice in the stories reflects the problem of abuse toward women and their sexuality because that is the primary means by which the *Heptaméron* showcases institutional corruption, redirecting the idea of the labyrinth toward pro-woman objectives.

With these delimitations in mind, we find that when characters in the tales attempt to redress some form of wrongdoing that implicates female sexuality—a central theme in sixty-eight tales—the vast majority of characters combine multiple response types in how they address injustice. Thirty-four of the sixty-eight pertinent stories, or 50 percent, fall into this category. Trickery or deceit constitutes the next most frequent response type, figuring in fourteen of sixty-eight tales for a total of slightly more than 20 percent. The categories of physical retribution and justice through non-violent or official channels contain three and five stories, respectively, whereas six stories fall under the heading of verbal reproach. In two tales, societal dictates or the absence of the perpetrator make it impossible for the wronged party to seek justice. One story features mercy as the only response the protagonist makes to injustice, and two show passive acceptance. Only one depicts withdrawal unaccompanied by another form of response. Examining each category of reaction to injustice in turn, beginning with the least numerous, working through the various categories, and ending with the most frequent, will help account for these tendencies, as well as for the frequency of certain response types.

i. Withdrawal, Mercy, and Passive Acceptance

Because so few stories feature passive acceptance, mercy, and withdrawal as sole responses to injustice, these labyrinthine pathways prove short and can therefore be considered in a single subsection. Although several stories feature some variation on withdrawing from a person who has caused harm, only one does so without also including other well-developed responses. Story 64 recounts how a nobleman from Valencia courts a lady he desires to marry. She rebuffs his advances to test whether he actually loves her. Unfortunately, her strategy backfires when the suitor becomes a cordelier. When she writes to him to explain her true intentions, the cordelier asks a friend to tell her that he has decided to subsume his pain in the love of God. At story's end, the young woman arrives at the monastery, decked out in her finest, in an effort to win him back, but his reaction is to flee: "n'ayant autre pouvoir, que par fuyr" ("flight was his only recourse").[37]

The primary injustice in this scenario involves patriarchal norms surrounding marriage, as perpetuated by the Church and aristocracy. Because parental approval and political alliances tended to hold greater weight in matchmaking than actual affection, and because the discourses of courtly love and parfaicte amitié combined to deceive women, the story's heroine endeavors to determine her suitor's true intent. Both parties end up having to forgo a marriage they would otherwise have desired, all because institutions have created a toxic scenario in which men and women cannot communicate openly or exercise an independent will.

This same societal ill underlies tales 7 and 57, which portray passive acceptance as a response to injustice. Whereas tale 57 describes an English lord who carries around a lady's glove to remind him of his beloved, with whom he could never establish a relationship, story 7 highlights sexual wrongdoing against two different women: a daughter and her mother. In this nouvelle, a merchant pursues an affair with a young woman to cover up his affections for a highborn lady. The young woman loves him sincerely and does not hesitate to pursue a physical relationship with him. When the young woman's mother nearly discovers the two together, the merchant pretends to press the mother for sex in order to create a diversion during which the daughter can escape. The tale features many forms of deceit, which we might consider the merchant's means of circumventing society's prohibition against his relationship with a wealthier woman. At the same time, the gravest injustice and threat to the social order in the story comes from the merchant's behavior toward women and his treatment of their sexuality. In order to cover up his own affair, he not only seeks to deflower a young woman who will afterward lose her marriage prospects, but also to terrorize an older woman with the threat of rape. The mother receives no explanation or justice for the merchant's behavior toward her.[38] The tale also offers no explanation as to why this should be the case.

Finally, one tale portrays mercy as the protagonist's lone response to injustice. In story 67, Captain Roberval sets out to people the New World with French Christians. One of the men aboard, most likely a former convict, attempts to get Roberval assassinated by the native peoples of the region. The plan fails, and as the king's representative, Roberval has the right to enforce the death penalty, but the man's wife intervenes and has his sentence commuted to marooning on a remote island "où n'habitoient que bestes sauvages" ("inhabited only by wild animals"), a fate in which she joins him, despite her innocence.[39] During their time on the island, she aids him in defending against wild animals and capturing food. She also reads to him from scripture. In time, he can no longer tolerate the local water and food sources. His swollen belly harkens back to Numbers 5:11–31 as Margaret Ferguson notes, alluding to the ancient practice by which a husband who suspected his wife of adultery could make her drink bitter water, and if she became swollen and died, she was considered guilty.[40] The guilt in this case rests with the husband, who has already demonstrated spiritual impurity. The wife manages to restore him to faith before he dies, but his fate contrasts pointedly with that of his wife, who is rescued after showing him mercy that he did not deserve.

Although mercy demonstrates Christian principles in interpersonal relationships, on its own, it cannot guarantee justice or right behavior in wider society, especially as not everyone ascribes to the same moral code. Neither does passive acceptance promote societal and institutional reform. Withdrawal from society and its injustices likewise counters the aim of positive change. In this first category, then, we see that one response—mercy—is morally sound from a Christian perspective, but none of the responses proves universally effective at the level of governance. The model reader, having walked these three paths, will not yet discover a clear direction toward reform. Several false starts may reveal to the discerning student that this assignment will prove perplexing and time consuming.

ii. Verbal Reproach

The next type of response to wrongdoing that the model reader may consider is verbal reproach. Six of the sixty-eight stories that address abuse toward women and their sexuality fall into this group: stories 9, 11, 26, 42, 44, and 71. These tales recount such scenarios as a dying lover's last embrace,[41] a wayward young man and a woman's secret love for him, a girl's outrage over a suitor's sexual imposition, a noblewoman's encounter with a monastery privy, an ailing wife's anger at her husband's infidelity, and a bourgeoise's resistance toward a prince's advances. Tale 42 is especially well known and has been treated elsewhere.[42] However, stories 26 and 71 also develop prominent examples of verbal reproach that provide insights into gender-based injustice in the text.

Story 26 describes the behavior of two women—one foolish, one wise—in such a way as to render ambiguous which woman deserves each title.[43] The story thereby prompts reflection on the part of the model reader, especially when it comes to institutions and the norms they promote around women's sexuality. In the tale, Lord d'Avannes develops feelings for the wife of a wealthy older gentleman who has taken d'Avannes as his adoptive son. The wife fulfills her society's requirements for feminine virtue by hiding her interest. The tale then contrasts the wife's behavior with that of a woman of looser morals, whom d'Avannes pursues successfully. When he cannot keep up with her sexual appetites, he falls ill and is forced to return to his adoptive father's household, where his old love interest nurses him back to health. The wife instructs him in virtue, and although this education prompts d'Avannes to repent of his misdeeds, it also inspires love and admiration for his teacher. In time, he attempts to seduce the wife, but she reproaches him sharply, stating that if he wishes to remain in contact with her, he can never again broach this topic.[44]

Ironically, the wife's determination to deny her desire makes her sicker than the nobleman's affair had made him. On her deathbed, she confesses that her refusal of him is "cause de ma mort" ("the cause of my death").[45] Saffredent, the male narrator of the tale, uses this assertion to argue in favor of rape, a fact that further underscores the toxicity of aristocratic attitudes toward women's sexuality. In the tale, though, the ultimate injustice stems yet again from the fact that marriage is a political and economic institution that does not take sexual compatibility sufficiently into account. The wife in the story can have no happy outcome to her situation. Either she persists in adhering to aristocratic behavioral norms for women, or she follows her inclination, but in either case, she will suffer. Her verbal reproach both reflects and questions the prevailing discourse of chastity during her time.

Tale 71 offers a different take on verbal reproach. Instead of concealing her emotions surrounding sexuality, the wife in the story expresses herself openly. When she falls ill, her condition deteriorates quickly, and her husband, a saddler, rushes to her side. After she has received the last rites, he begins to accost his chambermaid. Despite having not spoken for days beforehand, the wife regains the power of speech when she sees what her husband is doing. She shakes her fist and shouts, "Meschant, je ne suis pas morte" ("Swine! Brute! I'm not dead yet!").[46] Although brief, the wife's reprimands prove effective in separating the maid and the husband. The fact that she is holding the cross in her hand as she chastises her husband's inappropriate behavior only adds further weight to her words. Moreover, the wife's anger revives her strength and cures her of her illness. Anger literally saves her life in addition to the fidelity of her marriage. In the end, her husband pays dearly for his attempted misdeed since she reprimands him frequently for the lack of love he demonstrated toward her.[47]

In this second story, then, a verbal reproach proves effective at stopping unjust behavior in the moment, but the larger issue of a husband's lack of sincere love toward his wife derives from ideological influences surrounding gender and marriage, as previously noted. Such ideologies shape the thoughts and behaviors of the populace, even if they originate in the aristocracy and the Church. Whether women oppose social mores in an unambiguous way or not, these tales suggest that an active, even angry, posture might prove helpful to restoring women's well-being in the face of institutionally propagated abuse. The model reader may find this pathway slightly longer and more promising than those in the previous category. Still, it is but one path in a larger structure, and following it leads to additional choices as well as wanderings down uncertain avenues. The model reader's education on the topic of reform is only beginning.

iii. Nonviolent and Official Channels of Justice

Whereas many *Heptaméron* tales combine official or nonviolent forms of justice with other response types, only five consider official channels of justice on their own. Channels of justice might include the judicial system or the intervention of figures assumed to execute justice, such as high-ranking aristocrats and Church officials. Tales in this category include 30, 34, 56, 60, and 72. Anecdotes range in content from a cordelier pretending to be secular so as to marry a woman, a mother accidentally committing incest with her son, a clergyman coercing a nun into having sex with him, a pair of friars panicking and accidentally wounding themselves in fear of punishment, and a woman carrying on a public affair with a cantor. In some of the stories, an official agent of justice administers a punishment. In other cases, characters unwittingly punish themselves or must assuage their guilt by following the directives of those in authority. Stories 72 and 56 show how in many cases it is Church representatives themselves who promote wrongdoing; therefore, secular individuals, and especially influential women, must intervene to respond to injustice.

In tale 72, a young nun helps care for an ailing patient at the hospital that her order runs. We see a glimpse here of the world that Vives analyzed when he talked about conditions in hospitals, where nuns and clergy cared for the sick and the poor. Marguerite invested in such establishments and ensured their cleanliness and funding, as seen in chapter 2. It is therefore logical that her stories would bear the mark of her observations and real-world advocacy. In story 72, the patient in question suffers a slow decline. The nuns go to bed one by one until the only people left in the room are the youngest sister and the abbey's most austere priest. When he begins to preach about the joys of heaven, she listens respectfully, and before long, he has violated her.[48] Dagoucin, the male narrator, describes his female protagonist as timid. According to him, she does not dare to refuse such a devout man.[49] Although Dagoucin conveys some level of sympathy toward the nun, he also implicates her in her own objectification, as if she had actually desired the priest's advances. The text negates that reading by specifying that her subsequent grief stems not from having committed a sin, but from having allowed the priest to intimidate her.[50]

The nun only receives justice when, on a journey to the Vatican in search of help, she crosses paths with Marguerite de Navarre (then the duchess of Alençon).[51] She is able to confide in the textual Marguerite, who ensures that justice will be served, sending letters to the bishop to "faire chasser ce religieux scandaleux" ("have the scandalous monk removed").[52] The duchess's authoritative presence restores order and prevents the perpetrator from repeating his offense. She intervenes on behalf of other women, creating a network of solidarity within the confines of patriarchal society.

Tale 56 implies that women of lesser authority than the king's sister can still follow her example by contesting injustice within their spheres of influence. The story relates how a noblewoman in Padua asks her confessor's help in finding a suitable husband for her daughter. The mother explains that she will be living with the couple but will provide their home, furnishings, and food, as well as a considerable dowry. The corrupt confessor decides to enlist the help of his young companion, a fellow cordelier. The latter agrees to pretend to be secular in order to marry the daughter and receive room and board, while the former will take the money. To proceed with the plan, the confessor tells the mother that the marriage must take place in secret because the prospective husband is wrongly wanted by the law for having been present at a crime scene. The irony is that the young friar will soon engage in an act of fraud that will merit his being sought after by the justice system. With the marriage completed, the mother and daughter accept that in order to hide his identity, the "husband" must pretend to be a student and will only be home in the evenings after his daily lectures have ended.

One day, the mother and daughter happen to attend mass at the church where the young friar actually spends his time, and they espy him from afar. To test their suspicions, they remove his head covering later that evening and confirm that he has a monk's tonsure, at which point the mother and daughter respond like the countess in story 41: "Appellerent des serviteurs de leans, pour le faire prendre et lier" ("They called the servants and had him seized and tied").[53] The mother then calls her confessor to come visit, and when he arrives, she binds him up, as well. She then hands the clergy over to the justice system, and the tale specifies that the confessor, at least, winds up in prison.[54] Much as in previous tales, the mother in story 56 adopts a proactive stance within her sphere of influence. Although she cannot hand down justice the way the queen of Navarre could do by ordering the expulsion of a corrupt clergyman, she can seek out those who are in a position to issue such a punishment. As a widow, she has no husband to assist her in taking on two men, but she succeeds, with the help of her household staff and her daughter, in immobilizing them with ropes. The binding serves not as a violent form of retribution, but as a means of preventing escape so that an appropriate judicial action can then be taken.

These two tales, when read together, offer the strongest endorsement yet for the feasibility of institutional reform. Although they do not propose a specific set of agenda items, they present women as empowered to respond effectively to injustice and punish institutional leaders who harm women. This tendency exists in many other *Heptaméron* stories across response categories, such as in tale 5, as well as in story 42, which shows how Françoise's verbal reproach converts the heart of a prince. Because tales in other response groups also show women effecting justice, the *Heptaméron* suggests that it is not necessarily the strategy that a woman takes in redressing corruption that leads to success but rather the inherent justice of her cause, which many tales explicitly frame as supported by God. Like Marguerite herself, the *Heptaméron*'s female characters can participate actively in creating a more just society. Here, the model reader can derive hope even amid the fatigue and confusion of wandering the many paths of the tales; even though the model reader cannot yet perceive the way out of the labyrinth and name the precise solution to the problem of reform, the text suggests that the sovereignty of God ensures a coherent outcome for the believer, who perseveres in faith through a difficult process.

iv. Situations That Preclude the Pursuit of Justice

One phenomenon that the model reader may note from the previously analyzed tales is that an important factor in women's success as they combat institutional and ideological corruption is solidarity. Women who have a support system of other women fare well in the aforementioned tales and in other stories as well, such as when a countess saves a girl from an ill-meaning confessor in story 41.[55] However, not all women in the *Heptaméron* have such a support system. Women who are isolated physically or socially may find their pursuit of justice barred, either because they are caught in seemingly impossible situations or because the perpetrator gets away before he can be apprehended. Stories in this category include 45 and 62.

These nouvelles recount a neighbor's unsuccessful attempt to warn a friend of her husband's infidelity and a man's rape of a woman who refused him.

Although chapter 4 treated the last tale in that sequence, story 62, it is worth returning briefly to that tale to add that the story's heroine had no support system based on female solidarity. She was asleep alone in her room when the attacker arrived. After the assault, societal dictates prevented her from revealing what was considered the loss of her chastity, even though she had done nothing to deserve the attack. Indeed, the tale reveals that societal norms can actually divide women among themselves. We see this principle at work when other noblewomen hear the protagonist's story and assume she must have actually invited the man's behavior since she had recounted what had happened. Patriarchal mores that silence women also provoke fear and division, thus impeding solidarity and a concerted approach to reform.

Story 45, seen in chapter 4, likewise demonstrates the importance of solidarity among women. The husband in the story rapes his chambermaid repeatedly, but since she gets the mistaken impression from her mistress that the latter does not actually disapprove of her husband's behavior, she cannot obtain help. When the next-door neighbor sees the husband naked with the maid outside in the snow, she is outraged on her friend's behalf and decides to tell her everything, hoping that it will lead to justice.[56] Unfortunately, the deceptive husband comes up with a scheme to fool his wife and convinces her that her friend is mistaken. She never learns that she has been tricked because her support system has been rendered ineffective through division.[57]

Although there are few tales in this category, they offer an important reminder that community is a condition for success when it comes to institutional reform. Marguerite demonstrated her belief in this idea through her participation in a group of non-schismatic reformers, but in her *Heptaméron*, the concept extends to female solidarity, as well. The model reader, who has been charged with walking the text's paths toward reform, might well identify with the desire for community and solidarity that underlies these tales. Treading a multicursal labyrinth is an isolating and at times unsettling experience; without a sympathetic companion, there can be no collaboration, and the walker must bear the whole burden of problem-solving alone. Like a labyrinth walker, the model reader depends on independent powers of observation, memory, and strategizing to identify a path forward, but the individual cannot achieve anywhere near as much as a united community, whether in intellectual tasks or in governance.

v. Physical Retribution

Alongside such topics as female solidarity and justice through nonviolent and official channels, the *Heptaméron* provides another path for the model reader to explore: that of physical retribution. Some forms of institutionalized wrongdoing toward women are ideological in scope, but others are physical, and so the question arises as to whether physical reactions to corruption are ever appropriate, and if so, whether they prove effective. This question calls to mind both the queen of Navarre's faith, which emphasizes mercy while also announcing a future judgment, and early modern attitudes toward violence, which were far more permissive than is typical in twenty-first-century democracies. Unsurprisingly, then, three tales depict physical responses to institutional corruption and its societal echoes: stories 23, 48, and 50. These narratives recount a cordelier's rape of a woman who then kills herself, the punishment of two friars who conspire to take the groom's place on his wedding night, and the death of a lover who had undergone bloodletting to treat lovesickness.

Tale 23 offers important insights into the ways in which physical wrongdoing begets physical consequences for far more people than the perpetrator and the target of abuse. At the beginning of the story, a nobleman asks his spiritual director how long he should wait to have sex with his wife after she has given birth to their first child. The clergyman replies that since he has already waited three weeks, he must only wait until two o'clock in the morning. The corrupt adviser arrives in advance of the indicated time and snuffs out the candle in his victim's bedroom. Although the nobleman's wife expresses surprise that her "husband" has arrived early, the cordelier makes no response. Predictably, the wife chastises her spouse when he arrives later that night, accusing him of excessive libido. When the two characters realize they have been duped, the husband sets out to catch the fleeing cordelier, while the wife contemplates the great injustice she has suffered. She considers herself guilty, even though she has done nothing wrong.[58] Consequently, she descends into a crushing state of despair from which she will never recover. Since the cordeliers—whom she had trusted until so recently—never taught her the basic precepts of Christian theology, she concludes that no recourse remains except suicide. Worse still, she accidentally kicks her newborn baby as she lies dying and kills him, as well.[59]

Unfortunately, the violence does not stop there. The wife's brother finds her and her son and wrongly assumes that the husband killed them both. He races off after the husband and injures him severely, ultimately leading to his death. Physical violence abounds in the story, but the only person who never experiences it is the perpetrator, not because punishing him physically would have been impossible, but because a series of miscommunications distracted those who thought they were acting for justice. In tale 23, violence begets more violence while failing to ensure either justice or reform.

Many tales combine some element of physical retribution with other means of responding to injustice, but among those that deal only with physical reactions, tale 48 offers a different perspective than tale 23. In story 48, a pair of cordeliers crash a wedding and concoct a plan to take the place of the groom in the marriage bed. Because of his youthful immaturity, the groom stays out dancing late into the night, after his new wife has already retired and lies in bed awaiting his arrival. In the interval, the older clergyman visits the bride pretending to be her husband while the younger remains on the lookout for the groom. By the time the groom finally arrives, the young woman expresses irritation at his excessive libido, much as in tale 23. Also similarly to tale 23, the groom and a group of male wedding guests storm off after the offenders. However, unlike in tale 23, they actually catch up with the perpetrators and manage to punish them. Not only do they beat the clergymen ferociously, but they also make a horrifying example of them and leave them on display in a vineyard, a symbolically fitting location for debauched clergy: "leur coupperent les bras et les jambes, et les laisserent dedans les vignes" ("[The wedding guests] cut off their arms and legs, and left them in the vines").[60] The public exposure of both their shame and its punishment functions as a warning to their comrades, lest they consider a similar path. The two maimed clergymen will not be able to violate anyone in the future; they will likely die of blood loss, and even if they manage somehow to survive, they will lack the mobility to pursue wicked schemes.

Yet the trouble is that although these two particular individuals are punished, many other clergymen remain mobile and inclined toward corruption. The problem is not so much the ability to sin, but rather the desire to do so, since as the *Heptaméron* asserts, sin creates its own opportunities. Similarly, it is not the existence of multiple paths in the multicursal labyrinth that causes the walker to err; rather, it is the walker's decision-making and free will that the choices in the labyrinth's structure serve to underscore. Walkers are free to take whichever path they choose, just as learners can explore different concepts at length and individuals can behave in whatever way they decide. Still, the freedom to choose and to act, though liberating in some senses, nevertheless opens up the individual to error and wrongdoing. As a result, those who respond to injustice may become as unjust as the original perpetrators. In tale 48, then, we can consider physical retribution an unsatisfactory solution, one that achieves limited short-term results while also sitting poorly with the queen's Christian morality. Moreover, in tale 23, violence failed to achieve any justice at all; on the contrary, it led to an innocent man's untimely death. Physical retribution does not emerge as a top contender for effecting morally sound reforms.

vi. Trickery or Deceit

The second most frequent response to wrongdoing in the *Heptaméron* is one that features prominently in the multicursal labyrinth's many dead-end walkways: trickery or deceit. Although the two terms are synonyms, both have their place in this section heading, given that trickery connotes less serious forms of deception, whereas deceit implies a more malicious brand of dishonesty. Both varieties of dishonesty exist in the text. As previously stated, fourteen of the sixty-eight pertinent tales foreground deception as a response to injustice: stories 3, 18, 25, 27, 29, 49, 53, 54, 55, 58, 59, 63, 68, and 69.[61] Listing the contents of every tale would prove cumbersome given the quantity of them, though some motifs emerge, including infidelity, wives tricking unfaithful husbands, women testing would-be suitors, and women and young people circumventing the authority of those who are older or more powerful than they are. In tales of deception, characters contest power dynamics and ideologies surrounding gender. They seek to assert their agency in the face of unjust restraints or against threats and insults to their self-worth. As the above summary suggests, many tales involving trickery or deceit foreground female sexuality. Consequently, deception becomes a tool that enables women to subvert patriarchal power structures.

For example, in story 3, the king of Naples strikes up a liaison with a nobleman's wife. At first, the betrayed husband grieves the loss of his wife's love, but then it occurs to him that the queen must also feel mistreated. He therefore speaks with her privately, addressing amorous words to her and persuading her that the best solution for them both is to start an affair of their own, concealing their infidelity from those who have wronged them. The queen resists his argumentation initially, as she recognizes her society's double standard for women, which makes it impossible to have "l'honneur et le plaisir ensemble" ("both honour and pleasure").[62] In this statement, the queen summarizes the impossible dilemma that aristocratic notions of gender create: women can have either honor or pleasure but not both. As seen in many other tales, the female protagonist must either abide by patriarchal dictates handed down to her by the aristocracy and the Church or risk losing her standing in society and her sense of moral decency in order to meet her sexual and relational needs. The most basic aspects of a romantic relationship—emotional and sexual intimacy—were often absent or strained in arranged marriages. Whereas noblemen in Marguerite's time were judged for their bravery, not their fidelity, and could thus pursue extramarital affairs in response to this unsatisfying arrangement, a woman's worth depended on the repression of her sexual desires. The only situation in which chastity and fulfillment could coexist was in the rare and fortunate case of a compatible marriage. Still, a man's relative freedom to engage in adultery meant that even compatibility could not guarantee a wife's long-term fulfillment.

Although adultery breaks one of the Ten Commandments and was not a behavior that a devout Christian such as Marguerite could have recommended, it is interesting to note that the queen in story 3 eventually cedes to the nobleman's pursuit because he says that she is honorable in and of herself, not because of societal standards, and that she is also worthy of companionship and fulfillment. On the one hand, his assertions are based first on her high rank.[63] On the other hand, he makes clear that he believes her innate qualities confer honor on her separately from her social status: "Mais vostre beauté, grace, et honnesteté a tant merité de plaisir" ("But you are also beautiful, charming and refined, and you deserve to have your pleasures as well").[64] Regardless of the man's level of sincerity, he pinpoints a crucial problem that subtends the attitude that institutions promoted toward women. Instead of focusing on the queen's relational roles and how she serves patriarchal society through them, by bearing children or appearing respectable, he speaks to her in such a way as to suggest that he views her as fully human. He demonstrates awareness of her need for relationship, love, esteem, and sexual fulfillment, whereas most people likely viewed her as a political figurehead tasked with procreation. Through the establishment of a new relationship, the tale generates a happy outcome for the queen and her suitor. Both succeed in finding happiness after having been betrayed, and in an old trope of medieval literature, the original deceivers—the king and his mistress—are themselves deceived.

Because threats to women's sexuality can take either ideological or physical forms, it is likewise worth considering how trickery enables women to defend against physical infractions. Story 27 offers a valuable example. In the tale, a secretary lodges at the home of his companion, a valet de chambre. The valet and his wife have a harmonious marriage, but the secretary lusts after the wife and accosts her on numerous occasions. In response, she concocts a plan to shame him. Instead of refusing him, she pretends to welcome his advances. One day, she agrees to sleep with him and suggests that he go upstairs to the attic, saying she will follow him shortly. When he reaches the top of the stairs, she announces that because she knows his friendship toward her husband is so great, she has no doubt that he would want her to tell her husband about the plan. Despite his protests, that is what she does. Not only does she succeed in humiliating her pursuer, who flees the house, but she also augments her husband's esteem for her, as he is impressed by her "honneste tromperie" ("virtuous little trick") and values her loyalty and cleverness.[65] Paradoxically, in the story, the wife demonstrates her virtue by behaving dishonestly. Her trickery enables her to put an end to the secretary's harassment while also preventing an even graver injustice against her. Her strategy thus incorporates both reactive and proactive elements. Moreover, she preserves her positive relationship with her husband, a relatively rare occurrence in the sixteenth century and thus one worth protecting.

Stories 27 and 3 contrast with each other to highlight the moral ambiguities surrounding deception in sixteenth-century France. In the case of the valet's wife, trickery serves to reinforce marital bonds and promote well-being for each spouse. On the contrary, tale 3 suggests that arranged marriage and patriarchal mentalities toward women render marital concord very difficult to achieve and that as a result, deception proves the most viable option for achieving relational happiness. In comparing the two nouvelles, one notes the distance between real-world suffering and an ideal of companionable marriage. This contrast between spiritual ideals and earthly corruption recalls the idea of the labyrinth; indeed, the model reader's laborious efforts to correctly navigate the paths that the tales create harken back to suffering and difficult process in a fallen world. The conflict between the real and the ideal proves a challenging aspect of the model reader's education. Still, in a hopeful way, the *Heptaméron* suggests that the ideal could be more achievable than conflicting notions of gender might appear to assert. The key, as nouvelle 3 implies, is to reframe honor not as a social construct but as a moral one and to define it as fidelity for both spouses. This ideological shift is in keeping with Marguerite's faith as well as her attempt to revalorize marriage in the *Heptaméron*, as critics have noted.

vii. Combinations

The moral complexities raised by tales involving deception also inform stories that combine two or more responses to injustice, a gesture that calls to mind the labyrinth's polysemous character and combination of in bono and in malo meanings. Thirty-four of the sixty-eight tales that discuss female sexuality fall into this category. This means that 50 percent combine multiple reactions to wrongdoing. One reason for the sheer quantity of tales in this group is that the process of envisioning solutions to institutional corruption entails trial and error, creative thinking, and the dissecting of multilayered, systemic problems. A single solution will not likely suffice for such a large task, especially not when one considers that a response to injustice that proves effective in one situation may not in another, or that a solution, however impactful, may contradict Christian morality. Might combining response types enable the model reader to pursue reform in a way that is both successful and Christian, while also combating threats to women's sexuality?

Statistical information about this category provides some preliminary insights. The thirty-four tales in this group are stories 1, 2, 4, 5, 6, 8, 10, 12, 13, 14, 15, 16, 19, 20, 21, 22, 24, 31, 32, 33, 35, 36, 37, 38, 39, 40, 41, 43, 46, 47, 51, 61, 66, and 70.[66] Prominent themes, in addition to abuse toward women, include infidelity, scandalous behavior by religious officials, jilted lovers withdrawing from society, and the frustration of lovers' desire to be together. The characters in the stories employ many combinations in response to their specific circumstances. For instance, a wife who suspects her husband of infidelity might trick him and then chastise him verbally when she confirms his pursuit of her chambermaid (story 8). To fend off a predatory nobleman, a lady might employ verbal reproach, trickery, and withdrawal from his presence (tale 10). Other stories combine official channels of justice and physical retribution, such as when an incestuous priest and his sister are tried and burned at the stake (tale 33). Some characters blend verbal reproach with the threat of physical retribution before ultimately showing mercy, as seen in the story of Madame de Loué, who nearly kills her cheating husband by arson (story 37). In some instances, mercy, though pure in itself, can be read as having a manipulative effect on an errant spouse's psyche and thereby introduce an element of trickery into the narration (tale 38). The fact that characters can mix response types that might at first appear incompatible—such as violence and mercy or mercy and trickery—underscores the need for a morally acceptable approach to reform that does not merely perpetuate new forms of injustice in response to institutional abuse. A closer look at stories 37 and 38, similar in scope but different in approach, will help illuminate this conundrum.

At the outset of tale 37, the male narrator Dagoucin claims that he will praise the aptly named Madame de Loué, who won over her cheating spouse.

The wife in Dagoucin's story must confront a scene of wrongdoing, as she discovers her husband with the chambermaid. Her response to this discovery suggests that she employs aristocratic notions of social class, virtue, and gender to parse the situation. As a noblewoman, she believes that she merits her husband's affections more than any chambermaid could, especially considering her careful stewardship of her husband's wealth.[67] Her offense at the situation is class based and not merely moral.

Although she sets fire to the room in which her husband and his mistress are sleeping with the aim of teaching her husband a lesson, rather than in an attempt to kill him, her actions remain threatening and destructive, as a fire once set may rage more quickly than anticipated.[68] As the fire spreads, the wife intervenes to save her husband, shouting to wake him.[69] She then delivers a speech in which she admonishes him to return to his prior faithfulness and issues this warning: "Je ne sçay si une seconde fois, je vous pourrois retirer du danger comme j'ay faict" ("I do not know if I shall have it in my power a second time to save you from danger").[70] By making threats, the wife exhibits mercy, but only conditionally, and so not in a Christian sense. She intimidates her spouse into accepting a second chance. In the end, he does change his ways, and the marriage is saved. This unusual happy ending suggests that threatening behavior achieves justice for women and that its efficacy outweighs its dubious morality—an idea that the model reader may recognize as diverging from Christian moral thought.

Tale 38 reconsiders this scenario, as the female storyteller Longarine relates how a bourgeoise from Tours responds to the same injustice but in a different way. From the outset of her tale, Longarine makes clear that her story will furnish a rewriting of Dagoucin's,[71] saying that she will provide an even more praiseworthy example.[72] The distinction between the two protagonists becomes evident in their reactions to sin. Whereas Dagoucin's character reacts violently and only later extends conditional mercy, Longarine's heroine interprets her husband's errancy through the lens of her faith. When she locates the hovel where her husband goes to visit his sharecropper mistress, she responds with pity because the room is so filthy and cold.[73] Her interpretive stance becomes even more apparent when she demonstrates, by taking constructive action, that she believes divine love and charity can transform this unappealing circumstance. Instead of accepting wrongdoing at face value, she makes the surprising choice to redecorate, bringing in a new bed, hanging up decorations and tapestries, and providing "une pipe de bon vin, des dragées, et des confitures" ("a cask of good wine, and a supply of sweetmeats and preserves").[74] By reworking the scene, the bourgeoise practices a form of Augustinian exegesis, bringing the city of the world closer to the City of God.

The protagonist's remarkable decision to react in faith has a transformative impact that extends beyond the scene itself to implicate the behavior of the characters. When the mistress and the unfaithful husband reconvene after the home renovation, the latter asks how this transformation has occurred, and his mistress replies that his wife directed it. Immediately, the husband is struck with a remorse proportionate to the great kindness his wife has shown him and decides to return to her. Ironically, the bourgeoise's choice to forgo explicit retribution provides positive and immediate results for her, as well as for those who wronged her. Not only do she and her husband benefit from the renewed integrity of their marriage, but the former mistress also gains new surroundings that may help to inspire in her a sense of dignity, despite the tendency of wealthier men to view working women as sexually available.

Nevertheless, it is important to note that this tale can be read as containing an element of trickery because it employs what we would now call reverse psychology. Instead of opposing her husband's behavior, the wife says nothing to him about it. Given that part of the affair's appeal to him was likely its illicit and secretive nature, the wife's behavior removes his primary motivations for infidelity. The story does not state outright that the wife intended her actions to function manipulatively; however, the husband perceives her as planning and implementing an "honneste tour," a phrasing that recalls the virtuous trick by the wife of the valet de chambre in story 27.[75] It therefore seems prudent to place story 38 in the "combinations" category as opposed to under the heading of "mercy" alone. Ultimately, however, Longarine's tale encourages her peers and the model reader to view injustice from a faith-based perspective. She implies that in the written word and the world, divine love and charity are always present and await an exegete who can employ strategies to make them visible.

What lessons can the model reader learn not just from these two tales but from the approach of combining response types? First, the stories show that in some cases, wrong begets wrong; in responding to injustice, characters adopt immoral postures. Unfortunately, such behaviors may in fact yield results, whether in the short or long term. The trouble for the model reader is that in the view of the évangéliques whom Marguerite supported, no approach to reform that rejects Christian principles is viable. The question is not only whether a reaction to injustice redresses the original problem but whether it does so in a morally responsible way and whether it fosters the public good, improving women's circumstances. That last point likewise entails multiple considerations since righting a single inter-personal wrong helps one woman, but it does not address the ways in which patriarchal institutions and their ideologies create toxic scenarios that target women's sexuality. Both the macro and the micro shape reform efforts.

III. Conclusion

The relationship between the micro and the macro in the *Heptaméron* calls to mind the multicursal labyrinth, with its numerous paths and disorient-ing shifts. On the micro level of the tales, the text offers a dizzying number of approaches to reform.[76] Each example gives way to a counterexample or to a different perspective that throws its predecessor into question. One sees instances of mercy, withdrawal, verbal reproach, official and nonviolent forms of justice, physical retribution, trickery or deceit, passive acceptance, the impossibility of recompense, and various combinations thereof. The model reader may initially imagine that analyzing these options will reveal the one best approach to reform. However, when weighed against the criteria of Christian morality, effectiveness in promoting the public good, and the defense of women and their sexuality at all levels of society, no one response functions as a panacea. Even those reactions that come closest to meeting all the criteria fall short of effecting large-scale change. What is needed is a higher vision that surpasses the limits of human cognition, a fact that the text prompts the model reader to recognize and accept in humility. This, more than anything else, is the outcome of the model read-er's education—not the obtaining of information, not the formulating of a particular opinion, not the display of intelligence, but rather the recogni-tion of the need for external assistance to guide the model reader onto the correct path.

Such guidance would have to derive from an encompassing vision of societal and individual realities, one that resembles the idea of the labyrinth as complex, artistic product; from an aerial view, one perceives how the walkway's meandering avenues form a coherent whole. To gain this higher vision, the model reader will need to grasp that education alone cannot pro-vide a sufficiently holistic perspective to reconcile the fallen world and the City of God. Instead, chapter 6 will show that for the model reader, engag-ing in the redemptive work of God's city entails learning to think differ-ently. What matters is not formal education or the honing of intellect, but rather, an individual's overall mindset. This is because justice and reform depend on the frameworks through which the model reader perceives human society, frameworks developed by an errant institutional Church and by the aristocracy. Since both institutions suffer from corruption, a new framework will need to replace the old ones. In essence, the model reader must become a new person in order to effect positive change from his or her position of influence, and as numerous tales in chapter 5 suggested, women help lead this process from a standpoint that reveals flaws in patriarchal institutions and their norms.

6

Above the Labyrinth

A Higher Vision for Reforming the Self and Society

Like a labyrinth, the *Heptaméron* combines spirituality with earthly concerns via tales of, and characters' reactions to, wrongdoing. Yet, as chapter 5 demonstrated, no one approach to redressing injustice emerges as both effective and morally flawless in the stories, and that outcome leaves the model reader disoriented, like a person wandering a multicursal labyrinth. Chapter 6 responds to this problem by contending that the model reader can determine how to respond to iniquity by looking upward, above the tales, to consider the frame. Indeed, the frame provides an alternative source of guidance for the model reader. It is in the frame that we see how Marguerite's text reworks elements of literary genre, including the nouvelle, as seen in chapter 5, and the debate genre, to which this chapter will devote particular attention. The debates form a second level of instruction for the model reader, but just as with the tales, the model reader requires guidance in parsing the storytellers' many opinions in their discussions. Someone with knowledge of the correct path must take the model reader by the hand and show the way forward, just as Christ harrowed hell at Easter in medieval theology, leading the just out of imprisonment and into freedom. In the scriptures that Marguerite and her évangéliques studied, Christ is described as the Way and more specifically as the one way to God the Father and thus to paradise and eternal life.[1] To exit the textual labyrinth in malo, which risks imprisoning the model reader in an endless proliferation of approaches to reform, the model reader must follow the steps of Christ-Theseus. Christ becomes the one way out—a unicursal path superimposed onto what at first resembled a multicursal labyrinth. Free will makes many paths possible, but in Marguerite's faith, Christ is the path that Christians take, the only path by which one leaves the city of the world and journeys toward the City of God.

In the *Heptaméron*'s frame, then, we see the idea of the labyrinth in bono, as both salvation and intricate artistic product. Just as the idea of the labyrinth encompasses in malo components such as sin, the fallen world, confusion, and difficult process, as chapters 3 and 4 demonstrated, so too does it incorporate product, order, divine sovereignty, and salvation into its in bono meanings. The fact that the idea of the labyrinth encompasses both in malo and in bono readings helps explain why scholars have tended to view the *Heptaméron* as either chaotic or spiritually coherent. Some critics assert its undecidability.[2] Others mark it as évangélique.[3] As we have seen, however, both in bono and in malo features are in fact present. What chapter 6 will show is how the in bono components of the labyrinth inform the *Heptaméron*'s structure as well as the model reader's education, which seeks to take institutional representatives from disorientation and distress to transcendent understanding and a newfound appreciation. To gain this new vantage point, which looks down on the *Heptaméron*'s complex design from above, the model reader will have to adopt a new way of thinking and a new standard against which to measure ideas, outcomes that aspects of the *Heptaméron*'s frame promote.

In the frame, we see two genre-related strategies that point the model reader toward the divine.[4] First, the frame manipulates genre to attract and then reform the model reader, an institutional representative who, as a learned and worldly individual, would have been apt to enjoy texts by Marguerite's male predecessors, such as Giovanni Boccaccio and Baldassare Castiglione.[5] Second, the frame highlights the topics of God and scripture through Oisille's Bible study, which takes place each morning. By putting the study of scripture before storytelling in the day's sequence, the *Heptaméron* establishes faith as its first priority. Even the storytelling venture reflects the primacy of faith, as the storytellers admit when they cite the Bible to evaluate the tales they hear. The text further indicates that it espouses the cause of the évangéliques through its characterization of Oisille. A wise, older woman, Oisille acts as a spiritual teacher and a trusted maternal figure. Unlike the incestuous mother in tale 30 or Rolandine's abusive relative, the queen of France, in tale 21, Oisille uses her authority to empower her friends to think critically and work for justice.[6] She seeks to reform institutions by prompting a reformation of the self and making God's presence known.

In the *Heptaméron*, then, the solution to systemic injustice is found in God, rather than in political maneuvers, vigilantism, or the legal system alone. The queen of Navarre's *foi engagée* bridges the gap between self and society, with justice being a top concern.[7] The text suggests that by being reformed on a spiritual level, like the storytellers at Oisille's Bible study, the model reader can hope to develop a higher vision rooted in faith. From this elevated vantage point, the unicursal labyrinth in bono, or salvation in Christ, becomes visible in the *Heptaméron*'s frame and thereby transcends and subsumes the in malo components present in the tales. This outcome derives from the belief system of the évangéliques in which the Kingdom of God will reach full fruition when Christ returns for the Final Judgment. Until then, sin persists in the fallen world, but redemption has nevertheless begun and continues to unfold, with Marguerite and her fellow non-schismatic reformers seeking to participate in that redemptive work, the ultimate outcome of which is already known. The *Heptaméron* can be read as inviting the model reader to join the work of redemption by first being redeemed and undergoing a change of perspective. Consequently, the frame takes on an evangelizing function.[8]

Within this framework, how might the *Heptaméron* encourage readers to reorient their interpretive efforts toward the faith of the évangéliques and away from the confusion that the numerous ideological pathways in the text might otherwise cause? Modern and historical understandings of the reading process can combine to offer insights into this question. As in the accounts of reading that Umberto Eco and Yves Citton describe, the queen of Navarre's text seeks to challenge the model reader's preconceived notions. However, instead of managing that feat through literal content, as Eco suggests, the *Heptaméron* does so through genres and the ideological orientation of the frame.[9] It thereby communicates a belief that texts can actively promote a given interpretation rather than merely discouraging impertinent readings. This difference of perspective stems from Marguerite's faith, according to which scripture is "living and active" (Hebrews 4:12) and can impact a person's motivations.

To make this case, the remainder of the present chapter illustrates how the genres in the frame point the model reader toward God and how questions of interpretation shape the model reader's education and Marguerite's vision for justice. The first section, divided into multiple subsections, compares Marguerite's use of the nouvelle and debate genres in her *Heptaméron* to their iterations in Boccaccio's *Decameron* and Castiglione's *Book of the Courtier*, respectively. As previously explained, the *Heptaméron*'s prologue names the *Decameron* as its primary source of inspiration; moreover, the devisants launch discussions that engage with aspects of Castiglione's *Book of the Courtier*. The second major section in the chapter analyzes the role of Oisille and her Bible study sessions in the spiritual development of the storytellers, including how Oisille's behavior responds to certain arguments in Juan Luis Vives's *Education of a Christian Woman*. The second section also considers how Oisille's instructional role factors into the model reader's education in addition to that of the storytellers. Taken together, the two primary sections of the chapter highlight how in the frame, we see that the idea of the labyrinth in bono prevails and that Marguerite's text depicts women's power to advocate for in bono outcomes through their active involvement in institutional reform.

I. Gendering Genres: Marguerite, Boccaccio, Castiglione

Because the *Heptaméron*'s frame both contains and reworks literary genres, it is important to interrogate the concept of genre and its relation to ideology. Doing so will set up an analysis of how Marguerite's text differs from those of Boccaccio and Castiglione. The first concept to consider is that notions of literary genre depend on reception. As Thomas Beebee argues, genre can be understood in terms of use-value, a concept that encapsulates the text's affective impact on the reader and, in turn, the reader's predictions about how texts will influence him or her in the future.[10] Texts can create particular use-values by participating in multiple genres at once.[11] Moreover, use-values convey ideology; differences between genres and among texts said to participate in the same genre derive from contrasting ideologies.[12] A reader's impression of a text's use-value stems from his or her sociohistorical context; but even if a reader is aware of the norms that informed the original readership of an older text, he or she may be surprised by the text's actual treatment of genre. That is why genre theorist Amy Devitt argues that we should "see genre as both/and rather than either/or, to encompass both the conformity and the resistance."[13] Thus understood, genre facilitates the complex intermingling of worldviews, a phenomenon that harkens back to the labyrinth's polysemous in malo and in bono symbolism.

The coexistence of diverging viewpoints, and especially of conventional and exceptional components in a single text, constitutes a major topic of inquiry for gender and genre scholar Christine Planté, who examines literature as a site for interrogating gender norms.[14] The circumstances that lead women to practice certain genres also help determine the value placed on women's writings. In Planté's view, feminist scholars should take these factors into account by analyzing not only texts that seem unusual for their time but also ones that may appear more conventional.[15] She argues that this approach helps critics to avoid perpetuating a conventional versus exceptional binary that fails to acknowledge the comingling of patriarchal and (proto)feminist impulses within individual texts.[16] After all, tensions in female-authored works provide insight into the challenges women face and the strategies they adopt when they take up the pen.

The *Heptaméron* contributes to such discussions by suggesting that the literary text can influence readers' perception of use-value by manipulating expectations for genre and gender. This process depends on the identity of a text's model reader, who in the case of the *Heptaméron* is an institutional representative. Although both clergy and aristocrats can identify with that title, the text implies through its foregrounding of the nobility that it considers aristocrats to be its primary audience. As the model reader turns toward the *Heptaméron*'s frame in the search for a path toward reform, allusions to Boccaccio's *Decameron* and Castiglione's *Book of the Courtier* should become apparent, given the model reader's level of education and orientation toward material concerns, two criteria that would make the model reader appreciative of such texts. Because the model reader may be inclined to read the *Heptaméron*'s frame through the lens of its male-authored predecessors, the queen of Navarre's text must challenge the reader's assumptions in order to inaugurate an ideological shift.[17]

We see this shift in the three texts' treatment of women in relation to literary genre. Although there is at times a tone of sympathy toward women in Boccaccio's and Castiglione's works, overall these texts convey a more complacent attitude toward women's role in the social order and the injustices that occur in connection with that role than the *Heptaméron* does. This is not to say that there are not examples of women who at times speak up for themselves in either male-authored text, nor is it to say that there are no male characters in either text who can be read in a sympathetic light. The *Heptaméron* likewise contains some male characters who can be interpreted sympathetically, even if, as we have seen, systemic injustice against women as a result of corrupt male leaders in the Church and in the aristocracy, as well as toxic ideologies that derive from those institutions, figure in sixty-eight out of seventy-two tales. The concern here is less the individual characters and whether they can be read in a sympathetic manner, although that is one point of analysis; rather, the main focus of this chapter's examination of gender and genre is larger systemic issues, which can be read as filtering down to the words and actions of narrators and of individual characters. The blending of systemic and personal components in each text will necessarily result in some measure of polyvalence, but that polysemy is contained within a larger framework that brings the parts into relation with the whole, a gesture that recalls the symbolism of the labyrinth. Given such complexities within individual tales and debates, it is useful to consider the larger frame that contextualizes the texts' component parts.

What this section interrogates, then, is the ways in which the frames of the *Decameron*, the *Book of the Courtier*, and the *Heptaméron*, as well as the genres those frames employ, suggest certain use-values to the model reader and how those use-values might be said to intersect with the topics of women's sexuality, justice, and reform. Whereas genre and the frame can be said to downplay the impact of systemic abuse on women in Boccaccio's and Castiglione's texts, the *Heptaméron* reorients these same genres, as well as the frame, toward the revelation of that abuse and its spiritual implications. What the *Decameron* and the *Book of the Courtier* appear to frame as seduction, the *Heptaméron* considers injustice. The queen's text thus prompts the model reader to identify ideologies that prove harmful toward women and to rethink them in light of Christian spirituality and women's ability to further reform.

The *Heptaméron* can be read as directing the genres in Boccaccio's and Castiglione's texts toward a program of Christian education in which women play a key role. By appearing to emulate male literary genius, the text avoids censure, a perennial threat for Marguerite, all while conveying different ideas from those of its predecessors. The *Heptaméron* mimics in some senses the male authors' strategy of seduction, but rather than meditating on worldly pleasures, it attracts a model reader who finds that topic alluring, only to redirect the ideological focus toward spiritual concerns. Here, we see a delicate balance between the revelation and concealment of subversion. This strategy fosters the development of a higher, in bono perspective on the labyrinthine subject of reform, one that subsumes the in malo moments of injustice toward women in the nouvelle and debate genres as practiced by Boccaccio and Castiglione.

i. Gender, Genre, and Justice: How Frame Narrators and Use-values Engage the Model Reader in the Decameron and the Heptaméron

The *Heptaméron*'s vision of reform responds to Boccaccio's *Decameron*, and as such, a brief word on Boccaccio is in order. Although Boccaccio lived and wrote before Marguerite's time, his use of the vernacular and his innovation surrounding literary genre made him a renowned writer throughout early modern Europe. Boccaccio's choice to write in the vernacular meant that those who did not read Latin could access his works. This category often included merchants and women. Indeed, Boccaccio dedicated several of his texts to women in particular, and many women writers in the ensuing centuries would produce literary innovations of their own in response to his works.[18] Marguerite de Navarre is a famous example of this trend since her *Heptaméron* explicitly names Boccaccio's *Decameron* as its original source of inspiration.

Yet ideological influences on the two authors prompt us to question the exact nature of the relationship between the two texts. For example, Boccaccio promoted the study of ancient languages, especially Greek, but he did so primarily out of an interest in the mythology and culture of antiquity,[19] rather than out of particular support for the teaching of ancient languages in connection with biblical exegesis, as Marguerite encouraged her brother to do in his founding of the Collège de France. Although Boccaccio had read and admired the work of Aquinas, in his *Decameron*, he drew more on the pleasures and sorrows of earthly life and the notion of fortune than on religious devotion.[20] The motif of fortune diverges from the discourse of divine sovereignty coupled with free will that one sees in the *Heptaméron*, a text in which Christian spirituality is of the utmost importance.

Boccaccio's emphasis on fortune also suggests a certain fatality in the unfolding of events, as if to imply that human action cannot change earthly realities or correct injustice. Rather than highlighting the distance between the city of the world and the City of God, Boccaccio's *Decameron* presents a focus on earthly pleasures as a response to suffering, thus presenting an alternative to religious discourses on paradise as the realm of the afterlife.[21] Amid the painful realities of human existence, such as the plague epidemic, the company seeks to escape not only from physical danger but also from the negative emotions it provokes. Escaping to the villa enables them to redirect their attention toward amusing pastimes that begin to counterbalance the suffering they have witnessed and experienced. This ideological orientation gestures toward the in malo half of the labyrinth's symbolism; instead of foregrounding spiritual redemption—the labyrinth's most theologically important in bono reading from a Christian point of view—the text proposes earthly pleasure as an antidote for earthly pain. When coupled with its dedication to female readers, the text's treatment of pleasure raises important questions as to how a devoutly Christian and reform-oriented author such as Marguerite would respond to Boccaccio's writing in her *Heptaméron* and what ideological revisions her text might propose through the use of literary genre in relation to gender.

An analysis of how the *Decameron*'s frame and formulation of the nouvelle genre treat the topics of women and injustice will lay the groundwork for textual comparison. The *Decameron*'s frame and nouvelles can be said to cultivate a use-value of pleasure that aims to seduce the model reader.

This goal entails casting the model reader in a receptive and permissive role that ultimately fosters complacency toward systemic injustices. The process begins in the prologue, which contextualizes the frame and the tales. The prologue's narrator adopts the persona of the author and claims to pity women because they lack a diversion from the torments of love.[22] This frame narrator, whom we might equally call the model author,[23] presents his *Decameron* as a gift to lovesick ladies: "les dames qui les lyront pourront prendre (des plaisantes choses en icelle montrées) plaisir" ("In reading them, the ladies of whom I have been speaking will be able to . . . derive pleasure from the entertaining material they contain").[24] In making such a prediction, the model author assigns a use-value of pleasure to his text, casting himself as a kind of literary lover.

Yet despite the model author's sympathetic stance and awareness of the wrongs that society commits against women, he accepts societal norms as they are. Instead of advocating for change, he invites the model reader to leave behind life's sufferings, which the city of Florence and its plague epidemic represent, and to focus on gratification. To underscore this idea, he situates the utopic villa where the storytellers gather atop a small mountain that contrasts with the ever-deepening grave in the city's churchyard. As the citizens of Florence descend to the depths, the soon-to-be storytellers ascend to a place of perfect yet earthly enjoyment in which neither plague nor death can reach them.[25]

Although the palace's elevation recalls the association between high altitudes and divinity found in Greco-Roman mythology (Mount Olympus), the Hebrew Bible (Mount Sinai and Mount Zion), and the New Testament (the ascension of Christ into heaven), the frame narrator indicates that the company's paradise teems with material pleasures.

> Lequel lieu estoit sur une petite montaignette, ung peu loing de toutes partz du grand chemin, pleine de divers arbrisseaux et d'entes toutes feuillues de vertes branches, plaisantes à regarder, sur la syme de laquelle y avoit ung palays avec une belle et grande court au meilieu accompaigné de galleries, salles, & chambres toutes & chascune d'icelles a-part soy, tresbelles & enrichies de plaisantes painctures à veoir: & les preaulx estoient à lentour, & les jardins beaulx à merveilles avec puyz de tresfresches eaues: aussi les caves plaines de vins excellentz, choses plus à estimer à curieux buveurs que à sobres et honnestes femmes.

> The place in question was some distance from any road, situated on a little mountain that was quite a pleasant sight to see with all its shrubs

and trees decked out in their green foliage. At the top there was a palace, built around a large, lovely courtyard, containing loggias, great halls, and bedchambers, all of which were beautifully proportioned and adorned with charming paintings of happy scenes. Surrounded by meadows and marvelous gardens, the palace had wells of the coolest water and vaulted cellars stocked with precious wines, wines more suitable for connoisseurs than for honest, sober ladies.[26]

In this passage, the model author repeats positively connoted adjectives that communicate beauty, such as *plaisantes* and *beaux/belles*, while also emphasizing wholeness and vibrancy through his use of the word *pleine* and natural images. The fact that gardens and meadows surround the palace reminds readers that while death reigns in the city, life thrives elsewhere. The text thus suggests that the company will find vitality in their new environment.

References to life and the senses soon take on an erotic cast. When detailing the villa's interior, the model author pays special attention to the bedrooms: "ladicte compaignie trouva tout nettoye & bien en ordre, & les lictz dedans les chambres faictz & dressez. Si estoit tout seme de fleurs, telles qu'on pouvoit avoir en la saison entremeslées de jonchée, qui ne fut sans grand plaisir de toute la compaignie" ("When they got there, the company discovered to their great delight that the palace had been swept clean from top to bottom, the beds had been made up in their chambers, every room had been adorned with seasonal flowers, and the floors had been carpeted with rushes").[27] Initially, the text justifies its interest in bedrooms by incorporating it into a commentary on the palace's well-ordered cleanliness, but the presence of flowers and plants adds a symbolic dimension. It brings the natural world's pleasures indoors, marking the bedroom as a hedonistic space.

Although the text may employ such images to foreground the sexual tension between several of the women in the company and their serviteurs, no one in the group initiates sexual activity while at the villa.[28] Instead, the frame's insistence on pleasure works its way into the nouvelles that the storytellers recount. Sex constitutes an important motif in numerous tales, appearing as an unavoidable reality in which satisfaction ultimately overrides moral concerns. The text's rendering of the nouvelle genre reinforces this thematic emphasis on pleasure by identifying fortune (*Fortuna*) as the plot's impetus. Because of the nouvelle's use-value of pleasure, which the model author established, many tales portray sex as harmless and desirable and suggest that because Fortuna decides a person's fate, women should respond receptively to men's seductive advances. The trouble is that, as the *Heptaméron*'s many stories of abuses against women make clear, women's sexuality can be targeted for oppressive aims and not only out of mutual romantic interest. Systemic injustices toward women can color interpersonal relations.

In Boccaccio's text, the tale of Alatiel, daughter of the Babylonian sultan, sheds lights on the differences in ideology that subtend the *Decameron*'s use of the nouvelle genre, as opposed to the *Heptaméron*'s. In the story, fortune assures male dominance by presenting sex as adequate compensation for women's function as objects of exchange within patriarchy. The story's female protagonist becomes the property of nine strangers in succession after a shipwreck separates her from her fiancé. While Alatiel mourns her fate each time she passes from one man to the next, her focus on pleasure enables her to accept quickly that which Fortuna dictates. Furthermore, although premarital abstinence helped safeguard the line of succession and was therefore considered a feminine virtue, the text offers no moral commentary on Alatiel's decision to enjoy each man's sexual imposition instead of resisting.[29] Instead, the tale implies that women are by nature perpetually aroused and that Fortuna serves as their ally in forcing sex on them. The female listeners' reaction bolsters that assertion since rather than object to the tale's implications, the women sigh with envy: "Les dames souspirerent fort des divers cas advenuz à la belle dame: mais qui scet quelle occasion mouvoit ces souspirs? Paradventure y en avoit il de celles qui non moins souspiroient du desir de faire si souvent telles nopces, que de pitie qu'elles eussent d'elle" ("The ladies sighed repeatedly over the lovely lady's various misadventures, but who knows what may have moved them to do so? Perhaps some of them sighed as much out of a desire for such frequent marriages as out of pity for Alatiel").[30] Alatiel's story can be said to prime women to accept men's aggression since in the *Decameron*, they can escape neither destiny nor desire.

Given that the text identifies women as its intended audience, stories such as Alatiel's suggest to the female model reader that sex is an inherently positive experience for women and that therefore they ought to adopt a complacent and permissive attitude toward men who make sexual advances toward them. This implied discourse proves dangerous not only for the well-being of the model reader but also for society writ large since the social order depended on women's sexuality, as the *Heptaméron* demonstrates through its many tales of the chaos that ensues as a result of sexual misconduct by men in positions of power.

Although Boccaccio's nouvelles became the standard for later writers,[31] including Marguerite de Navarre, the *Heptaméron* diverges from the *Decameron*'s stances on women and gender relations. It reassigns to the nouvelle genre a use-value of truthfulness, which undergirds both the tales themselves and the entire storytelling venture, as the prologue attests. This focus on the notion of truth combines the in malo and in bono components of the labyrinth's symbolism since the New Testament affirms both the fallen world and Christ's victory over it. Still, the in bono readings of the labyrinth prevail because instead of presenting earthly pleasures as a corrective to the fallen world, the *Heptaméron* points toward divine truth and redemption through its emphases on faith and scripture. It is therefore not only the city of the world with its secular ideologies that the text examines but also the City of God, as well as the distance between the two cities, and the need to bring the former more in line with the latter. Parlamente, an outspoken female storyteller, begins to unveil such ideas when she explains that the narrators' guiding principle will be to tell true stories.[32] This new use-value for the nouvelle distinguishes the *Heptaméron*'s agenda from the *Decameron*'s. The fact that the storytellers reference actual people and events and occupy a real location (Notre Dame de Sarrance) suggests that the quest for truth in all senses will become the text's focus.

An emphasis on truthfulness likewise figures in the model author's narration of the prologue, which sets up the text's treatment of the nouvelle genre. Unlike the model author in Boccaccio's frame, the *Heptaméron*'s frame narrator omits all references to her identity and motivations.[33] She limits self-referentiality to rare uses of the first person, as can be found in the text's second sentence: "Ma fin n'est de vous declarer la situation ne la vertu des bains [de Caulderets], mais seulement de racompter ce qui sert à la matiere que je veux escrire" ("But it is not my purpose here to expatiate on the power of these waters and their fine situation. I wish merely to relate those details which will serve the subject I have in hand").[34] This citation contains the only instance of first-person narration in the entire prologue. Immediately afterward, the narration assumes an omniscient perspective and makes no direct attempt to influence the reader's interpretation.[35] On the contrary, the *Heptaméron*'s model author maintains the appearance of obedience toward sixteenth-century notions of feminine virtue by remaining "silent." Nevertheless, her reticence enables the *Heptaméron* to implement substantial revisions to the nouvelle genre. Through subversive means, the queen's text can be read as countering the seductive schemes of its male-authored predecessor.

Yet another device from the *Decameron* that the *Heptaméron* reworks is the use of a tragic impetus to propel the characters toward reclusion and storytelling. Like Boccaccio's characters, Marguerite's devisants face uncontrollable forces in the prologue that push them toward a secluded location; however, in the *Heptaméron* the catalyst is a flood. Unlike in the *Decameron*, God remains present in the disaster and uses it to draw the nobles to the abbey of Notre Dame de Sarrance; here, again, we see the in bono assertion of divine sovereignty in the face of apparent chaos. Furthermore, the austere environment contrasts pointedly with the self-indulgent materialism that dominates at the Florentine villa. Whereas the *Decameron* provides elaborate descriptions of the villa's natural setting, the *Heptaméron* mentions only one aspect of the abbey's grounds: its meadow. The model author declines to describe the meadow in detail and merely states that it is "si beau et plaisant, qu'il avoit besoing d'un Bocace, pour le depeindre à la verité" ("so beautiful and fair that it would take a Boccaccio to describe it as it really was").[36] Through this statement, the frame narrator supposedly defers to Boccaccio's skill while omitting an essential component of the text she claims to imitate, since the *Decameron*'s setting, tone, and thematic preoccupations coalesce in descriptions of nature's sensual appeal. The *Heptaméron*'s frame narrator implies through this divergence that the text as a whole will not valorize the natural world and its pleasures as its predecessor did, nor will it celebrate the same "beauté de rhetoricque" ("rhetorical ornament").[37] Instead, it will valorize truth telling.[38]

Like the labyrinth, with its in bono and in malo connotations, the search for truth in the *Heptaméron* operates on two levels: that of harsh realities and that of spiritual revelation. As a text founded in a pro-woman vision of Christianity, the *Heptaméron* reaffirms divine sovereignty rather than the notion of Fortuna in Boccaccio's text. God remains a guarantor of truth and meaning and intervenes in many tales on behalf of righteous women. The text likewise subverts the *Decameron*'s promise of gratification. Instead of depicting sex as inherently enjoyable, Marguerite de Navarre's nouvelles reveal the prevalence of sexual violence at court and in the Church. In recounting instances of attempted rape, the devisants provide a series of case studies through which the company can test their understanding of Christian morality and its application to social interactions. The women's narration of tales alongside men participates in this endeavor by addressing the subject the men find appealing—sex—but reframing it as a channel for aggression.[39] The sharing of nouvelles, presented as a concession, fuels the search for solutions to injustice.

Through such strategies, the *Heptaméron* replaces the *Decameron*'s project of seduction with spiritual conversion, an objective that implies a shift from distress to awe, process to product, in malo to in bono. To prompt the model reader to recognize and combat wrongdoing, the *Heptaméron*'s nouvelles present examples for evaluation, as chapters 4 and 5 discussed at length. This gesture reflects the nouvelle's close affinity with the exemplum, the ecclesiastical genre from which it is often said to derive.[40] Just as medieval clergymen used everyday anecdotes when preaching, the devisants' tales demonstrate the problem of sin, the influence of corrupt institutions, and the difficulty of determining the correct response to systemic issues. Tales about people outside the immediate group enable the storytellers to discuss problems with a measure of affective distance and to consider what behaviors they deem appropriate in a given situation. Within this context, examples support the text's overarching goal of reform, not only by prompting the model reader to walk down numerous paths and thus yearn for the one way out but also by providing fodder for the storyteller's discussions, which revise elements of Castiglione's *Book of the Courtier*.

ii. Smooth Talkers and Truth Seekers: The Dialogue Genre in the Book of the Courtier and the Heptaméron

The call to self-assessment and reform becomes possible both through the *Heptaméron*'s reworking of the nouvelle and through its response to the dialogue genre as practiced by Castiglione in *The Book of the Courtier* (1528).[41] As a word of introduction, Castiglione lived and wrote during Marguerite's lifetime. He received an education that blended humanism with military training and social etiquette, a trend that would later influence all of Europe, in large part thanks to *The Book of the Courtier*, on which the author had begun working by the time François Ier became king of France in 1515.[42] Alain Pons asserts that Castiglione most likely drafted his book in three phases. As a result of this lengthy time span, the author's political leanings evolved alongside the book and shifting power dynamics in Europe, given that François Ier remained locked in an ongoing conflict with Charles V from his ascendancy until his capture at Pavia in 1525. Castiglione hesitated between dedicating his *Book of the Courtier* to the French king or to the Holy Roman emperor but eventually decided on the latter, whose power and prestige had seen considerable gains in the intervening period.[43] Because Castiglione's text discusses the traits of the ideal courtier as well as his attitudes toward women and the behaviors appropriate to women, his choice of dedicatee was not neutral, especially considering that François Ier's court had become known as a haven of learning and refinement and was so full of women as to be nicknamed "la cour des dames." Although Castiglione's allegiance was to Charles V, the spirit of *courtoisie* that marked François Ier's own court figures prominently in the text.

Given their ideological focus, the dialogues in the *Courtier*, like Boccaccio's nouvelles, can be read as positing a use-value of pleasure; however, for Castiglione, pleasure is associated primarily with erudition. As such, the *Courtier*'s implied use-value of pleasure suggests to the model reader, a man or woman of the court, that power and happiness stem from intellect. The text implies that both enjoyment and influence are normal outcomes of masculine intelligence rather than temptations to unjust behavior. To support this idea, the text praises intellectual noblemen and depicts women accepting unequal treatment. In this way, the *Courtier* can be said to repeat the same underlying ideological orientation as Boccaccio's *Decameron*. The text portrays the city of the world, in this case the Urbino court—which the *Heptaméron*'s tale 51 associates with deception and brutality—as a place in which intellectual endeavors offer an escape from suffering.[44] Instead of contemplating spirituality as a means of redeeming the fallen world, as the in bono labyrinth implies, Castiglione's text reinforces Boccaccio's suggestion that an escape from earthly suffering can be found in pleasure. While the *Courtier* does allude to Christianity, it does so obliquely and as an interdiction, claiming that it is not appropriate to discuss spiritual matters and courtly life in tandem. Consequently, courtly intrigue and the roles of men and women according to secular ideologies become the dominant themes of the work.

Although Castiglione and Boccaccio practiced different genres and although the former presented his project as departing from the *Decameron*, multiple similarities invite further comparison between the two texts. In Castiglione's dedication and introduction, one finds a frame narrator identified as the author, a sumptuous setting, and an emphasis on pleasure. Like Boccaccio, the model author explains his motivation for writing, stating that the duke's passing prompts him to publish his text so that the frame narrator's friend, the bishop of Viseo, may come to know the members of the Urbino court secondhand. Castiglione's choice of dedicatee reflects the fact that in addition to his time at court, he served as the Vatican's ambassador to Spain and as bishop of Ávila. The dedication acknowledges the overlap between politics and religion in early modern Europe, even if courtly norms and intellectual pastimes constitute the text's main focus.

The *Courtier*'s use-value of pleasure inflects the setting and thematic preoccupations of the frame, revealing further similarities with the

Decameron. Indeed, the model author situates his characters' discussions in the bucolic countryside: "Alentour la campagne est la plus fertile du monde et pleine de fruits, de manière qu'outre la salubrité de l'air, il y a abondance de toute chose nécessaire à la vie humaine" ("[Urbino] has been blessed by Heaven with a most fertile and bountiful countryside, so that, besides the wholesomeness of the air, it abounds in all the necessities of life").[45] The shortness of this description does not prevent it from dialoguing with the idyllic setting of the *Decameron*; the connotations of nature in Boccaccio's text—abundance, life, enjoyment—also qualify Castiglione's.

Unlike in the *Decameron*, however, the *Courtier*'s model author situates the company's games indoors, providing a detailed account of the duke's abode. Among the duke's many treasures, one finds statues from antiquity, musical instruments, rare artwork, and gold-adorned books in Latin, Hebrew, and Greek.[46] The model author states that the duke prizes his books above all else, "estimant que c'était là la suprême excellence de son grand palais" ("deeming these to be the supreme excellence of his great palace").[47] From these objects, one infers the duke's appreciation of high culture and intellectualism, two indicators that the *Courtier* will privilege the court over nature.

The motifs that accompany courtly life in the text also recall Boccaccio's *Decameron.* Just as Boccaccio's storytellers convey joie de vivre, Castiglione's discussants punctuate their remarks with laughter, highlighting the themes of games and pleasure. Every evening, the nobles partake in amusements, including games of wit: "[À] côté des passe-temps agréables, comme la musique et les danses, qui étaient ordinaires, on proposait parfois de belles questions, d'autres fois on se livrait à des jeux d'esprit, au gré de l'un ou de l'autre, dans lesquels, sous des voiles divers, les assistants découvraient souvent par allégorie leurs pensées à ceux qui leur plaisaient le plus" ("Amid the pleasant pastimes, the music and dancing which were continually enjoyed, fine questions would sometimes be proposed, and sometimes ingenious games, now at the behest of one person and now of another, in which, under various concealments, those present revealed their thoughts allegorically to whomever they chose").[48] Just as in the description of the duke's palace, the narrator links culture with intellectualism. The foregrounding of cognitively oriented vocabulary within the context of games demonstrates the interconnectedness of wit, social life, and pleasure at court.

This dynamic informs the primary activity in which Castiglione's aristocrats engage: describing the ideal courtier and *dame de palais.* The company's project provides "un plaisir merveilleux" ("a marvelous pleasure") and a chance to showcase intelligence.[49] All discussants aim to please the highest-ranking player, and due to the duke of Urbino's chronic illness and absence, his wife replaces him as leader of the game. In endowing the duchess with this role, the *Courtier* might appear to advance a pro-woman agenda, but because the men in the group do the vast majority of the talking, and because conversation between men and women carried erotic undertones in Italian court culture, the courtiers' arguments can be read as attempts at ideological and amorous seduction.[50] Much like in the *Decameron*, the male speakers construct their interjections carefully with a female audience in mind. These efforts help reinforce the valorization of male intellect that the description of the duke's antique statues and books implied. The model author further emphasizes the link between masculinity and intelligence when he lists out all the learned people who took part in games of wit at Urbino, such as Ottaviano Fregoso, Pietro Bembo, Cesare Gonzaga, and Julien de Médicis le Magnifique. In ending his list with the phrase "et une infinité d'autres très nobles gentilshommes" ("and countless other very noble gentlemen"), he omits women from the group of superior intellects.[51] Against a backdrop of erudition, the *Courtier*'s repetition of Boccaccio's setting, tone, and motifs can be read as attempting to seduce the model reader into accepting masculine preeminence.

The duchess reinforces this idea by using her authority to impose silence on the women, even during the debate on the ideal dame de palais.[52] Her decision carries over from the *Courtier*'s first pages, when her second-in-command, Madame Emilia, declines to begin the discussion as the duchess requests, calling speaking a "peine" ("trouble") and silence a "privilège" ("ease").[53] Even as the text acknowledges that Emilia possesses lively intelligence, it silences her and bars her from the list of great minds. The text's false protofeminism becomes even more apparent when Emilia enlists Julien le Magnifique to plead the women's case during the debate on the ideal noblewoman. Le Magnifique contends that women should be judged based on their adherence to gendered standards of virtue, such as beauty, composure, and modesty.[54] His focus on appearances gestures toward the text's preoccupation with social status. Moreover, aspects of Le Magnifique's diction and bearing suggest that he desires to appear authoritative in his erudition.[55] When Margherita Gonzaga asks him to tell stories about virtuous women, he responds by citing anecdotes from antiquity in an authoritative tone that recalls the instructional stance that a teacher might adopt toward a student. Although Le Magnifique does not openly espouse misogynist ideals, his comments about women and interactions with them imply sexist power dynamics.

Much as the men in Alatiel's tale objectify her and deny her agency, so the *Courtier* condones the silence of women, a pointed gesture in the context of the debate genre. In so doing, the text suggests that women should be seen (by men), but rarely heard, and that they ought to gratify men's desires, either by accepting sexual advances, as was more overtly the case in the *Decameron*, or by listening to their well-worded seductive arguments. In either case, these male-authored texts can be said to promote a complacent and permissive mindset in the female model reader.

The *Heptaméron* redresses that injustice by enabling active female participation in debates about conduct for aristocratic men and women. To achieve the promise of equity on which the *Courtier* fails to deliver, Marguerite de Navarre's text grants men and women equal speaking rights within a polyphonic dialogue. This genre choice entails different consequences than it would in a male-authored text. First, women did not typically practice the polyphonic dialogue genre because women who spoke extensively in mixed company were considered less virtuous than those who, through their silence, suggested their chastity and obedience.[56] Most women writers opted for the diphonic dialogue, in which one female character addresses another. By choosing polyphony, Marguerite appears to bow to masculine literary genius even as she defies expectations for women's use of the dialogue.

Moreover, the *Heptaméron*'s implementation of the polyphonic dialogue opposes the *Courtier*'s use-value of pleasure by attracting a worldly model reader into debates about abuse against women and strategies for effecting change. It realizes its goal by affording women the opportunity not only to narrate stories but also to engage in discussion on equal terms with men. The text's concern for gender equality begins in the prologue, which specifies that when several high-ranking aristocrats originally suggested the project, they forbade learned men from participating.[57] The prologue's admonition against erudition for erudition's sake recalls the queen's belief in the fallibility of human cognition. Her text can be read as invalidating masculine intellectualism and instead suggesting that the devisants must all access the same God and scriptures for understanding.[58]

The text furthers that egalitarian initiative through the contributions of outspoken and quick-witted women and through the reworking of the medieval *débat* tradition and the Platonic dialogue.[59] The débat genre, practiced in the medieval universities, was a type of Socratic exchange in which a teacher tested a student's knowledge. The Platonic dialogue, in contrast, was more concerned with the development of sound judgment. It raised an abstract topic and included several perspectives with a view to advancing a general understanding of the subject. The *Heptaméron* combines elements of each debate type. The text's cyclical structure in which tales and debates perpetuate each other depends on a storyteller raising a question that he or she will address through the narration of a tale. At the end of the story, he or she delivers a moral lesson with a tone of authority. However, unlike Socratic disciples, the devisants debate, rather than accept, the ideas presented to them. By melding debate types, the *Heptaméron* enables women to examine the implications of Christian spirituality for gender relations, especially given the pervasive reality of threats to women's sexuality in Marguerite's society.

Specifically, the *Heptaméron*'s dialogues bolster the use-value of truthfulness set forth in the nouvelles. Like the stories, the debates suggest that systemic injustices against women are neither inevitable nor warranted and that it is therefore necessary to reform both individuals and structures that support abuse. By adding questions of spirituality to Castiglione's model, the *Heptaméron* challenges the *Courtier*'s assertion that courtly topics should remain separate from religious ones. Instead, the *Heptaméron* brings religious principles to bear on politics, much as the labyrinth combines spiritual and earthly concerns. The text takes this approach because the storytellers share not only their social class and the secular ideologies it promotes but also their faith.[60] Moreover, the inclusion of religious discourse in the *Heptaméron*'s debates marks a departure from both Boccaccio and Castiglione and suggests that the model reader is not only a courtier or dame de palais, as in Castiglione's text, or women in general, as in Boccaccio's, but rather an institutional representative. This means that the topics discussed will be relevant to the clergy in addition to the nobility. In an era of Church reform, the inclusion of the clergy within the role of the model reader is significant because it indicates that the *Heptaméron*, unlike its male-authored predecessors, does not seek merely to affirm what already is but instead aims to reconcile what is with what should be. In malo and in bono aspects of the labyrinth's symbolism interact, with the in bono aim of transformation ultimately taking precedence. Reform becomes the text's ideological orientation rather than the defense of the status quo, although the text does make recourse to the concept of the social order to present its objectives in a manner palatable to the model reader. Ultimately, the *Heptaméron* reflects the view of the évangéliques, who put faith into conversation with politics in order to bring the city of the world into closer alignment with the City of God.

The debate following tale 14 illustrates these concepts. The tale follows the vengeful schemes of Bonnivet, who tricks a woman who once refused his advances into sleeping with him. In the story, Bonnivet pretends to advise the woman's serviteur on strategies for seducing her. As soon as the serviteur secures a date and time for the tryst, Bonnivet takes his place. In the end, he succeeds in duping the woman, who unlike Alatiel, contemplates suicide. The tale's initial emphasis on seduction strategies calls to mind the *Courtier* and the *Decameron* before revealing that destructive behavior underlies courtly discourses of seduction and gender. This destructiveness stems from the lies that those in positions of power, such as men at court, tell to pursue their own desires at their subordinates' expense.

The *Heptaméron*'s discussions unveil such lies to the characters and the model reader as part of the search for truth, as the debate following the story helps demonstrate. The tale's misogynist narrator, Simontault, opens the discussion with an apology of deception, claiming that the nobleman's actions were warranted because of the woman's hypocrisy.[61] Here, Simontault echoes Bonnivet's mindset by suggesting that men have an inherent right to women's bodies. However, the oldest male storyteller, Guebron, dissects Simontault's assertions. Guebron claims that because he desires to atone for predatory behaviors in his youth, he must warn the ladies that noblemen view them in terms of selfish pleasure.[62] In stating an ugly truth, Guebron insists that the use-value of pleasure and the project of seduction benefit the male originator of discourse.[63]

Although Guebron presents himself as coming to the ladies' aid, much like Julien le Magnifique, the *Heptaméron*'s female storytellers refuse merely to listen; instead, they think critically and elaborate their own defense. Longarine, for instance, considers her own life experience before agreeing with Guebron: "tous les serviteurs que j'ay eu, m'ont tousjours commencé leurs propos par moy . . . mais la fin en a esté par eulx" ("Every man who's ever wanted to be *my* devoted servant has always started by declaring that my life, my welfare and my honour were all he truly desired. But in the end it's always their own interests that count").[64] Emarsuitte, another devisante, brings up the notion of bons tours, which figured in the *Courtier* and the *Decameron*. She insists that Bonnivet's ploy is a "tour meschant" ("mean trick") and asks, "Est il dict que si une dame en aimoit un, que l'autre la doive avoir par finesse?" ("If a woman is in love with one man, does that make it alright for some other man to take her by trickery?").[65] Unlike in Castiglione's text, the devisantes reveal through their comments that notions of seduction and pleasure are couched in terms of masculine dominance.

Reflections on courtly gender norms become even more apparent when the tale 14 debate references the *Courtier*, which states that ladies should refuse to believe their suitors' professions of love and should deliberately misinterpret what they say to discourage their pursuit of sex. The motivation behind these recommendations is to preserve women's reputation at court since the ideal dame de palais must avoid scandal.[66] The queen of Navarre's storytellers examine these rules by breaking one of the *Courtier*'s requirements for courtly conversation, which is to avoid mixing worldly and spiritual topics.[67] Parlamente, for instance, alludes to Le Magnifique's advice when she says, "une femme ne doibt jamais faire semblant d'entendre où l'homme veult venir" ("[A] lady should not let it appear that she understands what he is driving at").[68] Yet spiritual questions soon intervene when Nomerfide asks whether it is in fact a sin to judge one's neighbor.[69] In raising a question rooted in the scriptures, Nomerfide refuses to accept societal dictates at face value. Instead, she references another text whose spiritual focus renders it more authoritative in her eyes.

Indeed, despite their varying opinions, the storytellers have frequent recourse to scripture as an authority on truth when they analyze the stories they hear. This is significant given the divergences in the devisants' ages, genders, and romantic experiences, to name only a few criteria that shape their opinions. The storytellers' varying viewpoints offer insights into broader trends in sixteenth-century society, marked by the comingling of discourses we might now term misogynistic or pro-woman, as well as numerous philosophical and literary influences. We can read this plethora of perspectives as a window into how individuals grappled with opposing ideologies, sometimes internalizing mentalities we would now term toxic alongside less harmful ideas. An example of this phenomenon is when the outspoken devisante Parlamente affirms a man's authority over his household, alluding to a commonly accepted understanding of Paul's writings on marriage in her day. Such statements do not negate the text's attention to abuses against women; rather, they render, in a complex way, the reality that all women exist within patriarchy and process numerous and at times conflicting messages about gender relations.

Whereas the male storytellers Hircan, Saffredent, and Simontault, for example, tend to espouse a more hedonistic and misogynist view on women and sex, Parlamente, Emarsuitte, and Longarine often chastise them for their mentalities.[70] Oisille and Guebron are the oldest members of the company. Guebron claims that he desires to reveal ugly tendencies in masculine attitudes toward women so as to protect the women in the group, although he also enjoys criticizing the clergy. Oisille, as we have seen, acts as surrogate mother and also as religious educator to the others, who respect her authority on spiritual matters. Dagoucin, an idealistic male storyteller, tends to speak in Neoplatonic terms on the topic of romance, although

several of the other men accuse him of using this chaste persona to manip-
ulate women. Finally, Nomerfide, the youngest devisante, has a reputation
for immaturity, but the others appreciate that she tells stories they find
amusing.

Nomerfide is the storyteller who, in response to tale 14, alludes to the
principle of nonjudgment in James 4:12, Luke 6:37, and Matthew 7:1. Because
she has a reputation for being too generous with suitors, her citation can
be interpreted as a defense of her past behavior, about which we read in the
discussion following tale 5. When Nomerfide says that had she been in
the ferrywoman's place, she would have jumped into the river to preserve
her chastity, Oisille responds jokingly, "Vous sçavez doncques bien nager"
("So you're a strong swimmer, are you then!").[71] Paul Chilton, in his
English translation of the *Heptaméron*, notes that in the De Thou manuscript from 1553 the verb was *nouer*, as opposed to *nager*, and that the term
nouer meant both "to swim" and "to tie," with the latter carrying sexual
connotations.[72] Regardless of whether we accept this word play as penned
by Marguerite, given De Thou's editing of the manuscript, we see that
Oisille questions Nomerfide's assertions. Through her comments, she urges
the company to develop a sincere, undivided heart.

Oisille can be considered a teacher not only to Nomerfide and her friends
but also to the model reader, who likewise requires guidance to move
beyond diverging opinions and toward ideological stability. After all, the
Heptaméron's use-value of truthfulness supports a project of reform that
includes the model reader, who occupies a similar role in society as the storytellers or the monks. Whatever changes the storytellers may need to
make to their thinking, the model reader is prompted to make as well. If
the devisants cannot, based on secular ideologies or their own experiences,
agree on a single correct interpretation of each tale, then they must look to
a higher source for clarity, a gesture that prompts a similar response in the
model reader.

II. God of the Labyrinth: Reform through Oisille, Exegesis, and Multilayered Narration

Oisille, in her role as spiritual educator, provides direction to the aristocrats and the model reader as they struggle to find truth amid competing
ideologies. Her spiritual authority features prominently in the frame, beginning in the prologue. When the flood forces the company to flee Cauterets,
we glimpse a symbolic reminder of Noah and the flood, a topic that Augustine treated in *The City of God*, arguing that the ark and its inhabitants

represent the Church, whom Christ saved from destruction.[73] One might also see in this flood an allusion to the waters of baptism or to the promise that God makes to Israel in Isaiah 43:2: "When you pass through the waters I will be with you; and through the rivers, they shall not overwhelm you; when you walk through fire you shall not be burned, and the flame shall not consume you." In the Book of Isaiah, God makes this promise specifically so that Israel will not fear, saying, "Fear not, for I have redeemed you; I have called you by name, you are mine." Taken together, all of these meanings of the flood waters point toward membership in the people of God, as well as divine protection and new beginnings in the life of faith.

Amid such symbolism of unity and new beginnings, it is significant that all of the storytellers initially panic and set out on conflicting routes except for Oisille, who heads straight for Notre Dame de Sarrance. Oisille is the only member of the company who adopts a singular, secure path; the others embark on multicursal wanderings at first, encountering danger and exhaustion along the way. Might we see here a first glimpse of a refining process, such as the refiner's fire or the rushing waters in Isaiah 43? In that case, the multicursal allusion becomes a form of initiation, a refining trial that precedes a deepening of faith. This labyrinthine symbolism proves significant, as Oisille's decisiveness foreshadows the cohesion that she will bring to the group by advocating for a single path of truth.[74] Indeed, Oisille's faith, wisdom, and practical life experience enable her to serve as the storytellers' mentor as they seek to understand how to live a life of faith in a fallen world. In place of an outspoken frame narrator, the *Heptaméron* holds up Oisille as the one who will guide the aristocrats and the model reader. Her leadership has different implications for the latter depending on institutional affiliation, but the larger objective is to inspire individual reform that can lead to integrity in institutions and justice in society.

Oisille takes up her goal of reform in the context of sixteenth-century France, in which widows were encouraged to provide spiritual insights. In many ways, Oisille embodies Vives's exhortations for Christian widows as found in *The Education of a Christian Woman*, a text written to detail how education ought to inform each stage in a woman's life,[75] and as encapsulated in 1 Timothy 5. Indeed, as Paula Sommers observes, Oisille takes on an educational role, makes faith her top priority, and serves as an example to others.[76] Yet Oisille lives a more joyous life than the widow Vives depicts because as part of the court, she has access to social events and lighthearted pastimes, both of which she can direct toward instructional purposes.[77] Unlike the widow in 1 Timothy 5:5, who lacks family, Oisille is surrounded by members of the court, who serve as her surrogate children. Furthermore, she is anything but "a child deprived of its tutor," an analogy in which Vives compares the husband to a teacher and the wife to a student.[78] Although we know nothing about Oisille's married life, we do know that she is now her own tutor and that of the storytellers, as well. As such, she can participate in Christian community and exercise authority in her maternal role.[79]

Moreover, Oisille's instructional approach proves broader than the one Vives recommends for women in her situation as it combines rules for widows with rules for mothers of young children. For instance, Vives asserts the importance of mothers reading literature and pious works in order to teach them to their children: "A pious mother will not think it a burden to consecrate some moments of leisure to literature or to the reading of wise and holy books, if not for her own sake, at least for the sake of her children, so that she may teach them and make them better."[80] Oisille adopts this approach by studying the Bible each morning before reading passages aloud to her audience. She likewise permits the creation of "literature" in the afternoon storytelling sessions, with an emphasis on forming moral discernment, as Vives recommends when he says that mothers should "have on hand pleasant stories and edifying tales that lead to the commendation of virtue and the deploring of vice."[81] By combining Vives's advice for mothers with modifications to his vision of widowhood, Oisille provides a spiritual education for her companions as well as a practicum.[82] Her educational role is important because through it, she seeks to inculcate a moral perspective in her "students" and to prompt them toward reform, a course of action that will defend against threats to women's sexuality and thus promote societal stability. Indeed, the well-being of the social order was one of the arguments that Vives advanced in favor of universal women's education; he contended that educated women would be moral wives and mothers and thus benefit the state.[83]

Although Vives makes this argument from the perspective of a man in patriarchal society, Marguerite de Navarre's text redirects the same idea toward the larger goal of women assuming prominent roles in reform efforts. Her *Heptaméron* can be read as seeking to secure not only the safety of women and the inviolability of their sexuality but also their active participation in shaping the future course of the Church and the state as well as the discourses they disseminate. Marguerite's text also depicts Oisille as including both men and women among her students, much as famous regents—such as Louise de Savoie and before her, Blanche de Castille—directed the education of their sons and daughters.[84] As an avatar of powerful, faith-motivated women, such as Marguerite herself, Oisille uses storytelling to help her students build a bridge of their own between the written Word and the world as God's text.[85]

Although no one in the company is a child, the characters' reactions to hardship reveal that they are "babes in Christ" and require Oisille's guidance.[86] In addition to serving as the group's instructor, Oisille represents both the aristocracy and, through her faith, the Church. Her attitude toward scripture and her observance of the Catholic mass suggest her allegiance to the évangéliques, and consequently, she incarnates the type of leadership that the *Heptaméron* wants the model reader to emulate: one rooted in a living faith ("foi vive"). Teaching was an important form of this charitable, living faith because it enabled people to draw near to God, so the évangéliques ensured access to scripture and commentaries in the vernacular, as well as to preachers who espoused their perspective. Such efforts aimed to recruit individuals to the cause while also purifying the institutional Church. Against this backdrop, Oisille's instruction proves invaluable.

The present chapter focuses on Oisille's teaching rather than on the related question of whether she preaches and, if so, in what style.[87] Although those questions are important, the cornerstone of charity for the évangéliques was spiritual education. Whether one interprets Oisille's lessons as preaching, as would be clearest in a formal and public setting, or as offering a commentary to a group of like-minded individuals, her lessons promote the principle of living faith. Moreover, this section contends that Oisille's instructional role continues during the afternoon storytelling and debate sessions, thus reinforcing connections between the tales and Christian themes, such as the fallen world, the redeeming grace of God, and scripture as revealed truth—all of which are reflected in the symbol of the labyrinth. The effect of Oisille's teaching at both levels of narration is to direct the model reader toward personal and institutional reform.

This reform is needed because the model reader, as embodied by the aristocrats and monks, is torn between spiritual life and worldly pursuits, hesitating between in malo and in bono components of human experience. The aristocrats' divided hearts are on display in a more central way, although the monks' temptation to worldliness also features in the frame narrator's comments. Each group must learn through Oisille's instruction that they need to take up a more resolutely spiritual view. For the noblemen and women, the process unfolds through Oisille's Bible study and interpretive exercises. The monks, however, receive a more secondhand education. Their exclusion from scripture lessons and full participation in storytelling has important implications to which we will return.

For now, let us consider the group of aristocrats, whom the text foregrounds. Beginning in the prologue, the frame narrator demonstrates that among the devisants, Oisille is the most interested in spirituality. The others occupy a space of contemplation along with her but do not wish to assume a contemplative attitude.[88] Parlamente therefore asks Oisille to suggest activities to pass the time while the bridge is being built.[89] Oisille, who calls the company "mes enfans" ("my children"), responds that the only pastime that can meet their needs is Bible study.[90] In presenting spiritual activities as more fulfilling than physical ones, Oisille reverses the focus on earthly pleasures in the *Decameron* and the *Courtier* and thus begins to reorient the labyrinth of human life toward in bono meanings.

She makes this statement to a group of people she knows well, and as such, she can anticipate that they are unlikely to accept what she says. Hircan confirms that suspicion by asserting that aside from Oisille, no one else present is spiritually mature enough to find physical contentment in reading the Bible: "Nous ne sommes encore si mortifiez qu'il ne nous faille quelque passetemps et exercice corporel" ("We have not yet become so mortified in the flesh that we are not in need of some sort of amusement and physical exercise").[91] The exchange between Oisille and Hircan establishes the thematic tension of spirit versus world that produces the *Heptaméron*'s ideological complexity. That tension finds resolution in the goal of reform, in which spirituality empowers people to redress society's injustices such that in malo experiences give way to in bono transformations.

Ironically, the company's division between spirit and world actually enables Oisille to pursue her program of spiritual education in an unthreatening manner. In the compromise between exegesis and storytelling, we see Oisille's political acumen. She knew to ask for more than what the company would allow because when they inevitably bargained with her, she would still have the instructional opportunity she required. Whether the company is aware of it or not, for Oisille, the storytelling and debates will constitute a practicum that supports the pedagogical objectives she pursues in the daily prologues. Moreover, as a wise, older woman, Oisille has surely observed the half-heartedness of the abbey's monks as well as the hypocrisy of the abbot.[92] At Notre Dame de Sarrance, ecclesiastical officials display as worldly a mindset as the least spiritual courtier. The frame narrator notes, for instance, that the abbot is filled with anticipatory greed as he watches the bridge being built that will allow the company to return home, since he knows that the bridge will enable more pilgrims to visit the site and donate money.[93] Against this backdrop, Oisille can imply that she has no choice but to claim the educational role that the clergy should fill, while also suggesting that as a mother well versed in Christian precepts, she is more qualified than anyone else to instruct her companions. She thus represents what Mary McKinley terms "la mère saincte Eglise," or the convergence of ecclesiastical and maternal authority.[94] Ultimately, Oisille functions as an amalgam of all the protective mother figures in the nouvelles.

Through her maternal and instructional influence, Oisille spearheads a subversive campaign to reform individuals and favor positive change to the institutions they represent. In displaying her capacity to teach scripture, Oisille positions herself as spiritually and intellectually superior to the clergy, who avoid critical thinking. This gesture has numerous consequences. First, by evoking her moral authority as a mother, Oisille implies that the Church requires parental surveillance. Like the quarrelsome aristocrats who cannot decide on an occupation, the Catholic clergy resemble unruly children in need of direction. Second, by placing herself in the role of spiritual adviser, Oisille relegates ineffectual clergymen to a submissive position, a gesture that implies the need to undo the damage patriarchy has wrought within the Church. Rather than excluding women from full membership in Christian community by demanding they remain silent or placing them under male tutelage, the *Heptaméron* suggests that the Church requires outspoken female leadership in order to realize its full potential.[95] The queen of Navarre's text likewise points to the necessity of greater lay participation in religious life since a member of courtly society demonstrates a more spiritual outlook than those who profess to devote their lives to their faith.

How has Oisille attained such spiritual heights when religious officials adopt a worldly perspective and marginalize women? The answer lies in one of the évangéliques' key aims: providing more widespread access to the scriptures. Because Oisille studies the Bible herself, she has been able to pursue her religious education proactively rather than depending solely on the clergy. She explains that she begins each day by reading the Bible.[96] By presenting the study of scripture as a means to spiritual maturity, Oisille asserts the primacy of faith over ritual and recommends that her "children" take full advantage of their access to sacred texts.

Still, Oisille acknowledges the importance of community by proposing that the company congregate each morning to hear her exposition of a given passage.[97] Surrounded by vice both at court and at the abbey, the storytellers remain vulnerable to ideologies that encourage wrongdoing. Without the support of community, they may revert to their previous temptations, such as power, wealth, learning, conquest, and courtly notions of romance. Oisille must ensure that her students resist such reversions because the goal of reform depends on the storytellers caring more about the spiritual than about the material. They need to use their position to benefit others, as Erasmus implied in *The Education of a Christian Prince* and as Vives argued in both *On Assistance to the Poor* and, to a certain extent, *The Education of a Christian Woman*. Although no one in the group expresses as much seamlessness as Oisille, they can nevertheless safeguard each other by investigating whether the moral of each tale aligns with Oisille's lessons. This approach recalls the évangéliques' tendency to combine real-world references with scripture and to empower the laity.[98] In exercising their faith, the company can make a positive impact on the Church via a bottom-up reform process.

To obtain these results, Oisille needs to teach the company that scripture is the ultimate source of truth and also inspire in her students the desire to apply what they learn to daily life. We see her objectives in the morning lessons and also in the debates, although for the former, the company's growing enthusiasm is especially evident, as critics have noted.[99] Christine Martineau-Génieys, in particular, analyzes the days' prologues to show the impact of Oisille's teaching.[100] What matters most for our purposes is to consider how this spiritual awakening replaces a use-value of pleasure with one of truthfulness and urges the storytellers and model reader to promote reform.

This project is slow to take hold at first; over the first four days, the storytellers show limited interest in Bible study. Only on day three does exegesis truly begin to interest them. They are so engrossed that they would have forgotten to go to mass if a monk had not come to collect them, as they did not notice the bell tolling.[101] Despite their increased attention to spirituality, however, the company remains tempted by material comforts; on day four, Parlamente and Hircan claim to have overslept, insinuating all the while that they were distracted by more intimate pastimes. They must choose whether to take up the spiritual perspective that Oisille desires.

The prologue to day five shows the characters forging on with Oisille and embracing her teaching with gusto. Indeed, the storytellers appear so enthused about the lesson that it brings them physical well-being—a feat that Hircan had declared impossible: "Ma dame Oisille leur prepara un desjeuner spirituel, d'un si tresbon goust, qu'il estoit suffisant de fortifier le corps et l'esprit" ("They broke their fast with a spiritual meal prepared for them by Oisille, a meal so nourishing that it sufficed to fortify both body and soul").[102] No longer babes in Christ, the devisants can now take solid food.[103] The notion of scripture as nourishment harkens back to Deuteronomy 8:3 and Isaiah 55, as well as the Last Supper, when Jesus, whom John calls "the Word," inaugurates the Eucharist. The group's hunger for truth has become more substantial to them than the pleasures of storytelling.

The devisants rush to Oisille's next lesson on day six, when she elucidates 1 John, a text that exhorts believers to lead a life of truthful and constructive action.[104] The storytellers find John's emphasis on love in action especially appealing, even if they appreciated Oisille's previous analyses of Paul's letter to the Romans, a favorite text of reformers, as it presents salvation as dependent on grace and faith as opposed to works.[105] The pairing of a controversial text with a traditional one recalls the middle path that the évangéliques walked between orthodox Catholicism and schismatic reform and suggests that, having received charity from Oisille in the form of instruction, the company must now further personal and institutional purification.

On day seven, Oisille continues to push her listeners toward action as she teaches on the Book of Acts. This choice suggests that her primary aim is to inspire her audience not only to hear the Word but also to do it,[106] like the apostles after Pentecost. She focuses on the Book of Acts and the stories of the early Church, which she says should make them "desirer veoir un tel temps, et plorer la fortune de cestuy-cy" ("long to live in such an age, and weep for the corruption of the present").[107] In her presentation of Acts, Oisille declares that the sixteenth-century Church lacks the empowered action that the early Church displayed. She also presents the acts of the apostles as a set of powerful stories—an important rhetorical gesture given that the devisants engage in a storytelling venture of their own. Here, Oisille underscores the distance between the reality of corruption and the ideal of spiritual purity. As a result of this comparison, one senses that in her eyes, the next step in the devisants' spiritual development is for them to see themselves as empowered in the Spirit to effect change, thus emulating the apostles. The text reinforces that idea by stating that the company attends the mass of the Holy Spirit after the lesson.

This detail sets up the last day in Marguerite's unfinished work, when news of the outside world arrives; the bridge will soon be finished, and the aristocrats will return to court. When Oisille delivers her final lesson, her listeners are set ablaze with inspiration, and they sense that the Holy Spirit is speaking through her.[108] The progression at work in the daily prologues seems to indicate that the storytellers have been preparing, with Oisille, to be sent forth with a different perspective into the courtly society from which they came; after all, the reason they are at Sarrance in the first place is that they are awaiting an opportunity to return to their previous residences after the flood.

Although the text is unfinished in the sense that Marguerite died before completing the one hundred tales that one might assume she had in mind to write, given the prologue's allusion to the *Decameron*, cues in the text nevertheless indicate a circular arc. Like those who, in the present day, walk unicursal labyrinths, the text shows the devisants' entry into a spiritual process and their experience of that process. The reference to the completed bridge likewise implies that there will be an eventual outcome. Even though we do not possess a definitive ending to the *Heptaméron*, it seems reasonable to imagine that in the Christian framework of the évangéliques, which emphasized the importance of scripture and of teaching as a form of Christian charity, those who study sacred texts should undergo some measure of positive change through what they read, even if all human beings fall short of perfection. Positive change need not imply perfect harmony or agreement on every point among the devisants as the final result of their exchanges. A stronger and more sincere study of scripture, however, unites their time and efforts as much as the storytelling itself. Faith provides a unifying thread that binds the storytellers together despite their differing life experiences, exposure to ideologies, and components of identity.[109] Regardless, then, of what exactly each storyteller might say or do at story's end, the text suggests through its evangelizing frame the powerful impact that faith can have on willing individuals and on those with whom such individuals interact.

The idea of spiritual influence recalls Marguerite's strategic use of genre to draw in readers familiar with texts by Castiglione and Boccaccio. As the storytellers reenter society, they too can engage in instruction, bringing their peers into a community of laypeople who are being reformed together. Having been worldly, they can now see their former companions and activities in a new light. Having learned that they are meant to act on the Word and not merely hear it, they can use their positions of influence not for themselves, but for justice. In the prologues to the eight days of the *Heptaméron*, Oisille's teaching prepares them to work toward equity in the world.

While the text depicts the aristocrats' progress in an evident way through the daily prologues, a second group remains in the background: the monks. What effect might Oisille and the storytellers have on this secondary audience with whom the model reader—an institutional representative—may identify? After all, the monks do not narrate tales of their own, nor do they intervene in the debates. They are also excluded from Oisille's morning lessons, where the bulk of the storytellers' personal transformation occurs.

How, then, can they comprehend their need for individual reform and pursue it? One might imagine that as clergy, they have the requisite knowledge of scripture to recognize their own need for reform. However, the *Heptaméron* indicates that many clergy lack a sufficient understanding of the Bible to analyze their own actions or teach others. This proves all the more important given that Parlamente knows of religious officials who consider scripture no more authoritative than texts from Greco-Roman antiquity.[110] Moreover, the text presents these particular monks as physically and intellectually lazy. They enjoy listening to the company's stories but lose interest when the debates turn religious. The text implies that the monks should exhibit a foi vive that combines active and contemplative components and that fits the model the évangéliques adopted.[111] They require personal reform even more than the aristocrats, as faith is their calling.

They find the way forward in listening, as the storytellers—led by Oisille—collectively assume an instructional role. Through this reversal, the text marks the monks as unworthy to teach—a gesture meant to humble them into becoming more biblically literate and upright. Much as the storytellers had to face temptations deriving from their wealth and station, the monks will have to reject laziness and worldliness. The revelation of their unfitness to educate should cause them to recognize the high stakes of their attitude toward personal and institutional reform. If they fail to change, there are reform-minded aristocrats ready to usurp their role in spiritual education and, when possible, replace them with sympathetic clergy.

The storytellers, with Oisille acting as the spiritual and interpretive authority, help point the monks toward their need for personal reform as they witness their aristocratic counterparts navigating scripture and real-world scenarios. We see an example following tale 36, which recounts how a man murders his adulterous wife. The devisants begin by debating whether the husband's actions were justified. Saffredent contends that a man in love, which is how he frames the man in the story, can commit no more than a "pesché veniel" ("venial sin").[112] Saffredent's pronouncement over what counts as a sin shows his desire to pose as an ecclesiastical figure. His intervention into a debate that should be the purview of Catholic officials ought to get the monks' attention, even if they prefer the tales to the debates.

Predictably, scripture figures in another of Saffredent's assertions in which he paraphrases 1 John 4:19–21. He says that he does not believe God would be angered by this kind of sin and that on the contrary, people must love what they can see before they can love an invisible God: "Comment aimerez vous Dieu, que vous ne voyez point, si vous n'aimez celuy, que vous voyez?" ("How shall you love God, whom you see not, unless you love him whom you see?").[113] In this statement, Saffredent redirects a biblical passage to unrelated contexts. He implies that his selected verses excuse rape and that by extension, a man who commits murder in a fit of rage should not be judged for his actions. His failed interpretation of scripture takes place on day four, before he has received a full education from Oisille. Oisille's reaction proves severe; she not only corrects his interpretation but also accuses him of evil intent. Specifically, she likens him to a spider that converts its food into venom and warns him sharply against quoting the Bible unnecessarily.[114] In her exhortation, Oisille reinforces the association between scripture and nourishment, implying that just as food fuels action for good or for ill, individuals may use scripture to their own ends.

As the group's arbiter, not only in the morning Bible study sessions but also in the storytelling and debates, Oisille warns Saffredent that he is attempting to re-create the passage in his own image.[115] In her view, Saffredent's interpretation demonstrates an insufficiently reverential attitude, a temptation for Saffredent, at least as of day four. She states that there is not a single passage in scripture that "vous ne tiriez à vostre propos" ("you would not turn to your own ends").[116] We see that Oisille pays attention to her companions' individual needs and how they factor into the group's spiritual growth. She evaluates Saffredent's mindset and makes clear that he will not be able to apply scripture correctly or reap the benefits thereof until his outlook becomes less self-interested.[117] The listening monks, who focus primarily on their own pleasures, may find here a secondhand critique of their ways. Like Saffredent, they need to put knowledge of the Bible and personal integrity above selfishness. If not, they may find that even laypeople can offer greater expertise than they can.

The storytellers' debates, and Oisille's interventions in them, support this idea in the discussion following tale 72, which hints that aristocrats have the power to remove problematic clergy. As a brief reminder, in the story, a young nun is caring for a dying patient at a hospital when a male religious official sexually violates her. She only finds justice when she meets the duchess of Alençon, who orders the expulsion of the perpetrator. We see, then, that in the *Heptaméron*'s vision of reform, aristocrats wield power over the Church. The duchess of Alençon, a textual reflection of the author, conveys the idea that noblewomen can play critical roles in reforming institutions.

The duchess's intervention functions as a variant on Oisille's authority, and indeed, we see Oisille guiding the company's understanding of scripture in the subsequent debate. Through this indirect form of Bible study, the monks have the opportunity to explore a variety of perspectives, though

Oisille fulfills the role of religious educator for the company. The devisants' attempts to apply her teachings to the tales they hear result both from their religious education and their desire to remain in the good graces of their most venerable friend. Oisille wants to see evidence that their critical thinking is being honed by knowledge of the scriptures since she asserts that those who study the Bible will not be fooled by erroneous or deceitful arguments.[118] The company thus uses the Bible as a guide as they analyze the actions of individuals in the tales.

In the case of story 72, they do so by examining the following question: How could a religious official who just administered the last rites desire to sexually victimize a nun? Hircan responds by calling the priest's attack "les œuvres de la vie," or "the works of life," and lending it a positive connotation.[119] Saffredent reinforces Hircan's reading by arguing that the priest and the nun decided to have sex because they wanted to create new life in homage to the dead patient.[120] In Saffredent's view, the priest's behavior is laudable; moreover, Saffredent argues without evidence that the nun agrees to have sex with the priest. His reading twists not only the nouvelle but also scripture. To give his argument greater weight, Saffredent contends that like Lot's daughters, the nun and the priest considered it their duty to "conserver nature humaine" ("conserve the human race").[121] This reading takes the biblical passage out of context, even if it recognizes scripture as truth.

At this point, Oisille intervenes to correct the interpretations that Saffredent and Hircan propose. Whereas the two men attempt to ascribe some positive or neutral motive to the tale 72 protagonists, including the clergyman, Oisille invokes James 1:15 to declare his behavior sinful: "Ce n'est point œuvre de vie, dist Oisille, de pecher" ("'To commit a sin like that is not,' said Oisille, 'performing the works of life!'").[122] In this way, Oisille reverses her students' assertions about the relationships among life, death, and sin; she questions their use of the euphemism "œuvres de la vie" and urges them to rethink this phrase in light of scripture. Deeds that genuinely lead to life should be the company's focus in Oisille's view. By countering the noblemen's misuse of scripture, Oisille asserts her spiritual authority over the group as the monks observe the proceedings and as they listen to a pointed critique of clerical abuse. Although the story criticizes them, they are not part of the company and cannot respond to what the storytellers are saying. The text thus implies that they are not worthy to defend themselves because they are guilty of significant wrongdoing and must therefore listen rather than speak. In this way, Oisille's spiritual instruction reaches both the clergy and the aristocrats; all encounter scripture and God on some level, and a female teacher, Oisille, facilitates that process. Like the model author and the female characters who fight injustice in numerous tales, Oisille steers others toward God as a precondition for societal change. In place of selfishness and the will to dominate, Oisille's maternal leadership promotes moral education and care for others. The text shows God intervening through a female authority figure—yet another allusion to Marguerite—to prompt individual and institutional reform.

III. God in the Vision: From Beginning to End

God is at work through Oisille, establishing her in an instructional position, but God is also the origin of the company's meeting at Notre Dame de Sarrance and the end of the model reader's journey. For the newly inspired aristocrats, God becomes their mission in society, in accordance with the views of the évangéliques. For the clergy, a return to God becomes essential, lest they lose their position. Regardless of the model reader's station, he or she is called to be both contemplative and active, both spiritual and at work for justice.[123]

The frame suggests that God not only has an all-knowing perspective on the labyrinth of the world and the text but is also omnipresent in both.[124] God is above the labyrinthian chaos of the tales and debates but can also intervene at any level of narration—in the storytellers' circumstances and in the tales themselves. God likewise inhabits the discussions as the storytellers consider scripture and religious topics. Ultimately, the *Heptaméron*'s frame shows that God is the beginning and the end, of the text as of the universe—an in bono reading that encapsulates the text's many components. The *Heptaméron* thus implies that in its model of reading, the written word retains the ability to act on the reader in transformative ways, like the scripture the évangéliques cherished.

Yet the person who, in the twenty-first century, holds the *Heptaméron* in hand is removed from the model reader in time and space. What, then, does the *Heptaméron*'s vision of reform mean for flesh-and-blood readers—a category whom Eco refers to as the "empirical reader"[125]—since such individuals may have personalities, interests, and ideologies that shape their response to the text in diverging ways? The answer lies in the notion of leadership, as the empirical reader, regardless of his or her standing in society, rubs shoulders with institutional representatives and ponders alongside them the reality of injustice and the potential for change. As the next and final chapter argues, the *Heptaméron*'s vision for reform intersects with modern-day activist causes in surprisingly fruitful ways, regardless of one's opinions on religion and social class.

Conclusion

The Empirical Reader at Labyrinth's End

Responding to Marguerite's Vision

The *Heptaméron* imagines a model reader as part of its vision for institutional reform; yet the twenty-first-century empirical reader may embody any number of intersecting identity components. Today's empirical reader of the *Heptaméron* is not likely a Church official or a government representative. The probability of empirical readers hailing from the aristocracy falls even further, given the prevalence of democracy today, at least in the Western world. Within a democratic context, empirical readers in the twenty-first century might best understand themselves as engaging with the words and actions of the *Heptaméron*'s leaders as a general category of people.

Just as the queen of Navarre's text can be said to urge its model reader to lead from a mindset of service and to work for the betterment of society, with a particular emphasis on combating injustice against women, the text implicates empirical readers in those same discussions by allowing them to observe the educational process in which the model reader engages. This extension outward from the model reader to the empirical reader provides yet another example of what Nicolas Le Cadet has called fictional evangelism.[1] *The Visionary Queen* adds a political component to the evangelism that Le Cadet describes, however, since the *Heptaméron* can be said to encourage the model reader to promote reform efforts as a second course of action that follows the spiritual conversion more closely associated with the term *evangelism*. The question remains as to how empirical readers might respond to the spiritual and political transformation that the text posits for the model reader via its emphasis on religious education and approaches to reform.

After all, empirical readers have access to the same labyrinthine elements of the *Heptaméron* as the text's model reader does. These labyrinthine elements may feature in the experiences of empirical readers who analyze

Marguerite's text, regardless of whether they recognize them as connected to the idea of the labyrinth. When empirical readers open the queen of Navarre's text, for instance, they enter a foreign and potentially disorienting setting based on sixteenth-century France and its realities. Some empirical readers may know very little about French society during this period; others may know more, especially if they have read other early modern works. This is one sense in which empirical readers may differ from the model reader, who possesses all the historical and cultural knowledge necessary to interpret the text. Still, whether an empirical reader knows a great deal about sixteenth-century France or very little, the places, people, and customs that comprise the text's backdrop represent, in many ways, a divergence from twenty-first-century life. Early on, then, the *Heptaméron* can be said to destabilize its empirical readers to varying degrees, just as a person who enters a labyrinth may experience discomfort when navigating the first twists and turns, all the more so if they have never walked such a structure previously.

This initial departure from the familiar may well intensify for empirical readers as they persist in the difficult process of interpreting Marguerite's multivalent work. Like the labyrinth, the *Heptaméron* weaves together many individual parts within its design; it depicts numerous forms of injustice and reactions to it, as well as diverging opinions about aspects of sixteenth-century society, including gender and institutional norms. The text's ideological polyvalence opens it up to different analyses by both specialist and nonspecialist readers. These interpretations reflect the broader polysemous symbolism of the labyrinth, with its melding of in malo and in bono connotations. At first glance, the text's rich polysemy recalls the chaos of the labyrinth in malo, as well as the experience of walking a multicursal structure. Empirical readers may choose to wander down one path or another, but they cannot be assured as they make their selection that their chosen direction will guide them out of uncertainty and toward a vision for reform, which constitutes the model reader's aim. Neither the tales nor the debates alone can provide the necessary guidance to solve the puzzle.

What empirical readers do in response to this confusion and difficult process will vary. Some readers in the twenty-first century may see in the proliferating pathways an echo of modern anxieties, not just in terms of political turmoil in the current historical era but also in terms of the crisis of meaning documented by such schools of thought as existentialism, deconstruction, and postmodernism. Readers can certainly find in malo components of the *Heptaméron* that resonate with such twenty-first-century concerns. Still, those elements represent one half of the labyrinth's symbolism. In bono readings also exist, even amid sights of chaos. Indeed, the duality of the labyrinth as process and product highlights the ultimate subsuming of disorientation within order and coherence. Viewing the text from above, at the level of the frame, provides the vantage point from which to perceive the text's in bono meanings. When the beholder perceives the complex design of this, or any, work of art, newfound understanding brings praise to the artist, who becomes a Daedalus figure. In the case of the *Heptaméron*, the artist is also a visionary queen, one whose faith enables her to acknowledge in malo and in bono influences in tandem and to contain them both within in a larger spiritual framework that privileged order over chaos, salvation over the fallen world. Like the unicursal labyrinth, Marguerite's life and writings can be said to form a path of faith amid the many possible avenues that one may, in free will, choose to walk.

Despite its allusions to the multicursal labyrinth, in the end, the *Heptaméron* is contained within one frame, and sooner or later, empirical readers will reach the final page. At that point, they will have undergone a difficult process and will have taken away lessons of various kinds from their experience. The next question that arises is how they will respond to the labyrinthine experience that the text has offered them. Standing at labyrinth's end, what will they understand about sixteenth-century France and its treatment of gender, religion, politics, injustice, and reform? What insights might these lessons provide as empirical readers close the book and reenter their twenty-first-century lives?

Some empirical readers may feel an immediate resonance with the *Heptaméron*'s invitation to spiritual renewal and a change of perspective, especially if they come from a Christian or otherwise religious background. For other readers, organized religion may not figure prominently in their lives at all. In either case, Marguerite's text can be said to encourage empirical readers, following the example of the model reader's journey, to self-examine, adopt a higher and more spiritual vision, and become less self-centered and more other-oriented in their outlook on human society. For all empirical readers, the *Heptaméron* offers a message of empowerment, prompting those who encounter the text to see themselves as leaders in their own right, capable of effecting change.

The text delivers this message primarily through influential female characters who belong to different social classes and who represent various ages and life situations. Oisille, for example, is both an aristocrat and a widow; her class, age, and relative independence for a woman of her time enable her to approach reform in both the political and religious senses from a particular angle that proves beneficial to her younger friends. The text identifies her as a teacher figure for all readers, whether model or empirical. Alongside Oisille, we see numerous other influential women in the text. One example from the bourgeoisie is a young, single woman named Françoise. Despite the fact that a future king of France attempts repeatedly to seduce and, failing that, rape her, she asserts her personhood and rejects his advances through well-worded speeches. Tale 42 indicates that it is because of her that the prince becomes a magnanimous king who forsakes his predatory behavior and adopts an attitude of service and justice in his reign. Of course, Françoise should never have had to suffer the prince's threats to her sexuality in the first place. The narrator makes that clear, and God's intervention in the tale to thwart the prince's rape plot adds further confirmation. Nevertheless, within her sphere of influence—more restricted than Oisille's—her actions yield lasting results. The married ferrywoman in story 5 comes from a more modest background. Her physical labor combines with the same threats that her wealthier peers experience to make her life particularly challenging. She also lacks formal education, as the story's narrator points out. Still, her cleverness, self-worth, and faith in divine justice inspire her to oppose corrupt institutional representatives, and as a result, the entire town rallies to her cause, and the errant priests are punished.

Even women who choose to enter religious orders are not safe from predation in the *Heptaméron*. Story 22, about Sister Marie Héroët, makes that plain. Although she functions as a Church representative, just as Oisille represents the aristocracy, Sister Marie lacks clout within the ecclesiastical hierarchy. Her attacker, on the other hand, is a highly esteemed prior whom all the nuns fear. The prior uses his authority to menace Sister Marie and publicly humiliate her when she refuses his advances, but in the end, she receives vindication, at which point she is promoted to the rank of abbess, a status that will enable her to have even greater influence in the future. Through such stories, the *Heptaméron* can be read as encouraging empirical readers not only to develop empathy by analyzing societal injustice from the vantage point of numerous women but also to work for change, following their example.

The desire for positive change, especially when it comes to systemic injustices against women, may spark myriad associations in the minds of empirical readers, depending upon world events at the time of reading. Without negating the sociohistorical specificity of their own time or the text's, empirical readers can participate in a cross-temporal dialogue that leaves space for the familiar and the unfamiliar, as Carla Freccero and Yves Citton show.[2] The experiences of disorientation and revelation that underlie this kind of cross-temporal reading are also at work in the labyrinth's symbolism. It should prove unsurprising, then, that the labyrinth as a symbol and built structure continues to resonate with the work of female activists in numerous arenas as they seek to respond to the search for spiritual meaning, the pursuit of education, the threat of rape culture, and the intersecting forms of injustice that women of color face in numerous national contexts.

In the domain of spiritual life, the labyrinth's usefulness in envisioning responses to our troubled world prompted Dr. Lauren Artress,[3] an episcopal priest and canon of Grace Cathedral in San Francisco, to spearhead the Labyrinth Movement.[4] Inspired by her experience of walking the labyrinth at Chartres Cathedral, Artress created a canvas replica and invited the public to walk it, thereby launching what would become an international movement.[5] Artress's support for the labyrinth derives from what she terms "an open-minded Christian tradition," though scholars have called her and her fellow enthusiasts "'ecumenicalists' of the New Age."[6] For Artress, the goal of the Labyrinth Movement is for others to experience spiritual healing and wellness by walking the labyrinth and, in so doing, to reconnect with the aspects of spiritual life that she argues have fallen into neglect in our present time. In her view, the associations between masculinity and divinity in the Christian tradition, as well as the valorization of rationality and science in wider society, have alienated spiritual seekers from aspects of inner life that patriarchal societies have, in an essentializing vein, often coded feminine.[7] She refers to these discarded impulses in spiritual life as "the great-grandmother's thread" that has been "destroyed through centuries of patriarchal domination, through fears of creativity and of the traits associated with the feminine, such as empathy, curiosity, community, and holistic thinking."[8] As these comments might suggest, Artress's brand of spiritual practice incorporates numerous faith influences and traditions as well as theoretical perspectives and therefore diverges in some ways from the faith of the évangéliques.

Interestingly, however, on the website of Artress's foundation, Veriditas, anonymous individuals describe the labyrinth as facilitating many of the same goals and experiences as those that marked the queen of Navarre's life. Respondents speak of releasing grief and pain, feeling connected to others, gaining hope, and contemplating that which transcends the self. One respondent states that the labyrinth "gives me creative insight to solve the problem I'm working on."[9] This connection between creative insight or vision and spiritual and psychological well-being features prominently in Artress's writings on labyrinths, so much so that her most recent book sports the title *The Path of the Holy Fool: How the Labyrinth Ignites Our Visionary Powers* (2020). Although Artress walks the labyrinth in part through the vantage point of her Christian background, as a psychotherapist in addition to a priest, she is interested in spirituality and mental health together. The labyrinth, with its complex design, invites immanent experience as opposed to detached rationalization; it inspires humility and a tranquil pace, countering the desire to rush in and dominate that which seems complicated or unsettling.[10] The labyrinth thus encourages a mindset that acknowledges difficult realities all while promoting hope and creative thinking.

This same mindset can be found in numerous woman-led activist causes in recent years. Looking back at the last decade alone, we have seen advocacy for women's rights take many forms around the world, with influential women working for change, just as they do in the *Heptaméron*. In the early 2010s, Malala Yousafzai inspired the world with her courageous commitment to her education, even when faced with threats from the Taliban. Her defense of girls' instruction recalls the *Heptaméron*'s emphasis on education as charity, and her faith, although different from that of the évangéliques, informed her activist endeavors. Moreover, Malala explains that the reason she persists in telling her story is because it reflects the experiences of countless young women worldwide.[11] As in the *Heptaméron*, an individual example reveals larger dynamics that affect women from different walks of life.

Responding to the issue of girls' education, Michelle Obama launched the Let Girls Learn initiative in 2015.[12] Drawing on support from the Peace Corps, the Department of State, and the U.S. Agency for International Development, Let Girls Learn offered funding and guidance to help communities build schools, train teachers, and promote new attitudes toward girls and learning. Interestingly, the Let Girls Learn program employed similar rhetoric to that of Marguerite de Navarre's *Heptaméron*, advocating for female education and leadership in relation to societal outcomes by asserting that "a girl with an education can shape her own destiny, lift up her family, and transform her community."[13] Here, we see a rhetoric of self-direction and fulfillment on the part of educated girls combining with the argument that the social order depends on women, their sexuality, and their ability to make informed choices. Although not stated explicitly, references to bodily autonomy and education recall the topic of reproductive care for modern readers. In a historical vein, this focus on women's sexuality and educational opportunities finds echoes in Vives's *On the Education of a Christian Woman*, which advocates for the universal education of women as a means of securing societal stability. The rhetoric that Let Girls Learn employed is accessible to people of many different backgrounds. Much as in the *Heptaméron*, a pro-woman cause proceeds strategically, with particular audiences and aims in mind.

Still other pro-woman initiatives emerged throughout the 2010s, focusing on such issues as male involvement in feminist activism, the problem of rape culture, and the importance of intersectionality in addressing injustice against women. In 2014, for instance, Emma Watson launched the HeForShe movement in collaboration with the United Nations as a means of increasing male support for women's rights and encouraging people to self-identify as feminists.[14] Watson's goal recalls the *Heptaméron*'s attempt to recruit male institutional representatives to the cause of reform.

These discourses preceded the Me Too movement, which gained global participation, with the French iteration adopting the hashtag #BalanceTonPorc or #DenounceYourPig. Journalist Sandra Muller launched this French wing of Me Too in response to sexual harassment she had experienced at a work function. The outcome of that exchange at first seemed less encouraging than many verdicts seen in the United States, since in 2019, Muller was fined for defamation.[15] Although the French government did impose certain anti-harassment laws under the watch of then-secretary of state for gender equality Marlène Schiappa, cultural tensions within France became apparent not only over the course of Muller's case but also in the earliest days of the movement, when actress Catherine Deneuve asserted that men had the "right to pester" women as part of a French culture of seduction. In the end, Muller successfully overturned the defamation ruling in 2021.[16] In asserting the prevalence of sexual assault and abuse against women worldwide, Me Too in its various iterations spotlighted a harsh reality in order to affirm a larger message and enlist the support of all people, including men, for change. As in the *Heptaméron*, Me Too demonstrated that men target women's sexuality at all levels of society, from the wealthiest to the least well-to-do and including women of varying backgrounds.

This last point prompted further precision and attention in the movement, since the Hollywood voices that lent support to Me Too risked effacing its grassroots origins, as well as its noncelebrity founder, Tarana Burke.[17] Burke had founded Me Too in 2006, over a decade prior to 2017, when the hashtag came to dominate social media.[18] As stated on the Me Too movement's official website, "as someone who has been organizing within issues facing Black women and girls for more than three decades, Tarana has a commitment and vision that is bigger than any hashtag or viral moment."[19] Tarana's vision, which forms the core of Me Too, is to provide a space of solidarity in which to promote "empowerment through empathy" and to "[change] the way the world thinks and talks about sexual violence, consent and body autonomy." Me Too shares many of these goals in common with the *Heptaméron* while further highlighting the intersectional experiences that inform survivors' stories.

In underscoring the impact of race on women's lived realities, including sexual violence and abuse, Burke pointed toward the work of Black Lives Matter and Say Her Name. In 2013, three female activists, Alicia Garza, Patrisse Cullors, and Ayọ Tometi, founded Black Lives Matter. Although Black Lives Matter asserts the importance of all Black lives, its founders also affirm the need to prevent women from being marginalized within the activist community.[20] Say Her Name responded to this problem in 2014 to add amplification to stories about Black women who had died as a result of police brutality. In addition to posting the names of these women, the movement underscores the importance of sharing the life stories of individuals and has done so in the cases of Korryn Gaines, Breonna Taylor, and Tanisha Anderson, to cite only a few.[21] By emphasizing intersecting factors of identity in today's movements that seek justice for women, Say Her Name adds to the work of the Black Lives Matter movement while also foregrounding women's multifaceted experiences.

The work of these movements overlaps, in the French context, with La Vérité pour Adama or Truth for Adama. Spearheaded by female activist Assa Traoré, the movement originally sought justice for Adama Traoré, Assa's younger brother who died following an encounter with the French police in July 2016.[22] In 2021, after several years of activist work in her brother's memory, Traoré and the movement she created obtained confirmation that it was in fact a positional asphyxiation that had led to Adama's death.[23] The movement has acknowledged and supported its U.S. counterparts, Black Lives Matter and Say Her Name. From one country to another and ultimately around the globe, women have been at the forefront of social justice movements over the last ten years and continue to shape each movement's discourses and practices in the direction of greater inclusivity.

Marguerite de Navarre wrote in a different time and place than the ones that empirical readers encounter today, yet her push for justice within the limits of her time nevertheless resonates with aspects of twenty-first-century causes, all while developing a vision for reform that the idea of the labyrinth helps elucidate. With its in malo emphases on sin and the fallen world, the labyrinth underscores the realities of suffering and difficult process that underlie organized efforts to redress systemic injustice. Still, for Marguerite, as a Christian writer, the in bono assurance of divine sovereignty and salvation in Christ provided hope to help fuel the work of pursuing reform, an objective we see reflected in both her life and her creative output. In her writings, and especially in her *Heptaméron*, the queen of Navarre developed a creative vision for change that derived from a lifetime of political and religious endeavor. It is through the exploratory space of the literary text that this vision takes shape and constructs a textual labyrinth for the model reader, as well as today's empirical readers, to walk.

At labyrinth's end, empirical readers are poised to face the difficult realities of their own time from a new perspective, one informed by the relationship between writing and life, or as modern-day feminists might say, theory and praxis. As bell hooks argues, learning to theorize entails dissecting social interactions and the injustices that they perpetuate in the lives of individuals and communities.[24] Theory, in this sense, can be found in texts that do not necessarily self-identify as "theoretical." Literary texts can therefore offer a valuable example of how ideological perspectives colliding within an imaginary space generate new understandings of the social order. In the *Heptaméron*, the fight for justice and reform occurs within an environment of conflicting beliefs, just as misogynist and feminist worldviews continue to confront each other and evolve in different places and social groups today. Feminist thinkers can thus have recourse not only to texts that the canon labels theoretical, but also to female-authored literature, when considering how to redress systemic injustices against women. In contemplating or walking the labyrinth, they can, like Marguerite de Navarre, recall redemption in the face of suffering and work to bring positive change within their spheres of influence.

Notes

Introduction

1. Damien Plantey, *Les Bibliothèques des princesses de Navarre au XVIe siècle: Livres, objets, mobilier, décor, espaces et usages* (Villeurbanne, France: Presses de l'enssib, 2016), 8–9, https://doi.org/10.4000/books.pressesenssib.4840. For all references to Plantey in this chapter, paragraph numbers are given, as there are no page numbers in the open edition version of the book.

2. Plantey, *Les Bibliothèques des princesses de Navarre*, 18.

3. Plantey, *Les Bibliothèques des princesses de Navarre*, 24–25; Pierre Jourda, *Marguerite d'Angoulême, duchesse d'Alençon, reine de Navarre (1492–1549): Étude biographique et littéraire* (Paris: Champion, 1930), 1: 288.

4. Plantey, *Les Bibliothèques des princesses de Navarre*, 20.

5. Plantey, *Les Bibliothèques des princesses de Navarre*, 5.

6. Jourda, *Marguerite d'Angoulême*, 1: 298.

7. Jourda, *Marguerite d'Angoulême*, 1: 298.

8. For an overview of Marguerite's activities in relation to the évangéliques, see Jonathan Reid, *King's Sister—Queen of Dissent: Marguerite de Navarre (1492–1549) and Her Evangelical Network* (Leiden: Brill, 2009), 1: 17–28.

9. Reid, *King's Sister*, 1:103.

10. Patricia F. Cholakian and Rouben C. Cholakian, *Marguerite de Navarre: Mother of the Renaissance* (New York: Columbia University Press, 2006), 48–52.

11. Intersectionality, as developed by Kimberlé Crenshaw, offers important insights about the ways in which race and gender can compound oppression in the lives of women of color. Kimberlé Crenshaw, "Mapping the Margins: Intersectionality, Identity Politics, and Violence against Women of Color," *Stanford Law Review* 43, no. 6 (1991): 1244. Since Marguerite de Navarre was not a woman of color, I consider here the broader notion of intersecting factors of identity, focusing specifically on gender, class, and religion.

12. For more on Louise de Savoie's two regencies, see Cédric Michon, "Le Rôle politique de Louise de Savoie (1515–1531)," in *Louise de Savoie (1476–1531)*, ed. Pascal Brioist, Laure Fagnart, and Cédric Michon (Tours, France: Presses universitaires de Rennes and Presses universitaires François-Rabelais, 2015), 103–107, 110–114.

13. Barbara Stephenson, *The Power and Patronage of Marguerite de Navarre* (New York: Routledge, 2004), 7.

14. Elizabeth Chesney Zegura, *Marguerite de Navarre's Shifting Gaze: Perspectives on Gender, Class, and Politics in the* Heptaméron (New York: Routledge, 2017), 14.

15. Stephenson, *Power and Patronage*, 1–8.

16. See, for instance, Carla Freccero, "Queer Nation, Female Nation: Marguerite de Navarre, Incest, and the State in Early Modern France," *Modern Language Quarterly* 65, no. 1 (2004): 36–42, and "Voices of Subjection: Maternal Sovereignty and Filial Resistance in and around Marguerite de Navarre's *Heptameron*," *Yale Journal of Law & the Humanities* 5, no. 1 (1993): 154–157.

17. Laura Foxworth, for example, notes the difficulties that proponents of feminist theology faced in garnering both feminist and societal support for greater female leadership in organized religion. See Laura Foxworth, "'No More Silence!': Feminist Activism and Religion in the Second Wave," in *The Legacy of Second-Wave Feminism in American Politics*, ed. Angie Maxwell and Todd Shields (London: Palgrave Macmillan, 2018), 71–73. Maxwell and Shields provide an overview of the shift from a reproductive and social focus in second-wave feminism toward individuality and complex identities in the third wave. See Maxwell and Shields, introduction to *The Legacy*, 7–11.

18. Dawn Llewellyn discusses the uncomfortable relationship between religion and third-wave feminism, in particular: "Although the early stages of the women's movement are linked to Christian activism, a sacred/secular ideological structure has coded the wave metaphor and the development of feminism as a secular narrative. This has led to a disciplinary disconnection between feminist studies and religious feminism, seen in the (lack of a) relationship between feminist theology and third wave feminism." Dawn Llewellyn, *Reading, Feminism, and Spirituality: Troubling the Waves* (London: Palgrave Macmillan, 2015), 4.

19. In her new biography of Marguerite de Navarre, Patricia Eichel-Lojkine likewise seeks to present the queen of Navarre in a more multifaceted vein. She describes the goal of her endeavor as "aborder sous un angle biographique l'œuvre, la pensée et l'action de Marguerite de Navarre." Patricia Eichel-Lojkine, *Marguerite de Navarre. Perle de la Renaissance* (Paris: Perrin, 2021), 12.

20. See Reid, *King's Sister*, 1:13–15; Nicolas Le Cadet, *L'Évangélisme fictionnel: Les Livres rabelaisiens, le Cymbalum mundi, L'Heptaméron (1532–1552)* (Paris: Classiques Garnier, 2011), 1–4; Carol Thysell, *The Pleasure of Discernment: Marguerite de Navarre as Theologian* (Oxford: Oxford University Press, 2000), 4–13; and Catharine Randall, *Earthly Treasures: Material Culture and Metaphysics in the* Heptaméron *and Evangelical Narrative* (West Lafayette, IN: Purdue University Press, 2007), 2–11.

21. Christine Planté, "Femmes exceptionnelles: Des Exceptions pour quelle règle?" *Les Cahiers du GRIF*, no. 37–38 (1988): 92, 102.

22. Zegura, *Marguerite de Navarre's Shifting Gaze*, 4.

23. Zegura, *Marguerite de Navarre's Shifting Gaze*, 5. For more on concepts of authorship in early modern France, see Scott Francis, *Advertising the Self in Renaissance France: Lemaire, Marot, and Rabelais* (Newark: University of Delaware Press, 2019), 5–13.

24. "In the case of early modern female writers, however, Foucault's 'author question' strikes a false note." Zegura, *Marguerite de Navarre's Shifting Gaze*, 4.

25. Zegura, *Marguerite de Navarre's Shifting Gaze*, 5.

26. Carla Freccero, *Queer/Early/Modern* (Durham, NC: Duke University Press, 2006), 3.

27. Robert Estienne, *Dictionnaire françois-latin* (Paris: L'imprimerie de Robert Estienne, 1549; Geneva: Slatkine Reprints, 1972), s.v. "justice," accessed May 30, 2022, https://gallica.bnf.fr/ark:/12148/bpt6k4396v/f343.item.

28. James Morwood, ed., *Pocket Oxford Latin Dictionary: Latin-English*, 3rd ed. (Oxford: Oxford University Press, 2012), s.v. "iūstitia," https://www.oxfordreference .com/view/10.1093/acref/9780191739583.001.0001/b-la-en-00001-0005578.

29. I will retain Estienne's early modern French spellings throughout this chapter. English translations are my own and refer to both Estienne's dictionary and the *Pocket Oxford Latin Dictionary*.

30. Merriam-Webster Online, s.v. "justice," accessed May 27, 2022, https://www .merriam-webster.com/dictionary/justice.

31. Regarding laws and regulations in the Hebrew Bible, termed the Old Testament in the Christian tradition, see, for example, the books of Deuteronomy and Leviticus, which develop extensive regulations for sacrifices, the judging of cases between individuals, and rules for the priesthood. One could select any number of abundant passages from the New Testament regarding Jesus's merciful stance toward the marginalized, but a few representative examples include his healing of a Canaanite woman's daughter (Matthew 15:22–29), his calling of Matthew the tax collector (Matthew 9:9–13), and his multiplication of loaves and fishes to feed thousands of people who had come to listen to his teaching (Matthew 14:13–21).

32. Estienne, *Dictionnaire françois-latin*, s.v. "reformer," accessed May 30, 2022, https://gallica.bnf.fr/ark:/12148/bpt6k4396v/f517.item. Again, these English translations are my own and refer to the *Pocket Oxford Latin Dictionary*.

33. Merriam-Webster Online, s.v. "reform," accessed May 27, 2022, https://www .merriam-webster.com/dictionary/reform.

34. Merriam-Webster Online, s.v. "visionary," accessed December 11, 2020, https:// www.merriam-webster.com/dictionary/visionary.

35. Merriam-Webster Online, s.v. "vision," accessed December 11, 2020, https:// www.merriam-webster.com/dictionary/vision.

36. See chapter 3 for an overview of Marguerite de Navarre's life and literary endeavor as well as an analysis of the decades-long tradition of scholarship on her religion and social thought. This introduction will deal with more recent trends in criticism, especially those pertaining to Marguerite's political agency.

37. Zegura, *Marguerite de Navarre's Shifting Gaze*, 17–19.

38. See Theresa Brock, "A Love That Reforms: Improving Gender Relations by Contesting Typologies of Women in *La Comédie de Mont-de-Marsan* and *L'Heptaméron* 10 and 42," *Renaissance and Reformation/Renaissance et Réforme* 43, no. 1 (2020): 51–79.

39. Estienne, *Dictionnaire françois-latin*, s.v. "vision," accessed December 11, 2020, https://gallica.bnf.fr/ark:/12148/bpt6k4396v/f641.item. Estienne lists the terms *phantasia* (apparition), *visio* (the act of looking or seeing), and *visum* (vision) under the "vision" heading.

40. On this point, see Paula Sommers's analysis of the *Miroir de l'âme pécheresse*, "The Mirror and Its Reflections: Marguerite de Navarre's Biblical Feminism," *Tulsa Studies in Women's Literature* 5, no. 1 (1986): 35–37.

41. Robert Cottrell, *The Grammar of Silence: A Reading of Marguerite de Navarre's Poetry* (Washington, DC: Catholic University of America Press, 1986), 15. Andrea Frisch adds that "the nature of the substance of testimony, as well as the nature of its relationship to the signs that vehicle it, is a crux of theological debate between Catholics and Protestants in sixteenth-century France" in *The Invention of the Eyewitness: Witnessing and Testimony in Early Modern France* (Chapel Hill: Department of Romance Languages, University of North Carolina, 2004), 141.

42. Nora Martin Peterson likewise considers how another of Marguerite's contemporaries, John Calvin, understands the relationship between knowledge and what is visible. Nora Peterson, "The Impossible Striptease: Nudity in Jean Calvin and Michel de Montaigne," *Renaissance and Reformation/Renaissance et Réforme* 37, no. 1 (2014): 68–75.

43. Catharine Randall makes a brief connection between John Calvin's use of the labyrinth in malo to symbolize worldly deceit and the *Heptaméron*'s treatment of material goods, in "Objects of Desire: Reading the Material World Metaphysically in Marguerite de Navarre's *Heptaméron*," *Quidditas* 19 (1998): 170. Zegura uses the term *scopic maze*, in a general metaphorical sense, to describe the confluence of many ideological perspectives in the *Heptaméron*, in *Marguerite de Navarre's Shifting Gaze*, 14. However, neither scholar addresses the labyrinth as a physical or cultural reality in Marguerite's time or the accompanying topic of its influence on literary production.

44. Cholakian and Cholakian, *Marguerite de Navarre*, 43, 192–194.

45. Craig Wright, *The Maze and the Warrior: Symbols in Architecture, Theology, and Music* (Cambridge, MA: Harvard University Press, 2021), 38.

46. Penelope Reed Doob, *The Idea of the Labyrinth from Classical Antiquity through the Middle Ages* (Ithaca, NY: Cornell University Press, 1992), 130–131; Jeff Saward, *Labyrinths & Mazes: A Complete Guide to Magical Paths of the World* (New York: Lark Books, 2003), 99.

47. Daniel Connolly, "At the Center of the World: The Labyrinth Pavement of Chartres Cathedral," in *Art and Architecture of Late Medieval Pilgrimage in Northern Europe and the British Isle Texts*, ed. Sarah Blick and Rita Tekippe (Leiden: Brill, 2005), 305.

48. Wright, *The Maze and the Warrior*, 213. The only documented interaction between church labyrinths and laypeople in the Middle Ages, according to Wright, comes from Italy, where small-scale labyrinths etched in stone and sometimes mounted on church walls inspired visitors to trace the pathways with their fingers (36).

49. Several labyrinth scholars have commented on clerical dances that celebrated Christ's "harrowing of hell" at Easter. See, for example, Saward, *Labyrinths & Mazes*, 99; Wright, *The Maze and the Warrior*, 85; and Doob, *The Idea of the Labyrinth*, 124.

50. Hermann Kern, *Through the Labyrinth: Designs and Meanings over 5,000 Years* (Munich: Prestel, 2000), 226.

51. Saward, *Labyrinths & Mazes*, 154.

52. Saward, *Labyrinths & Mazes*, 154.

53. W. H. Matthews, *Mazes and Labyrinths: A General Account of Their History and Developments* (London: Longmans, Green, 1922), 112; Saward, *Labyrinths & Mazes*, 155.

54. As Marine Pajon-Héron explains, Louise de Savoie took up residence at Romorantin and launched large-scale renovations there beginning in the 1510s, around the same time that the historical record makes mention of her "maison de Dédalus." Marine Pajon-Héron, "Les aménagements architecturaux et paysagers réalisés par Louise de Savoie au château de Romorantin," in *Louise de Savoie* (1476–1531), ed. Pascal Brioist, Laure Fagnart, and Cédric Michon (Tours: Presses universitaires François-Rabelais and Presses universitaires de Rennes, 2015), 62. In her journal, Louise de Savoie refers to a large park on the castle grounds as "mon bois" (69). Given that neither Saward nor Matthews specifies the location of Louise de Savoie's park and thus of her garden labyrinth, available evidence suggests Romorantin as a possible location.

55. Saward, *Labyrinths & Mazes*, 155.

56. Cholakian and Cholakian, *Marguerite de Navarre*, 12, 164.

57. Kern, *Through the Labyrinth*, 220, 226.

58. Saward, *Labyrinths & Mazes*, 156–157.

59. Doob, *The Idea of the Labyrinth*, 1.

60. Doob, *The Idea of the Labyrinth*, 102.

61. Doob, *The Idea of the Labyrinth*, 2.

62. Doob, *The Idea of the Labyrinth*, 2.

1. The Labyrinth as Structure and Symbol

1. *Merriam-Webster Online*, s.v. "labyrinth," accessed December 11, 2020, https://www.merriam-webster.com/dictionary/labyrinth.

2. Craig Wright, *The Maze and the Warrior: Symbols in Architecture, Theology, and Music* (Cambridge, MA: Harvard University Press, 2021), 213.

3. Jeff Saward, *Labyrinths & Mazes: A Complete Guide to Magical Paths of the World* (New York: Lark Books, 2003), 99; Wright, *The Maze and the Warrior*, 85; Penelope Reed Doob, *The Idea of the Labyrinth from Classical Antiquity through the Middle Ages* (Ithaca, NY: Cornell University Press, 1992), 124.

4. Wright, *The Maze and the Warrior*, 45.

5. Jean-Baptiste Souchet, writing around 1650 as a historian and canon of Chartres, complained of laypeople walking the church labyrinth at all hours, a phenomenon depicted in a 1696 engraving. Wright, *The Maze and the Warrior*, 215.

6. Wright, *The Maze and the Warrior*, 210.

7. Doob, *The Idea of the Labyrinth*, 57–58.

8. Doob, *The Idea of the Labyrinth*, 50.

9. Doob, *The Idea of the Labyrinth*, 48–50.

10. Wright, *The Maze and the Warrior*, 225; Saward, *Labryinths & Mazes*, 155–157.

11. Matthews offers the example of the rostrum at the Hampton Court Maze. W. H. Matthews, *Mazes and Labyrinths: A General Account of Their History and Developments* (London: Longmans, Green, 1922), 189.

12. Saward, *Labyrinths & Mazes*, 11.

13. Doob, *The Idea of the Labyrinth*, 41.

14. See Tony Ullyatt for an in-depth analysis of critical debates surrounding the terms *labyrinth* and *maze* in "'Gestures of Approach': Aspects of Liminality and Labyrinths," *Literator* 32, no. 2 (2011): 107–108. In addition to citing the work of Kern, Artress, Doob, and Matthews, Ullyatt also alludes to Adrian Fisher's *The Amazing Book of Mazes* (New York: Abrams, 2006), 7.

15. Doob, *The Idea of the Labyrinth*, 3.

16. Doob, *The Idea of the Labyrinth*, 46–48.

17. Doob, *The Idea of the Labyrinth*, 59.

18. "Since medieval people called both uni- and multicursal mazes *laborinti*, they must have seen multi- and unicursality as accidental qualities (however useful and suggestive for metaphor). What makes a maze a maze for a medieval writer, however, is something else; there must be *essential* qualities shared by both kinds of maze, attributes a maze must possess to be a maze at all." Doob, *The Idea of the Labyrinth*, 45; emphasis in original.

19. Doob, *The Idea of the Labyrinth*, 52; emphasis in original.

20. Doob, *The Idea of the Labyrinth*, 41.

21. Doob, *The Idea of the Labyrinth*, 67, 74.

22. Doob, *The Idea of the Labyrinth*, 126.

23. Jeff Saward, *Magical Paths: Labyrinths and Mazes in the 21st Century* (London: Mitchell Beazley, 2022), 18–23.

24. Doob, *The Idea of the Labyrinth*, 150–151, 164.

25. Doob, *The Idea of the Labyrinth*, 130.

26. Doob, *The Idea of the Labyrinth*, 51. John 14:6.

27. Doob, *The Idea of the Labyrinth*, 102.

28. "I have coined the term 'labyrinthicity,' by which I mean the condition of possessing significant features habitually associated with labyrinths." Doob, *The Idea of the Labyrinth*, 2.

29. Theresa Brock, "Subverting Seduction: Gender and Genre in Marguerite de Navarre's *Heptaméron*," *Women in French Studies* 26 (2018): 13–14. See also Kathleen Long, "Teaching the Rhetoric of the Battle of the Sexes: Dialogues in and between the *Heptameron* and the *Decameron*," in *Approaches to Teaching Marguerite de Navarre's* Heptaméron, ed. Colette Winn (New York: Modern Language Association of America, 2007), 182.

30. Doob, *The Idea of the Labyrinth*, 169.

31. Anthony K. Cassell, introduction to *The Corbaccio* by Giovanni Boccaccio, trans. and ed. Anthony K. Cassell (Urbana: University of Illinois Press, 1975), xi.

32. Doob, *The Idea of the Labyrinth*, 170; Boccaccio, *The Corbaccio*, 55–56.

33. Doob, *The Idea of the Labyrinth*, 149–150.

34. Doob, *The Idea of the Labyrinth*, 161.

35. Doob, *The Idea of the Labyrinth*, 159–160.

36. Doob, *The Idea of the Labyrinth*, 287.

37. Dante Alighieri, *The Inferno*, trans. Robert and Jean Hollander (New York: Doubleday, 2000), 201.

38. Doob, *The Idea of the Labyrinth*, 271, 281–286.

39. Doob, *The Idea of the Labyrinth*, 182–183.

40. Doob, *The Idea of the Labyrinth*, 175.

41. Doob, *The Idea of the Labyrinth*, 176; Emphasis in original.

42. Doob, *The Idea of the Labyrinth*, 172–175.

43. Doob, *The Idea of the Labyrinth*, 219.

44. Pierre Jourda, *Marguerite d'Angoulême, duchesse d'Alençon, reine de Navarre (1492–1549): Étude biographique et littéraire* (Paris: Champion, 1930), 1:303.

45. François Rabelais, *Œuvres complètes*, ed. Jacques Boulenger (Paris: Gallimard, 1955), 456; François Rabelais, *Gargantua and Pantagruel*, trans. and ed. M. A. Screech (New York: Penguin, 2006), 546.

46. Rabelais, *Œuvres complètes*, 456; Rabelais, *Gargantua and Pantagruel*, 546.

47. Rabelais, *Œuvres complètes*, 461; Rabelais, *Gargantua and Pantagruel*, 551.

48. Scott Francis, "Marguerite de Navarre, a Nicodemite? 'Adiaphora' and Intention in *Heptaméron* 30, 65, and 72," *Renaissance and Reformation/Renaissance et Réforme* 39, no. 3 (2016): 6–7.

49. John Calvin, *Institutes of the Christian Religion*, trans. Henry Beveridge (Grand Rapids, MI: Eerdmans, 1964), 2:203.

50. Calvin, *Institutes of the Christian Religion*, 2:204.

51. Calvin, *Institutes of the Christian Religion*, 2:204.

52. "Let it, therefore, be our first principle that to desire any other knowledge of predestination than that which is expounded by the word of God, is no less infatuated than to walk where there is no path, or to seek light in darkness." Calvin, *Institutes of the Christian Religion*, 2:204.

53. Doob, *The Idea of the Labyrinth*, 162. Doob identifies Petrarch's *Liber sine nomine* and *Canzoniere* as prime examples of texts that achieve this balance between process and artifact in their labyrinthine qualities.

54. Doob, *The Idea of the Labyrinth*, 218.

2. From the Labyrinth, a Vision

1. Pierre Jourda, *Marguerite d'Angoulême, duchesse d'Alençon, reine de Navarre (1492–1549): Étude biographique et littéraire* (Paris: Champion, 1930), 1:24.

2. Jourda, *Marguerite d'Angoulême*, 1:3.

3. Jourda, *Marguerite d'Angoulême*, 1:6.

4. Barbara Stephenson, *The Power and Patronage of Marguerite de Navarre* (New York: Routledge, 2004), 80.

5. Jourda, *Marguerite d'Angoulême*, 1:46.

6. Stephenson, *Power and Patronage*, 16.

7. Stephenson, *Power and Patronage*, 129.

8. Stephenson, *Power and Patronage*, 137–138.

9. Stephenson, *Power and Patronage*, 131.

10. Jourda, *Marguerite d'Angoulême*, 1:296.

11. Stephenson notes that Marguerite founded her own convent in Essai. Stephenson, *Power and Patronage*, 105. Cholakian and Cholakian likewise provide several

examples of the queen of Navarre reforming individual religious establishments, such as the convents at Hyères and Poitiers, among many others. Patricia F. Cholakian and Rouben C. Cholakian, *Marguerite de Navarre: Mother of the Renaissance* (New York: Columbia University Press, 2006), 48, 55.

12. Cholakian and Cholakian, *Marguerite de Navarre*, 52.

13. Cholakian and Cholakian, *Marguerite de Navarre*, 175. Jonathan Reid asserts that Marguerite was the principal node in a network of individuals committed to religious reform; he calls this conglomerate "the Navarrian network." Jonathan Reid, *King's Sister—Queen of Dissent: Marguerite de Navarre (1492–1549) and Her Evangelical Network* (Leiden: Brill, 2009), 1:13.

14. Reid, *King's Sister*, 1:20–22.

15. Cholakian and Cholakian, *Marguerite de Navarre*, 175.

16. Stephenson, *Power and Patronage*, 175.

17. Cholakian and Cholakian, *Marguerite de Navarre*, 175.

18. On these points, see Nicolas Le Cadet, *L'Évangélisme fictionnel: Les* Livres *rabelaisiens, le* Cymbalum mundi, L'Heptaméron *(1532–1552)* (Paris: Classiques Garnier, 2011), 161–171 and Elizabeth Chesney Zegura, *Marguerite de Navarre's Shifting Gaze: Perspectives on Gender, Class, and Politics in the* Heptaméron (New York: Routledge, 2017), 12–15.

19. Marguerite de Navarre's political activities and their relation to her writing inform Stephenson, *Power and Patronage* (see pp. 1–14 for an overview); Leah Middlebrook, "'Tout mon office': Body Politics and Family Dynamics in the verse epîtres of Marguerite de Navarre," *Renaissance Quarterly* 54, no. 4 (2001): 1108–1141; and Carla Freccero's work, including "Patriarchy and the Maternal Text: The Case of Marguerite de Navarre," in *Renaissance Women Writers: French Texts/American Contexts*, ed. Colette Winn and Anne Larsen, 130–140 (Detroit: Wayne State University Press, 1994).

20. Jourda, *Marguerite d'Angoulême*, 1:288.

21. Jourda, *Marguerite d'Angoulême*, 1:102.

22. Jourda lists such figures as Antoine Héroët, Mellin de Saint-Gelais, Lazare de Baïf, Guillaume Budé, Gérard Roussel, and Jacques Lefèvre d'Étaples, among others, as influencing the queen of Navarre's intellectual activities. Jourda, *Marguerite d'Angoulême*, 1:290.

23. See the introduction for an in-depth explanation of the term *visionary* as it appears in this study.

24. Jourda, *Marguerite d'Angoulême*, 1:24.

25. Jourda, *Marguerite d'Angoulême*, 1:21–22.

26. Jourda, *Marguerite d'Angoulême*, 1:25.

27. Cholakian and Cholakian, *Marguerite de Navarre*, 16.

28. Cholakian and Cholakian, *Marguerite de Navarre*, 10.

29. For an explicit comparison between Marguerite's depiction of politics in the *Heptaméron* and Machiavelli's, see Zegura, *Marguerite de Navarre's Shifting Gaze*, 206.

30. Zegura, *Marguerite de Navarre's Shifting Gaze*, 36.

31. Zegura, *Marguerite de Navarre's Shifting Gaze*, 36–37.

32. Cholakian and Cholakian, *Marguerite de Navarre*, 19–20, 39.

33. Jourda, *Marguerite d'Angoulême*, 1:47.

34. Jourda, *Marguerite d'Angoulême*, 1:47.

35. Cholakian and Cholakian, *Marguerite de Navarre*, 40.

36. A noteworthy example that Jourda cites is when the duke of Suffolk advised King Henry VIII of England to write Marguerite a warmly worded letter because of her new influence at court. Jourda, *Marguerite d'Angoulême*, 1:46.

37. Cholakian and Cholakian, *Marguerite de Navarre*, 48, 52.

38. Cholakian and Cholakian, *Marguerite de Navarre*, 56–57.

39. Stephenson, *Power and Patronage*, 155.

40. Stephenson, *Power and Patronage*, 154.

41. Reid, *King's Sister*, 1:21.

42. Reid, *King's Sister*, 1:21.

43. Reid, *King's Sister*, 1:22.

44. Stephenson, *Power and Patronage*, 157.

45. Cholakian and Cholakian, *Marguerite de Navarre*, 91.

46. Reid, *King's Sister*, 1:22.

47. Cholakian and Cholakian, *Marguerite de Navarre*, 108–109.

48. Cholakian and Cholakian, *Marguerite de Navarre*, 114–115.

49. Cholakian and Cholakian, *Marguerite de Navarre*, 117.

50. Jourda, *Marguerite d'Angoulême*, 1:117–118.

51. Cholakian and Cholakian, *Marguerite de Navarre*, 118.

52. Cholakian and Cholakian, *Marguerite de Navarre*, 119.

53. Cholakian and Cholakian, *Marguerite de Navarre*, 119.

54. Cholakian and Cholakian, *Marguerite de Navarre*, 122.

55. Cholakian and Cholakian, *Marguerite de Navarre*, 130–132.

56. Cholakian and Cholakian, *Marguerite de Navarre*, 151.

57. Zegura, *Marguerite de Navarre's Shifting Gaze*, 45.

58. Zegura, *Marguerite de Navarre's Shifting Gaze*, 45.

59. Zegura, *Marguerite de Navarre's Shifting Gaze*, 45.

60. Zegura, *Marguerite de Navarre's Shifting Gaze*, 45.

61. Cholakian and Cholakian, *Marguerite de Navarre*, 129.

62. Cholakian and Cholakian, *Marguerite de Navarre*, 158–159.

63. Zegura, *Marguerite de Navarre's Shifting Gaze*, 44.

64. Stephenson, *Power and Patronage*, 7.

65. Stephenson, *Power and Patronage*, 7.

66. Stephenson, *Power and Patronage*, 7.

67. Jourda, *Marguerite d'Angoulême*, 1:184.

68. Jourda, *Marguerite d'Angoulême*, 1:184–185.

69. Jourda, *Marguerite d'Angoulême*, 1:185–186.

70. Cholakian and Cholakian, *Marguerite de Navarre*, 177.

71. Zegura, *Marguerite de Navarre's Shifting Gaze*, 50.

72. Cholakian and Cholakian, *Marguerite de Navarre*, 259.

73. Cholakian and Cholakian, *Marguerite de Navarre*, 223.

74. Zegura, *Marguerite de Navarre's Shifting Gaze*, 53.

75. Zegura, *Marguerite de Navarre's Shifting Gaze*, 53.

76. Zegura, *Marguerite de Navarre's Shifting Gaze*, 6.

77. Jourda, *Marguerite d'Angoulême*, 1:190.

78. Zegura, *Marguerite de Navarre's Shifting Gaze*, 52.

79. Cholakian and Cholakian, *Marguerite de Navarre*, 262.

80. Zegura, *Marguerite de Navarre's Shifting Gaze*, 54–55.

81. Zegura, *Marguerite de Navarre's Shifting Gaze*, 54.

82. Zegura, *Marguerite de Navarre's Shifting Gaze*, 55.

83. Jourda, *Marguerite d'Angoulême*, 1:314.

84. Jourda, *Marguerite d'Angoulême*, 1:315.

85. Zegura, *Marguerite de Navarre's Shifting Gaze*, 55–56.

86. Stephenson, *Power and Patronage*, 76.

87. Jourda, *Marguerite d'Angoulême*, 1:322.

88. Jourda, *Marguerite d'Angoulême*, 1:327.

89. Jourda, *Marguerite d'Angoulême*, 1:328.

90. Jourda, *Marguerite d'Angoulême*, 1:332.

91. Jourda, *Marguerite d'Angoulême*, 1:332.

92. Jourda, *Marguerite d'Angoulême*, 1:336–339.

3. *"We Walk by Faith, Not by Sight"*

1. As there is no English version, all translations are my own and reference Marguerite de Navarre and Guillaume Briçonnet, *Correspondance, 1521–1524*, 2 vols., ed. Christine Martineau, Michel Veissière, and Henry Heller (Geneva: Droz, 1975). The original reads, "La superceleste, infinie, doulce, debonnaire, vraie et seulle lumiere . . . vueille, Madame, par son excessive et insuperable amour vous aveugler et illuminer, à ce que soiez en cecité voyante et voiant aveugle, pour parvenir au chemin sans chemin" (1:34).

2. Jacques Lefèvre d'Étaples, *La Saincte Bible en francoys translatee* (Antwerp: Martin Lempereur, 1530), Gallica. English translations are my own and reference Estienne, *Dictionnaire françois-latin*. The original reads, "Nous sommes donc tousjours en confidence: cognoissons que quant nous sommes en corps, nous sommes pelerins du Seigneur car nous cheminons par foy, non point par vision." The phrase "pilgrims of the Lord" diverges from most modern versions in English and French, which employ some variant of "away from the Lord." In the early modern era, the term *pilgrim* had a literal definition but also meant "strange, foreign, other." Wes Williams, *Pilgrimage and Narrative in the French Renaissance: "The Undiscovered Country"* (Oxford: Clarendon, 1998), 11. This meaning echoes the word's acceptation in Paul's time, which reflected "the position of the Christian in, but not of the world" (24).

3. In Augustine's *De doctrina Christiana* (397–426), exegesis reinforces love for God and neighbor and thus inspires charity. Claude La Charité, "Rhetorical Augustinianism in Marguerite de Navarre's *Heptaméron*," *Allegorica* 23 (2002): 68. For more

on Briçonnet's teachings, see Ehsan Ahmed, "Guillaume Briçonnet, Marguerite de Navarre and the Evangelical Critique of Reason," *Bibliothèque d'humanisme et renaissance* 69, no. 3 (2007): 615–625 and Jacob Vance, "Humanist Polemics, Christian Morals: A Hypothesis on Marguerite de Navarre's *Heptaméron* and the Problem of Self-Love," *MLN* 120, no. 1 (2005): S181–S195.

4. See Nicolas Le Cadet, *L'Évangélisme fictionnel: Les* Livres *rabelaisiens, le* Cymbalum mundi, L'Heptaméron *(1532–1552)* (Paris: Classiques Garnier, 2011), 161–164.

5. Robert Cottrell, *The Grammar of Silence: A Reading of Marguerite de Navarre's Poetry* (Washington, DC: Catholic University of America Press, 1986), 33. This chapter does not revisit the extensive scholarship on Marguerite's religious beliefs, as recent monographs by Reid and Le Cadet, among others, have helped demonstrate her evangelical sentiment. See Jonathan Reid, *King's Sister—Queen of Dissent: Marguerite de Navarre (1492–1549) and Her Evangelical Network* (Leiden: Brill, 2009), 1:6 for an overview of previous scholarship on Marguerite's religion.

6. Reid, *King's Sister*, 1:41.

7. Penelope Reed Doob, *The Idea of the Labyrinth from Classical Antiquity through the Middle Ages* (Ithaca, NY: Cornell University Press, 1992), 1.

8. Doob, *Idea of the Labyrinth*, 130. Kern also foregrounds in malo interpretations when analyzing the number of concentric rings in a unicursal labyrinth. Hermann Kern, *Through the Labyrinth: Designs and Meanings over 5,000 Years* (Munich: Prestel, 2000), 186.

9. Doob, *Idea of the Labyrinth*, 130.

10. While Mary B. McKinley and Joshua Blaylock have analyzed *Heptaméron* 13, in which a couple plans a pilgrimage, scholars have yet to consider how the text engages with discourses surrounding pilgrimage and exegesis in Marguerite's time. Mary B. McKinley, "An Ottoman 'Fixer' in Marguerite de Navarre's *Heptaméron*," *L'Esprit Créateur* 53, no. 4 (2013): 10; Joshua Blaylock, "Intertextual Echoes: Emblems, Rabelais, and *Heptaméron* 13," *L'Esprit créateur* 57, no. 3 (2017): 86. According to F. Thomas Noonan, pilgrimage was primarily a literary phenomenon at the time of the Reformation, a fact that links pilgrimage and exegesis. F. Thomas Noonan, *The Road to Jerusalem: Pilgrimage and Travel in the Age of Discovery* (Philadelphia: University of Pennsylvania Press, 2007), 3.

11. Navarre and Briconnet, *Correspondance*, 1:3.

12. Navarre and Briçonnet, *Correspondance*, 1:25.

13. Navarre and Briçonnet, *Correspondance*, 1:25.

14. Navarre and Briçonnet, *Correspondance*, 1:33.

15. Navarre and Briçonnet, *Correspondance*, 1:33.

16. Navarre and Briçonnet, *Correspondance*, 1:31

17. Navarre and Briçonnet, *Correspondance*, 1:31

18. Navarre and Briçonnet, *Correspondance*, 1:31.

19. Cottrell, *Grammar of Silence*, 15.

20. Cottrell, *Grammar of Silence*, 23.

21. Augustine, *The City of God*, trans. Marcus Dods (Edinburgh, 1871; Project Gutenberg, 2014), 2:166, https://www.gutenberg.org/files/45305/45305-h/45305-h.htm.

22. Conrad Rudolph, ed., *Pilgrimage to the End of the World: The Road to Santiago de Compostela* (Chicago: University of Chicago Press, 2004), 6.

23. Augustine, *De doctrina Christiana*, ed. and trans. R. P. H. Green (Oxford: Clarendon, 1995), 17. Williams calls this quote "a conflation of 1 Cor. 7:31,2, 2 Cor. 5:6, and Rom.1:20." Wes Williams, *Pilgrimage and Narrative in the French Renaissance: "The Undiscovered Country"* (Oxford: Clarendon, 1998), 49.

24. Anna M. Silvas, ed., *Gregory of Nyssa: The Letters. Introduction, Translation, and Commentary* (Leiden: Brill, 2007), 121.

25. Williams, *Pilgrimage and Narrative*, 99.

26. Williams, *Pilgrimage and Narrative*, 99.

27. Daniel Connolly, "At the Center of the World: The Labyrinth Pavement of Chartres Cathedral," in *Art and Architecture of Late Medieval Pilgrimage in Northern Europe and the British Isle Texts*, ed. Sarah Blick and Rita Tekippe (Leiden: Brill, 2005), 305, 291.

28. Martin Luther, "Address to the Christian Nobility of the German Nation, concerning the Reform of the Christian Estate," in *Luther's Primary Works, Together with His Shorter and Larger Catechisms, Translated into English*, ed. Henry Wace and C. A. Buchheim (London: Hodder and Stoughton, 1896), 202.

29. Luther, "Address to the Christian Nobility," 202.

30. Luther, "Address to the Christian Nobility," 215-216.

31. Doob, *The Idea of the Labyrinth*, 164.

32. Doob, *The Idea of the Labyrinth*, 149-150.

33. For a Catholic perspective, see the account of Greffin Affagart's travels in Phillip John Usher, *Errance et cohérence: Essai sur la littérature transfrontalière à la Renaissance* (Paris: Classiques Garnier, 2010), 27-58.

34. As Silvia Evangelisti notes, some pilgrims sought out relics because they believed these objects could provide healing. Silvia Evangelisti, "Spaces for Agency: The View from Early Modern Female Religious Communities," in *Attending to Early Modern Women: Conflict and Concord*, ed. Karen Nelson (Newark: University of Delaware Press, 2013), 129.

35. For the French and English citations, see, respectively, Jean Calvin, *Traité des reliques suivi de l'excuse à messieurs les Nicodémites*, ed. Albert Autin (Paris: Éditions Bossard, 1921), 85; and John Calvin, *Treatise on Relics*, trans. and ed. Joe Nickell (Amherst, NY: Prometheus Books, 2008), 51.

36. Calvin, *Traité des reliques*, 85; Calvin, *Treatise on Relics*, 51.

37. John Calvin, *Institutes of the Christian Religion*, trans. Henry Beveridge (Grand Rapids, MI: Eerdmans, 1964), 2:204.

38. Calvin, *Institutes of the Christian Religion*, 2:204.

39. Frédéric Tinguely asserts that for Luther as well, pilgrimage should not enter into spiritual practice. Frédéric Tinguely, *L'Écriture du Levant à la Renaissance: Enquête sur les voyageurs français dans l'empire de Soliman le Magnifique* (Geneva: Droz, 2000), 68. Barbara Pitkin examines Calvin's approach to exegesis and faith in depth. Barbara Pitkin, introduction to *What Pure Eyes Could See: Calvin's Doctrine of Faith in Its Exegetical Context* (Oxford: Oxford University Press, 1999), 3-7.

40. John W. O'Malley, ed., *Collected Works of Erasmus* (Toronto: University of Toronto Press, 1988), xlii.

41. O'Malley, *Collected Works of Erasmus*, 65.

42. O'Malley, *Collected Works of Erasmus*, 72. According to Williams, Erasmus helped launch a new understanding of pilgrimage that promoted "reading in detail, and harnessing the movement of the imagination." Williams, *Pilgrimage and Narrative*, 8.

43. O'Malley, *Collected Works of Erasmus*, 65. By "angelic world," Erasmus means the invisible world "in which God dwells with the blessed spirits" (65).

44. As Tinguely explains, Erasmus's *Enchiridion* suggests that there is no merit in literal pilgrimage if in one's heart one harbors Sodom, Babylon, and Egypt. Tinguely, *L'Écriture du Levant*, 48.

45. Cholakian and Cholakian, *Marguerite de Navarre*, 47.

46. Cholakian and Cholakian, *Marguerite de Navarre*, 48.

47. Cholakian and Cholakian, *Marguerite de Navarre*, 145.

48. M. L'Abbé Louis Leroy, *Histoire des pèlerinages de la Sainte Vierge en France* (Paris: Louis Vivès, 1874), 2:125.

49. Thysell notes that Marguerite "corresponded with the Strasbourg reformer Wolfgang Capito, one of Luther's followers, who may have provided the French queen with copies of the German reformer's works." Carol Thysell, *The Pleasure of Discernment: Marguerite de Navarre as Theologian* (Oxford: Oxford University Press, 2000), 8. Thysell also recalls Marguerite's reflections on Luther's assertions about free will in her *Dialogue en forme de vision nocturne* (1533) (9).

50. Zegura and Reid both view Louise de Savoie as more conservative in her religion than Marguerite. See Elizabeth Chesney Zegura, *Marguerite de Navarre's Shifting Gaze: Perspectives on Gender, Class, and Politics in the* Heptaméron (New York: Routledge, 2017), 41; and Reid, *King's Sister*, 2:462.

51. Jourda describes Marguerite's spiritual education as follows: "Louise de Savoie s'inquiète de la formation religieuse de sa fille: elle lui achète des reliques, 'deux grandes et une moïenne', lui fait écrire des heures sur 'peaux de vellin'. Si la comtesse d'Angoulême descendait à ces humbles détails, il est permis de supposer qu'elle s'occupait des questions importantes,—et l'éducation morale de Marguerite était de celles-là: sa conduite irréprochable est la preuve qu'elle avait été fortement armée." Pierre Jourda, *Marguerite d'Angoulême, duchesse d'Alençon, reine de Navarre (1492–1549): Étude biographique et littéraire*, 1:25.

52. Marguerite de Navarre, *Œuvres complètes. Tome X: L'Heptaméron*, ed. Nicole Cazauran and Sylvie Lefèvre (Paris: Honoré Champion, 2013), 1:2–7. Faced with the fact that the *Heptaméron* was still in manuscript form when the queen of Navarre died and several print editions followed, Nicole Cazauran and Sylvie Lefèvre argue that scholars should cite the edition by Claude Gruget, which was read in the sixteenth century and had, over several centuries, what they consider to be the most substantial influence on perceptions of Marguerite's tales (LXXXI).

53. Gustave Bascle de la Grèze, *Les Pèlerinages des Pyrénées* (Paris: Jacques le Coffre, 1858), 27 and Joan Evans, *Monastic Architecture in France: From the Renaissance to the Revolution* (Cambridge: Cambridge University Press, 1964), 82.

54. Citations to the *Heptaméron* refer first to Navarre, *Œuvres complètes. Tome X: L'Heptaméron*, and second to Marguerite de Navarre, *The Heptameron*, trans. Paul Chilton (London: Penguin, 1984), 1:9, 65.

55. For an analysis of faith and sacred spaces, see Jennifer Mara DeSilva, "Introduction: 'Piously Made': Sacred Space and the Transformation of Behavior," in *The Sacralization of Space and Behavior in the Early Modern World: Studies and Sources*, ed. Jennifer Mara DeSilva (New York: Routledge, 2016), 1–32.

56. Navarre, *Œuvres complètes. Tome X: L'Heptaméron*, 1:2–3; Navarre, *The Heptameron*, 61.

57. "Au-dessus du maître-autel règne une petite tribune, où l'on aperçoit dans un portique une statuette en pierre, recouverte de mantilles brodées en or, devant laquelle viennent s'incliner, chaque jour, une foule de pèlerins." Leroy, *Histoire des pèlerinages*, 2:121.

58. Dzero argues that walking to a countryside setting "illustrates the experience of reading." Irina Dzero, "From Exile to Escape: Frame Narratives of the *Decameron* and the *Heptameron*," in *Topodynamics of Arrival: Essays on Self and Pilgrimage*, ed. Gert Hoffman and Snježana Zorić (Amsterdam: Rodopi, 2012), 170. Jeanneret views the *Heptaméron* as helping characters to constitute their subjectivity through reading. Michel Jeanneret, "Modular Narrative and the Crisis of Interpretation," in *Critical Tales: New Studies of the* Heptaméron *and Early Modern Culture*, ed. John D. Lyons and Mary B. McKinley (Philadelphia: University of Pennsylvania Press, 1993), 95.

59. The idea that life constituted a metaphorical pilgrimage appeared in Guillaume de Deguileville's *Pèlerinage de la vie humaine*, which was published through 1517. Philippe Maupeu, *Pèlerins de vie humaine: Autobiographie et allégorie narrative, de Guillaume de Deguileville à Octovien de Saint-Gelais* (Paris: Honoré Champion, 2009), 268.

60. Critics who argue that the author's Christian worldview informed her *Heptaméron* include Gérard Defaux, "De la bonne nouvelle aux nouvelles: Remarques sur la structure de *L'Heptaméron*," *French Forum* 27, no. 1 (2002): 23–43; Edwin Duval, "'Et puis, quelles nouvelles?': The Project of Marguerite's Unfinished *Decameron*," in *Critical Tales: New Studies of the* Heptaméron *and Early Modern Culture*, ed. John D. Lyons and Mary B. McKinley (Philadelphia: University of Pennsylvania Press, 1993), 241–262; Carol Thysell, "Gender and Genre: Marguerite de Navarre and the Tradition of Allegorical Rhetoric," in *Pleasure of Discernment*; Le Cadet, *L'Évangélisme fictionnel*; and Gary Ferguson and Mary B. McKinley, "The *Heptaméron*: Word, Spirit, World," in *A Companion to Marguerite de Navarre*, ed. Gary Ferguson and Mary B. McKinley (Leiden: Brill, 2013), 323–372.

61. Stanley Fish, "How to Recognize a Poem When You See One," in *Is There a Text in This Class?: The Authority of Interpretive Communities* (Cambridge, MA: Harvard University Press, 1980), 326.

62. Stanley Fish, "Interpreting the *Variorum*," *Critical Inquiry* 2, no. 3 (1976): 467–468.

63. Umberto Eco, *From the Tree to the Labyrinth: Historical Studies on the Sign and Interpretation*, trans. Anthony Oldcorn (Cambridge, MA: Harvard University Press, 2014), 129.

64. Eco, *From the Tree to the Labyrinth*, 36.

65. Eco, *From the Tree to the Labyrinth*, 584.

66. "In *The Role of the Reader*, both the empirical reader and author are cast out from the field of semiotics, to be replaced by their textual simulacra, specifically by the Model Reader and Model Author." Valentina Pisanty, "From the Model Reader to the Limits of Interpretation," *Semiotica* 206 (2015): 58, https://doi.org/10.1515/sem-2015-0014.

67. Eco conceives of the author as a ghostly presence in the text that represents style and historical era. Umberto Eco, *Role of the Reader: Explorations in the Semiotics of Texts* (Bloomington: Indiana University Press, 1979), 10. He further explains that "the 'author' is nothing else but a textual strategy establishing semantic correlations and activating the Model Reader" (11).

68. "To make his text communicative, the author has to assume that the ensemble of codes he relies upon is the same as that shared by his possible reader. The author has thus to foresee a model of the possible reader (hereafter Model Reader) supposedly able to deal interpretatively with the expressions in the same way as the author deals generatively with them." Eco, *Role of the Reader*, 7.

69. Yves Citton originally developed the notion of actualizing readings in *Lire, interpréter, actualiser. Pourquoi les études littéraires?* (Paris: Éditions Amsterdam, 2007). In an online article from 2012, he offers the following summary of his thinking: "Une interprétation littéraire d'un texte ancien est actualisante dès lors que a) elle s'attache à exploiter les virtualités connotatives des signes de ce texte, b) afin d'en tirer une modélisation capable de reconfigurer un problème propre à la situation historique de l'interprète, c) sans viser à correspondre à la réalité historique de l'auteur, mais d) en exploitant, lorsque cela est possible, la différence entre les deux époques (leur langue, leur outillage mental, leurs situations socio-politiques) pour apporter un éclairage dépaysant sur le présent." Yves Citton, "Détourner l'actualisation," *Fabula*, https://www.fabula.org/atelier.php?Limites_des_lectures_actualisantes.

70. Le Cadet, *L'Évangélisme fictionnel*, 15–16.

71. Zegura highlights the importance of sight in the *Heptaméron*. Zegura, *Marguerite de Navarre's Shifting Gaze*, 2. Blaylock likewise emphasizes visual perception through his studies on emblems and anamorphosis. Blaylock, "Intertextual Echoes"; Joshua Blaylock, "A Skeleton in the Closet: Secrecy and Anamorphosis in Marguerite de Navarre's *Heptameron*," *The Sixteenth Century Journal* 45, no. 4 (2014): 951–972. See also François Rigolot, "Magdalen's Skull: Allegory and Iconography in *Heptameron* 32," *Renaissance Quarterly* 47, no. 1 (1994): 57–73. The present analysis considers sight and faith as a conceptual pairing.

4. Into the Labyrinth

1. Penelope Reed Doob, *The Idea of the Labyrinth from Classical Antiquity through the Middle Ages* (Ithaca, NY: Cornell University Press, 1992), 211–212.

2. Joan Kelly-Gadol famously asked, in light of restrictions on women's sexuality, whether women had a Renaissance. Joan Kelly-Gadol, "Did Women Have a Renaissance?" in *Becoming Visible: Women in European History*, ed. Renate Bridenthal and

Claudia Koontz (Boston: Houghton Mifflin, 1977), 137–140. Regarding the *Heptaméron* specifically, Patricia F. Cholakian analyzes the many examples of sexual violence in the text, reading them from an autobiographical perspective. Patricia F. Cholakian, *Rape and Writing in the* Heptaméron *of Marguerite de Navarre* (Carbondale, IL: Southern Illinois University Press, 1991), 7. The present study examines the relationship between that motif and the larger project of reform.

3. Nancy Frelick alludes briefly to this tendency in "Speech, Silence, and Storytelling: Marguerite de Navarre's *Heptameron* and Narrative Therapy," *Renaissance and Reformation/Renaissance et Réforme* 36, no. 1 (2013): 78. She pursues the idea of the *Heptaméron* as a textual mirror in "Mirroring Discourses of Difference: Marguerite de Navarre's *Heptaméron* and the *Querelle des femmes*," *French Forum* 32, no. 3 (2017): 378. The present chapter seeks to develop at greater length the notion of the *Heptaméron* as a textual mirror.

4. Einar Már Jónsson, *Le Miroir: Naissance d'un genre littéraire* (Paris: Les Belles Lettres, 2004), 64–66.

5. Robert Cottrell, *The Grammar of Silence: A Reading of Marguerite de Navarre's Poetry* (Washington, DC: Catholic University of America Press, 1986), 98.

6. Nancy Frelick, introduction to *The Mirror in Medieval and Early Modern Culture: Specular Reflections*, ed. Nancy M. Frelick (Turnhout, Belgium: Brepols, 2016), 1.

7. Colette Winn shows that this tension is at the heart of Marguerite's work and thought. See Colette Winn, "'Trop en corps': Marguerite de Navarre and the Transgressive Body," in *Renaissance Women Writers: French Texts, American Contexts*, ed. Anne Larsen and Colette Winn (Detroit, MI: Wayne State University Press, 1994), 101.

8. John D. Lyons, "The *Heptaméron* and Unlearning from Example," in *Exemplum: The Rhetoric of Example in Early Modern France and Italy* (Princeton, NJ: Princeton University Press, 1989), 72–117.

9. Edwin Duval, "'Et puis, quelles nouvelles?': The Project of Marguerite's Unfinished *Decameron*," in *Critical Tales: New Studies of the* Heptaméron *and Early Modern Culture*, ed. John D. Lyons and Mary B. McKinley (Philadelphia: University of Pennsylvania Press, 1993), 256.

10. Duval, "'Et puis, quelles nouvelles?'" 250.

11. Catharine Randall, "Scandalous Rhetorics: Preaching Plain Style in Marguerite de Navarre," *Women in French Studies* 13 (2005): 13.

12. Stephenson, *Power and Patronage*, 7.

13. Marguerite de Navarre, *Selected Writings: A Bilingual Edition*, ed. and trans. Rouben Cholakian and Mary Skemp (Chicago: University of Chicago Press, 2008), 76–77.

14. Navarre, *Selected Writings*, 76–77.

15. Navarre, *Selected Writings*, 76–77.

16. Susan Snyder, "Guilty Sisters: Marguerite de Navarre, Elizabeth of England, and the *Miroir de l'âme pécheresse*," *Renaissance Quarterly* 50, no. 2 (1997): 445–446.

17. See Gary Ferguson for more on these analogies. Gary Ferguson, *Mirroring Belief: Marguerite de Navarre's Devotional Poetry* (Edinburgh: Edinburgh University Press, 1992), 40–41.

18. For an analysis of the poem's treatment of sisterhood, a topic of particular importance given Marguerite's relationship to the king of France, see Snyder, "Guilty Sisters," 450–453.

19. See Numbers 12.

20. This story features in 1 Kings 3:16–28.

21. For the full account, see chapters 1–3 of Hosea.

22. See Luke 15:11–32.

23. Snyder, "Guilty Sisters," 444.

24. For more on this principle in Marguerite's writings, see Theresa Brock, "A Love That Reforms: Improving Gender Relations by Contesting Typologies of Women in *La Comédie de Mont-de-Marsan* and *L'Heptaméron* 10 and 42," *Renaissance and Reformation/Renaissance et Réforme* 43, no. 1 (2020): 66.

25. Ferguson discusses this universalizing thrust in greater detail. Ferguson, *Mirroring Belief*, 65.

26. "Las! bon Jesus, voiant ma cecité, / Et que secours en ma necessité / Ne puys avoir d'aulcune creature / De mon salut avez faict l'ouverture" ("But sweet Jesus, seeing my blindness, / and seeing that no mortal / could help me in my dire need, / you came to my deliverance"). Navarre, *Selected Writings*, 82–83.

27. Ferguson, *Mirroring Belief*, 56.

28. Cottrell, *Grammar of Silence*, 98.

29. Cottrell, *Grammar of Silence*, 98.

30. Tanya Stabler Miller, *The Beguines of Medieval Paris: Gender, Patronage, and Spiritual Authority* (Philadelphia: University of Pennsylvania Press, 2014), 2.

31. Miller, *The Beguines of Medieval Paris*, 4.

32. Wojciech Falkowski shows that the mirror for princes genre was already flourishing in the French context as early as Charlemagne. Wojciech Falkowski, "The Carolingian *Speculum principis*—The Birth of a Genre," *Acta poloniae historica* 98 (2008): 6.

33. Falkowski, "The Carolingian *Speculum principis*," 6.

34. An example of this is Augustine's treatment of Jerusalem as a literal place, a symbol for the church and for redemption, and both at once. Augustine, *The City of God*, ed. Marcus Dods (Edinburgh: T. & T. Clark, 1871; Project Gutenberg, 2014), 168, https://www.gutenberg.org/files/45305/45305-h/45305-h.htm.

35. Augustine compares the city of the world to Babylon, saying that the term encompasses all those who glory in their own strength and think more highly of themselves than they should. Augustine, *The City of God*, 172–173.

36. Doob, *The Idea of the Labyrinth*, 116–117.

37. In the *Revised Standard Version*, Revelation 21:2–4 reads, "And I saw the holy city, new Jerusalem, coming down out of heaven from God, prepared as a bride adorned for her husband; and I heard a loud voice from the throne saying, 'Behold, the dwelling of God is with men. He will dwell with them, and they shall be his people, and God himself will be with them; he will wipe away every tear from their eyes, and death shall be no more, neither shall there be mourning nor crying nor pain any more, for the former things have passed away.'"

38. Augustine, *The City of God*, 481.

39. Augustine, *The City of God*, 342.

40. Valentina Pisanty, "From the Model Reader to the Limits of Interpretation," *Semiotica* 206 (2015): 44.

41. For Yves Citton, literature helps readers to "frayer de nouveaux possibles personnels, autour desquels peuvent venir se cristalliser de nouveaux possibles sociaux." Yves Citton, *Lire, interpréter, actualiser. Pourquoi les études littéraires?* (Paris: Éditions Amsterdam, 2007), 184.

42. Cazauran views the text as "fait pour les princes et leur entourage." Marguerite de Navarre, *Œuvres complètes. Tome X: L'Heptaméron*, ed. Nicole Cazauran and Sylvie Lefèvre (Paris: Honoré Champion, 2013), 1:XLV. Freccero also considers political education one of the text's preoccupations. Carla Freccero, "Archives in the Fiction: Marguerite de Navarre's *Heptaméron*," in *Rhetoric and Law in Early Modern Europe*, ed. Victoria Kahn and Lorna Hutson (New Haven, CT: Yale University Press, 2001), 87. However, critics have paid little attention to the monks as a second intended audience or to the connections between these two interpretive groups and institutional reform.

43. This idea reflects not only the queen of Navarre's real-world activities but also the close association between the nouvelle genre and the theme of justice, as Ullrich Langer has shown. Ullrich Langer, "The Renaissance Novella as Justice," *Renaissance Quarterly* 52, no. 2 (1999): 317–319. John Lyons also points out the judicial orientation of the nouvelles through his commentary on the term *cas* or "case." John D. Lyons, *Exemplum: The Rhetoric of Example in Early Modern France and Italy* (Princeton, NJ: Princeton University Press, 1989), 88.

44. In the Cazauran-Lefèvre edition of the *Heptaméron* cited throughout this study, the four tales that do not deal with female sexuality and sexual roles in a significant way, either directly or indirectly, are 17 (about an assassination attempt against François Ier), 28 (about a practical joke involving ham), 52 (about frozen excrement), and 65 (about an elderly woman who mistakenly believes a statue has come to life). I include tale 34 among those that deal indirectly with female sexuality because the *cordeliers* are represented as pigs, a comparison that finds echoes with their sexually abusive tendencies in many tales.

45. See stories 3, 4, 9, 10, 12, 13, 14, 15, 16, 18, 19, 20, 21, 24, 25, 26, 30, 32, 37, 39, 40, 42, 43, 47, 49, 50, 51, 53, 54, 57, 58, 59, 62, 63, 64, 66, and 70.

46. See tales 1, 5, 11, 22, 23, 29, 31, 33, 34, 35, 41, 46, 48, 56, 60, 61, and 72.

47. See stories 2, 6, 7, 8, 27, 36, 38, 44, 45, 55, 67, 68, 69, and 71.

48. Navarre, *Œuvres complètes. Tome X: L'Heptaméron*, 2:506; Navarre, *The Heptameron*, 368. For more on clandestine marriage in Marguerite's society, see Reinier Leushuis, "Mariage et 'honnête amitié' dans *l'Heptaméron* de Marguerite de Navarre: Des idéaux ecclésiastique et aristocratique à l'agapè du dialogue humaniste," *French Forum* 28 (2003): 30.

49. David LaGuardia offers an analysis of infidelity in stories involving one-eyed men, such as the *Heptaméron*'s tale 6. David LaGuardia, "Exemplarity as Misogyny: Variations on the Tale of the One-Eyed Cuckold," in *Narrative Worlds: Essays on the French Nouvelle in 15th and 16th Century France*, ed. Gary Ferguson and David

LaGuardia (Tempe: Medieval and Renaissance Texts and Studies, Arizona State University, 2005), 147.

50. Freccero offers a reading of this tale that examines governmental and familial hierarchies in the sixteenth century. Carla Freccero, "Voices of Subjection: Maternal Sovereignty and Filial Resistance in and around Marguerite de Navarre's *Heptameron*," *Yale Journal of Law & the Humanities* 5, no. 1 (1993): 155–156.

51. For a discussion of how lovesickness as a medical concept informs the stories, see Judy Kem, "Fatal Lovesickness in Marguerite de Navarre's *Heptaméron*," *The Sixteenth Century Journal* 41, no. 2 (2010): 357–365.

52. Navarre, *Œuvres complètes. Tome X: L'Heptaméron*, 2:694; Navarre, *The Heptameron*, 485.

53. Navarre, *Œuvres complètes. Tome X: L'Heptaméron*, 2:694; Navarre, *The Heptameron*, 485.

54. Navarre, *Œuvres complètes. Tome X: L'Heptaméron*, 2:694; Navarre, *The Heptameron*, 485.

55. François Cornilliat and Ullrich Langer underscore the parallel between this narrative revelation and the pulling away of the bed covers to reveal the woman's naked body in the tale. François Cornilliat and Ullrich Langer, "Naked Narrator: *Heptameron 62*," in *Critical Tales: New Studies of the* Heptaméron *and Early Modern Culture*, ed. John D. Lyons and Mary B. McKinley (Philadelphia: University of Pennsylvania Press, 1993), 133. Frelick likewise analyzes tale 62 to demonstrate the dangers the narrator faces in telling her own story. Nancy Frelick, "Speech, Silence, and Storytelling: Marguerite de Navarre's *Heptameron* and Narrative Therapy," *Renaissance and Reformation/Renaissance et Réforme* 36, no. 1 (2013): 73. On the same topic, see Cholakian, *Rape and Writing*, 215.

56. Lucien Febvre views the couple's honesty as a social mistake, arguing that if they had carried on a discreet affair, they would not have been separated. Lucien Febvre, *Autour de* L'Heptaméron. *Amour sacré, amour profane* (Paris: Gallimard, 1944), 259.

57. Navarre, *Œuvres complètes. Tome X: L'Heptaméron*, 1:273; Navarre, *The Heptameron*, 222. Nora Martin Peterson examines involuntary confessions of the flesh, such as this one, as a recurring phenomenon in the text. For commentary on Pauline's reaction in this tale, see Nora Martin Peterson, *Involuntary Confessions of the Flesh in Early Modern France* (Newark: University of Delaware Press, 2016), 32–35.

58. Navarre, *Œuvres complètes. Tome X: L'Heptaméron*, 1:284; Navarre, *The Heptameron*, 228–229.

59. Émile Telle, *L'Œuvre de Marguerite d'Angoulême, reine de Navarre, et la querelle des femmes* (Toulouse: Imprimerie Toulousaine Lion, 1937), 269.

60. Christine Martineau argues that the value of perfect friendship is in disappointing lovers so that they seek the perfect love of God instead. Christine Martineau, "Le Platonisme de Marguerite de Navarre," *Bulletin de l'Association d'étude sur l'humanisme, la réforme et la renaissance* 4 (1976): 27–28.

61. Navarre, *Œuvres complètes. Tome X: L'Heptaméron*, 2:543; Navarre, *The Heptameron*, 393.

62. Navarre, *Œuvres complètes. Tome X: L'Heptaméron*, 2:545; Navarre, *The Heptameron*, 394.

63. Navarre, *Œuvres complètes. Tome X: L'Heptaméron*, 2:547; Navarre, *The Heptameron*, 395.

64. Navarre, *Œuvres complètes. Tome X: L'Heptaméron*, 2:549; Navarre, *The Heptameron*, 396.

65. For more on desire and gendered behavior in tale 43, see Hope Glidden, "Gender, Essence, and the Feminine (*Heptameron* 43)," in *Critical Tales: New Studies of the Heptameron and Early Modern Culture*, ed. John Lyons and Mary B. McKinley (Philadelphia: University of Pennsylvania Press, 1993), 25–29.

66. One might read the lover's skull in story 32 as a further symbol of threats to both female sexuality and the social order.

67. Cholakian, *Rape and Writing*, 106–109.

68. See Zegura for an analysis of political authority in the tale as evidenced by the parallel between the king's role and that of the woman's husband. Elizabeth Chesney Zegura, "What the Monk's Habit Hides: Excavating the Silent Truths in Marguerite de Navarre's *Heptaméron* 31," *Renaissance and Reformation/Renaissance et Réforme* 38, no. 2 (2015): 79–80.

69. See 1 Corinthians 7, especially verses 1–11, in which Paul states the validity of both marriage and singleness while also saying that those who are single might choose to remain so in order to focus on faith since he believes Jesus will soon return.

70. Febvre, *Autour de L'Heptaméron*, 265–266.

71. In *La Comédie de Mont-de-Marsan*, one reads, "L'ame au corps joincte et unie, / C'est l'homme" ("[T]he soul by itself is not man. / It is the joining of the two / That should be called man"). Marguerite de Navarre, *Œuvres complètes. Tome IV: Théâtre*, ed. Nicole Cazauran (Paris: Champion, 2002), 464; Navarre, *Selected Writings*, 323

72. Navarre, *Œuvres complètes. Tome X: L'Heptaméron*, 2:423; Navarre, *The Heptameron*, 317. For an analysis of incest, governance, and lineages in the tale, see Carla Freccero, "Queer Nation, Female Nation: Marguerite de Navarre, Incest, and the State in Early Modern France," *Modern Language Quarterly* 65, no. 1 (2004): 40–42.

73. Navarre, *Œuvres complètes. Tome X: L'Heptaméron*, 2:495; Navarre, *The Heptameron*, 361.

74. Navarre, *Œuvres complètes. Tome X: L'Heptaméron*, 1:65–66; Navarre, *The Heptameron*, 99.

75. Zegura notes that one reason the ferrywoman could count on the townsmen's help is that they already held a negative opinion of friars before the attempted assault. Elizabeth Chesney Zegura, *Marguerite de Navarre's Shifting Gaze: Perspectives on Gender, Class, and Politics in the* Heptaméron (New York: Routledge, 2017), 79.

76. Gary Ferguson examines the debate following tale 5 to show that certain devisants wonder about the ferrywoman's motives for resisting and that their suggestion she was simply unattracted to the friars ends up raising important questions about female sexual agency. Gary Ferguson, "Puns, Exemplarity, and Women's Sexual Agency: Nomerfide and Oisille, *Heptaméron* 5 and 6," in *Itineraries in French Renaissance*

Literature: Essays for Mary B. McKinley, ed. Jeff Persels, Kendall Tarte, and George Hoffman (Leiden: Brill, 2018), 31–33.

77. Mary B. McKinley, "Telling Secrets: Sacramental Confession and Narrative Authority in the *Heptaméron*," in *Critical Tales: New Studies of the* Heptaméron *and Early Modern Culture*, ed. John D. Lyons and Mary B. McKinley (Philadelphia: University of Pennsylvania Press, 1993), 150.

78. Navarre, *Œuvres complètes. Tome X: L'Heptaméron*, 2:521; Navarre, *The Heptameron*, 378. Scott Francis argues that tale 41 provides a strong example of rhetorical notions of scandal in the sixteenth century. Scott Francis, "Scandalous Women or Scandalous Judgment? The Social Perception of Women and the Theology of Scandal in the *Heptaméron*," *L'Esprit créateur* 57, no. 3 (2017): 37–38.

79. McKinley, "Telling Secrets," 151.

80. Navarre, *Œuvres complètes. Tome X: L'Heptaméron*, 2:521; Navarre, *The Heptameron*, 378.

81. Navarre, *Œuvres complètes. Tome X: L'Heptaméron*, 2:330; Navarre, *The Heptameron*, 255.

82. Navarre, *Œuvres complètes. Tome X: L'Heptaméron*, 2:330; Navarre, *The Heptameron*, 255.

83. Navarre, *Œuvres complètes. Tome X: L'Heptaméron*, 2:333; Navarre, *The Heptameron*, 257.

84. Navarre, *Œuvres complètes. Tome X: L'Heptaméron*, 2:333; Navarre, *The Heptameron*, 257.

85. For more on Sister Marie's frank speech, see Cynthia Nazarian, "Honor and Gender in the *Heptaméron* of Marguerite de Navarre," *L'Esprit créateur* 60, no. 1 (2020): 96.

86. Langer, "The Renaissance Novella," 328.

87. Navarre, *Œuvres complètes. Tome X: L'Heptaméron*, 2:346; Navarre, *The Heptameron*, 265.

88. Navarre, *Œuvres complètes. Tome X: L'Heptaméron*, 2:552–557. Chilton does not include this tale in his translation because it is found in Gruget's edition, which Cazauran and Lefèvre use.

89. Navarre, *Œuvres complètes. Tome X: L'Heptaméron*, 1:34; Navarre, *The Heptameron*, 80.

90. Navarre, *Œuvres complètes. Tome X: L'Heptaméron*, 1:34–35; Navarre, *The Heptameron*, 80.

91. Mary B. McKinley develops a compelling reading of story 2 that focuses on the distinction between body and spirit and that highlights the protagonist's spiritual focus. The present analysis adds a political angle to show how religious and political discourses overlap in the text. Mary B. McKinley, "Agony, Ecstasy, and the Mulekeeper's Wife: A Reading of *Heptaméron* 2," in *A French Forum: Mélanges de littérature française offerts à Raymond C. et Virginia A. La Charité*, ed. Gérard Defaux and Jerry Nash (Paris: Klincksieck, 2000), 131–132.

92. Zegura, *Marguerite de Navarre's Shifting Gaze*, 12–13.

93. Navarre, *Œuvres complètes. Tome X: L'Heptaméron*, 3:991.

94. Navarre, *Œuvres complètes. Tome X: L'Heptaméron*, 2:564; Navarre, *The Heptameron*, 401.

95. Navarre, *Œuvres complètes. Tome X: L'Heptaméron*, 2:565; Navarre, *The Heptameron*, 403.

96. Augustine, *The City of God*, 323.

5. Down Tortuous Paths

1. Penelope Reed Doob, *The Idea of the Labyrinth from Classical Antiquity through the Middle Ages* (Ithaca, NY: Cornell University Press, 1992), 85.

2. Doob, *The Idea of the Labyrinth*, 86.

3. Marcel Tetel argued that in the *Heptaméron*, truth fails. Marcel Tetel, *Marguerite de Navarre's* Heptaméron: *Themes, Language, Structure* (Durham, NC: Duke University Press, 1973), 206. The present study contends that in Marguerite's religious worldview, truth and meaning were secure in God, as Carol Thysell asserts in *The Pleasure of Discernment: Marguerite de Navarre as Theologian* (Oxford: Oxford University Press, 2000), 41. Human cognition, on the other hand, proved limited and fallible, as evidenced by Briçonnet's remarks on the need to subsume the intellect in faith. On that last point, see Ehsan Ahmed, "Guillaume Briçonnet, Marguerite de Navarre and the Evangelical Critique of Reason," *Bibliothèque d'humanisme et renaissance* 69, no. 3 (2007): 619.

4. Numerous contributors to standpoint feminist theories have articulated this concept. See, for example, Sandra Harding, ed., *The Feminist Standpoint Theory Reader: Intellectual and Political Controversies* (New York: Routledge, 2004), 7–8; Donna Haraway, "Situated Knowledges: The Science Question in Feminism and the Privilege of Partial Perspective," *Feminist Studies* 14, no. 3 (1988): 581; Nancy Hartsock, "The Feminist Standpoint: Developing the Ground for a Specifically Feminist Historical Materialism," in *Discovering Reality: Feminist Perspectives on Epistemology, Metaphysics, Methodology, and Philosophy of Science*, ed. Sandra Harding and Merrill B. Hintikka (Dordrecht, Netherlands: Kluwer Academic, 1983), 285.

5. See, for instance, Patricia Hill Collins, *Black Feminist Thought: Knowledge, Consciousness and the Politics of Empowerment* (New York: Routledge, 2008), viii–ix; bell hooks, *Feminist Theory: From Margin to Center* (London: Pluto, 2000), 16.

6. Elizabeth Chesney Zegura, *Marguerite de Navarre's Shifting Gaze: Perspectives on Gender, Class, and Politics in the* Heptaméron (New York: Routledge, 2017), 5.

7. Stephenson summarizes the thinking of V. L. Saulnier and Margaret Mann on the topic. Barbara Stephenson, *The Power and Patronage of Marguerite de Navarre* (New York: Routledge, 2004), 179.

8. John D. Lyons, *Exemplum: The Rhetoric of Example in Early Modern France and Italy* (Princeton, NJ: Princeton University Press, 1990), 72.

9. Desiderius Erasmus, *The Education of a Christian Prince*, ed. and trans. Lisa Jardine (Cambridge: Cambridge University Press, 1997), 26.

10. Erika Rummel, *Erasmus* (London: Continuum, 2004), 58.

11. Rummel, *Erasmus*, 54–55.

12. Erasmus, *Education*, 26.

13. Erasmus, *Education*, 109.

14. Patricia F. Cholakian and Rouben C. Cholakian, *Marguerite de Navarre: Mother of the Renaissance* (New York: Columbia University Press, 2006), 77–83.

15. Cholakian and Cholakian, *Marguerite de Navarre*, 39. R. J. Knecht adds that François Ier also accosted Mary Tudor with an inappropriate insistency. R. J. Knecht, *Renaissance Warrior and Patron. The Reign of Francis I* (Cambridge: Cambridge University Press, 1994), 557.

16. For an in-depth look at the politics behind this event, see Knecht, *Renaissance Warrior*, 170–174.

17. Cholakian and Cholakian, *Marguerite de Navarre*, 62.

18. Cholakian and Cholakian, *Marguerite de Navarre*, 62.

19. Cholakian and Cholakian, *Marguerite de Navarre*, 64.

20. Cholakian and Cholakian, *Marguerite de Navarre*, 253. Interestingly, according to Knecht, this was not the first French attempt to cement a political alliance with the Turks. Louise de Savoie had written to Suleiman the Magnificent after the battle of Pavia requesting aid for François. Knecht, *Renaissance Warrior*, 244–245.

21. Fred R. Dallmayr, "A War against the Turks? Erasmus on War and Peace," *Asian Journal of Social Science* 34, no. 1 (2006): 69.

22. Pollie Bromilow offers insights into how Marguerite's approach to the exemplum genre differs from that of her male predecessors. Pollie Bromilow, *Models of Women in Sixteenth-Century French Literature: Female Exemplarity in the* Histoires tragiques *(1559) and the* Heptaméron *(1559)* (Lewiston, NY: Edwin Mellen, 2007), 41.

23. Sister Alice Tobriner, "Introduction and Commentary," in Juan Luis Vives, *On Assistance to the Poor*, trans. Sister Alice Tobriner (Toronto: University of Toronto Press, 1999), 20.

24. Tobriner notes that Vives had written commentaries on Augustine's *The City of God*. Vives, *On Assistance to the Poor*, 3.

25. Vives, *On Assistance to the Poor*, 13.

26. Vives, *On Assistance to the Poor*, 33.

27. Vives, *On Assistance to the Poor*, 38.

28. Vives, *On Assistance to the Poor*, 39.

29. Vives, *On Assistance to the Poor*, 45.

30. Vives, *On Assistance to the Poor*, 39–40.

31. Vives, *On Assistance to the Poor*, 42.

32. Vives, *On Assistance to the Poor*, 48.

33. Vives, *On Assistance to the Poor*, 47.

34. Vives, *On Assistance to the Poor*, 43.

35. Vives, *On Assistance to the Poor*, 55–56.

36. Nancy Frelick offers an in-depth analysis of infidelity in the tales and its relationship to feminist subversion. Nancy Frelick, "Female Infidelity: Ideology, Subversion, and Feminist Practice in Marguerite de Navarre's *Heptaméron*," *Dalhousie French Studies* 56 (2001): 23–25.

37. Marguerite de Navarre, *Œuvres complètes. Tome X: L'Heptaméron*, ed. Nicole Cazauran and Sylvie Lefèvre (Paris: Honoré Champion, 2013), 2:710; Marguerite de Navarre, *The Heptameron*, trans. Paul Chilton (London: Penguin, 1984), 495.

38. Navarre, *Œuvres complètes. Tome X: L'Heptaméron*, 1:78; Navarre, *The Heptameron*, 106.

39. Navarre, *Œuvres complètes. Tome X: L'Heptaméron*, 2:721; Navarre, *The Heptameron*, 503.

40. Margaret Ferguson, *Dido's Daughters: Literacy, Gender, and Empire in Early Modern England and France* (Chicago: University of Chicago Press, 2014), 243. For other analyses of this famous tale, see Carrie F. Klaus, "From *Désert* to *Patrie*: Marguerite de Navarre's Lessons from the New World," *L'Esprit créateur* 57, no. 3 (2017): 65; Leanna Bridge Rezvani, "Nature and Nourishment, Bodies and Beasts: The *Heptaméron*'s Portrayal of Marguerite de Roberval's Marooning," *Dalhousie French Studies* 102 (2014): 4–5; Claude La Charité, "Les Questions laissées en suspens par le *Brief recit* (1545) de Jacques Cartier et les réponses de la nouvelle 67 de *L'Heptaméron* (1559) de Marguerite de Navarre," *Œuvres et critiques* 36, no. 1 (2011): 96–108; Frank Lestringant, "La Demoiselle dans l'île: Prolégomènes à une lecture de la nouvelle 67," in *Lire L'Heptaméron de Marguerite de Navarre*, ed. Dominique Bertrand (Clermont-Ferrand, France: Presses Universitaires Blaise Pascal, 2006), 192–195; Michel Bideaux, "Marguerite de Navarre: L'Histoire contée par *L'Heptaméron*," in *Roberval, la demoiselle et le gentil-homme: Les Robinsons de Terre-Neuve* (Paris: Classiques Garnier, 2009), 19–28.

41. Richard Regosin examines how sexuality overlaps with the theme of death in the tale. Richard Regosin, "Death's Desire: Sensuality and Spirituality in Marguerite de Navarre's *Heptaméron*," *MLN* 116, no. 4 (2001): 776–780.

42. See, for example, Gary Ferguson, "Gendered Oppositions in Marguerite de Navarre's *Heptaméron*: The Rhetoric of Seduction and Resistance in Narrative and Society," in *Renaissance Women Writers: French Texts/American Contexts*, ed. Anne Larsen and Colette Winn (Detroit, MI: Wayne State University Press, 1994), 151–154; Theresa Brock, "A Love That Reforms: Improving Gender Relations by Contesting Typologies of Women in *La Comédie de Mont-de-Marsan* and *L'Heptaméron* 10 and 42," *Renaissance and Reformation/Renaissance et Réforme* 43, no. 1 (2020): 74–78; Patricia F. Cholakian, *Rape and Writing in the* Heptaméron *of Marguerite de Navarre* (Carbondale: Southern Illinois University Press, 1991), 179.

43. Gary Ferguson develops an analysis of gendered rhetoric in relation to story 26 as well. Ferguson, "Gendered Oppositions," 144.

44. Navarre, *Œuvres complètes. Tome X: L'Heptaméron*, 2:400; Navarre, *The Heptameron*, 301.

45. Navarre, *Œuvres complètes. Tome X: L'Heptaméron*, 2:403; Navarre, *The Heptameron*, 302.

46. Navarre, *Œuvres complètes. Tome X: L'Heptaméron*, 2:772; Navarre, *The Heptameron*, 538.

47. Navarre, *Œuvres completes. Tome X: L'Heptaméron*, 2:772; Navarre, *The Heptameron*, 538.

48. Navarre, *Œuvres complètes. Tome X: L'Heptaméron*, 2:776; Navarre, *The Heptameron*, 540.

49. Navarre, *Œuvres complètes. Tome X: L'Heptaméron*, 2:776; Navarre, *The Heptameron*, 540.

50. Navarre, *Œuvres complètes. Tome X: L'Heptaméron*, 2:776; Navarre, *The Heptameron*, 541.

51. Scott Francis interprets tale 72 from the angle of Marguerite's stance on *adiaphora*. See Scott Francis, "Marguerite de Navarre, a Nicodemite? 'Adiaphora' and Intention in *Heptaméron* 30, 65, and 72," *Renaissance and Reformation/Renaissance et Réforme* 39, no. 3 (2016): 27–30.

52. Navarre, *Œuvres complètes. Tome X: L'Heptaméron*, 2:779; Navarre, *The Heptameron*, 543.

53. Navarre, *Œuvres complètes. Tome X: L'Heptaméron*, 2:649; Navarre, *The Heptameron*, 454.

54. Navarre, *Œuvres complètes. Tome X: L'Heptaméron*, 2:644; Navarre, *The Heptameron*, 451.

55. For an analysis of scandal and judgment in relation to the confessor's actions, see Scott Francis, "Scandalous Women or Scandalous Judgment? The Social Perception of Women and the Theology of Scandal in the *Heptaméron*," *L'Esprit créateur* 57, no. 3 (2017): 37–38.

56. Gérard Defaux develops a reading of the tale based on the liturgical calendar and the structure of the *Heptaméron*'s daily prologues, arguing that this scene of sin precedes a renewed focus on salvation. Gérard Defaux, "De la bonne nouvelle aux nouvelles: Remarques sur la structure de *L'Heptaméron*," *French Forum* 27, no. 1 (2002): 35–36.

57. It is important to recall here that although trickery is present in the tale, it is not present as a response to patriarchal injustice, enacted by the wronged party. Chapter 5 is interested in investigating how those who are harmed by patriarchal norms and the behaviors they promote decide to respond to injustice. The wife in the story cannot take appropriate action of any kind because she does not understand that she has been wronged.

58. Navarre, *Œuvres complètes. Tome X: L'Heptaméron*, 2:355; Navarre, *The Heptameron*, 270–71.

59. Cholakian argues that although the cordelier behaves similarly to Lord Bonnivet, who rapes a Milanese woman, the storytellers are able to agree that his actions are reprehensible given that they all oppose the Franciscans. Cholakian, *Rape and Writing*, 165.

60. Navarre, *Œuvres complètes. Tome X: L'Heptaméron*, 2:586; Navarre, *The Heptameron*, 415.

61. I have placed story 66 in this category for a few reasons. Although an elderly woman shouts insults at a noble couple in the tale, she has mistaken them for two other people she knows and whom she believes to be having an affair. Despite this mistaken verbal reproach, the real injustice in the story is yet again the fact that

patriarchal dictates forbid people from choosing their partners. In response to this injustice, trickery abounds.

62. Navarre, *Œuvres complètes. Tome X: L'Heptaméron*, 1:42; Navarre, *The Heptameron*, 85.

63. Navarre, *Œuvres complètes. Tome X: L'Heptaméron*, 1:42; Navarre, *The Heptameron*, 85.

64. Navarre, *Œuvres complètes. Tome X: L'Heptaméron*, 1:42; Navarre, *The Heptameron*, 85.

65. Navarre, *Œuvres complètes. Tome X: L'Heptaméron*, 2:412; Navarre, *The Heptameron*, 308.

66. I place tale 47 in this category because it includes both verbal reproach and a form of physical retribution. While many forms of physical retribution in the tales are more obviously aggressive than the one seen in tale 47, the story nevertheless includes revenge through physical means, since after reproaching his friend, a man states that to obtain vengeance, he will pursue the friend's wife relentlessly until she agrees to sleep with him. The man has no romantic interest in the wife and is treating her body as a battleground for exacting revenge.

67. Navarre, *Œuvres complètes. Tome X: L'Heptaméron*, 2:490; Navarre, *The Heptameron*, 358.

68. For more on the functions of anger in story 37, see Emily Thompson, "Playing with Fire: Narrating Angry Women and Men in the *Heptaméron*," *Renaissance and Reformation/Renaissance et Réforme* 38, no. 3 (2015): 161–162.

69. Navarre, *Œuvres complètes. Tome X: L'Heptaméron*, 2:492; Navarre, *The Heptameron*, 359.

70. Navarre, *Œuvres complètes. Tome X: L'Heptaméron*, 2:493; Navarre, *The Heptameron*, 359.

71. Deborah Losse also reads stories 37 and 38 in tandem, comparing gender and psychonarration, specifically. See Deborah Losse, "Authorial and Narrative Voice in the *Heptaméron*," *Renaissance and Reformation/Renaissance et Réforme* 11, no. 3 (1987): 231–234.

72. Navarre, *Œuvres complètes. Tome X: L'Heptaméron*, 2:496; Navarre, *The Heptameron*, 361.

73. Navarre, *Œuvres complètes. Tome X: L'Heptaméron*, 2:497; Navarre, *The Heptameron*, 362.

74. Navarre, *Œuvres complètes. Tome X: L'Heptaméron*, 2:498; Navarre, *The Heptameron*, 362.

75. Navarre, *Œuvres complètes. Tome X: L'Heptaméron*, 2:498; Navarre, *The Heptameron*, 363. Paul Chilton renders "honneste tour" as virtuous behavior, but given the discussion of *bons tours* and *mauvais tours* in the *Heptaméron* and the *Book of the Courtier*, a reading that implies trickery is also possible.

76. Michel Jeanneret sees the tales as individual modules for this reason. Michel Jeanneret, "Modular Narrative and the Crisis of Interpretation," in *Critical Tales: New Studies of the* Heptaméron *and Early Modern Culture*, ed. John D. Lyons and Mary B. McKinley (Philadelphia: University of Pennsylvania Press, 1993), 89.

6. Above the Labyrinth

1. See John 14:6.

2. See Marcel Tetel, *Marguerite de Navarre's* Heptaméron: *Themes, Language, and Structure* (Durham, NC: Duke University Press, 1973), 208; John D. Lyons, *Exemplum: The Rhetoric of Example in Early Modern France and Italy* (Princeton, NJ: Princeton University Press, 1990), 106; Michel Jeanneret, "Modular Narrative and the Crisis of Interpretation," in *Critical Tales: New Studies of the* Heptaméron *and Early Modern Culture*, ed. John D. Lyons and Mary B. McKinley (Philadelphia: University of Pennsylvania Press, 1993), 89; and Philippe de Lajarte, "Amour et passion dans *L'Heptaméron*: Perspective éthique et perspective pathologique," in *La Poétique des passions à la Renaissance: Mélanges offerts à Françoise Charpentier*, ed. François Lecercle and Simone Perrier (Paris: Classiques Garnier, 2001), 371.

3. See Nicolas Le Cadet, *L'Évangélisme fictionnel: Les* Livres *rabelaisiens, le* Cymbalum mundi, L'Heptaméron *(1532–1552)* (Paris: Classiques Garnier, 2011), 102; Carol Thysell, *The Pleasure of Discernment: Marguerite de Navarre as Theologian* (Oxford: Oxford University Press, 2000), 7–8, 17–18; Colette H. Winn, "'Trop en corps': Marguerite de Navarre and the Transgressive Body," in *Renaissance Women Writers: French Texts/American Contexts*, ed. Anne R. Larsen and Colette H. Winn (Detroit, MI: Wayne State University Press, 1994), 101; Catharine Randall, *Earthly Treasures: Material Culture and Metaphysics in the* Heptaméron *and Evangelical Narrative* (West Lafayette, IN: Purdue University Press, 2007), 5; Gary Ferguson and Mary B. McKinley, "The *Heptaméron*: Word, Spirit, World," in *A Companion to Marguerite de Navarre*, ed. Gary Ferguson and Mary B. McKinley (Leiden: Brill, 2013), 361; Nicole Cazauran in Marguerite de Navarre, *Œuvres complètes. Tome X: L'Heptaméron*, ed. Nicole Cazauran and Sylvie Lefèvre (Paris: Honoré Champion, 2013), 1:XXXIII; and Jonathan Reid, *King's Sister—Queen of Dissent: Marguerite de Navarre (1492–1549) and Her Evangelical Network* (Leiden: Brill, 2009), 1:13.

4. Gérard Defaux argues that the text's frame alludes to the liturgical calendar. Gérard Defaux, "De la bonne nouvelle aux nouvelles: Remarques sur la structure de *L'Heptaméron*," *French Forum* 27, no. 1 (2002): 35–37.

5. Raymond Lebègue calls the *Heptaméron* an "attrape-mondains" for this very reason. Raymond Lebègue, "*L'Heptaméron*: Un Attrape-mondains," in *De Ronsard à Breton, recueil d'essais: Hommages à Marcel Raymond* (Paris: José Corti, 1967), 35.

6. For analyses of these tales, see Carla Freccero, "Queer Nation, Female Nation: Marguerite de Navarre, Incest, and the State in Early Modern France," *Modern Language Quarterly* 65, no. 1 (2004): 42, and Carla Freccero, "Voices of Subjection: Maternal Sovereignty and Filial Resistance in and around Marguerite de Navarre's *Heptameron*," *Yale Journal of Law & the Humanities* 5, no. 1 (1993): 151.

7. "In short, they saw *just rule* as an expression of *true belief*." Reid, *King's Sister*, 1:67; emphasis in original.

8. Le Cadet, *L'Évangélisme fictionnel*, 1–4.

9. Valentina Pisanty, "From the Model Reader to the Limits of Interpretation," *Semiotica* 206 (2015): 55.

10. Thomas O. Beebee, *The Ideology of Genre: A Comparative Study of Generic Instability* (University Park: Pennsylvania State University Press, 1994), 4.

11. Beebee, *The Ideology of Genre*, 27.

12. Beebee, *The Ideology of Genre*, 19.

13. Amy Devitt, "Integrating Rhetorical and Literary Theories of Genre," *College English* 62, no. 6 (2000): 705.

14. Christine Planté, "Genre, un concept intraduisible?" in *Le genre comme catégorie d'analyse. Sociologie, histoire, littérature*, ed. Dominique Fougeyrollas-Schwebel, Christine Planté, Michèle Riot-Sarcey, and Claude Zaidman (Paris: L'Harmattan, 2003), 133.

15. Christine Planté, "Femmes exceptionnelles: Des Exceptions pour quelle règle?" *Les Cahiers du GRIF*, no. 37–38 (1988): 92.

16. Planté, "Femmes exceptionnelles," 102.

17. Margaret Ferguson, "Recreating the Rules of the Games: Marguerite de Navarre's *Heptaméron*," in *Creative Imitation: New Essays on Renaissance Literature in Honor of Thomas M. Greene*, ed. David Quint (Binghamton, NY: Medieval and Renaissance Texts and Studies, 1992), 161.

18. Janet Levarie Smarr, "Introduction: A Man of Many Turns," in *Boccaccio: A Critical Guide to the Complete Works*, ed. Victoria Kirkham, Michael Sherberg, and Janet Levarie Smarr (Chicago: University of Chicago Press, 2014), 2.

19. Smarr, "Introduction," 3.

20. Smarr, "Introduction," 7.

21. Smarr, "Introduction," 5–6.

22. Endnote citations will refer first to the sixteenth-century French translation of *The Decameron* by Antoine Le Maçon, to which Marguerite had access. Boccace, *Le Décaméron de Messire Jehan Bocace Florentin* (Paris, 1545), https://gallica.bnf.fr/ark: /12148/btv1b8600071m/f7.image. The second citation in each sequence is from Giovanni Boccaccio, *The Decameron*, trans. Wayne A. Rebhorn (New York: Norton, 2013). For the allusion to suffering ladies above, see Boccace, *Décaméron* 2; Boccaccio, *Decameron*, 3.

23. I use the terms *model author* and *frame narrator* interchangeably when discussing the *Decameron*, the *Courtier*, and the *Heptaméron*, as the two roles overlap in these texts.

24. Boccace, *Décaméron*, 2; Boccaccio, *Decameron*, 3.

25. I use the term *utopic* because the version of the Florentine countryside that the frame narrator depicts excludes suffering and cannot therefore be said to reflect earthly reality.

26. Boccace, *Décaméron*, 8; Boccaccio, *Decameron*, 19.

27. Boccace, *Décaméron*, 8; Boccaccio, *Decameron*, 19.

28. Néiphile, a female storyteller, communicates her awareness of sexual tensions in the group: "pource qu'il est assez manifeste qu'ilz pourtent affection à aucunes qui sont icy: je crains si nous les menons qu'il s'ensuyve sans nostre coulpe ny la leur, quelque déshonneur ou reproche" ("since it is perfectly obvious that they are in love with some of us here, I am afraid that if we were to take them with us, through no fault

of theirs or of our own, we would be exposed to censure and disgrace"). Boccace, *Décaméron*, 7; Boccaccio, *Decameron*, 18.

29. "[Se] repentoit quasi n'avoir plustost consenty aux persuasions de Pericon; et sans attendre d'estre de la en avant invitée à si doulces nuictz, elle se invitoit souventesfois soymesme" ("She almost regretted not having given in to Pericone's solicitations. And from then on, she would no longer wait for an invitation to enjoy such sweet nights, but often issued the invitation herself"). Boccace, *Décaméron*, 44; Boccaccio, *Decameron*, 139.

30. Boccace, *Décaméron*, 50; Boccaccio, *Decameron*, 157.

31. See Nicole Cazauran, "*L'Heptaméron* face au *Décaméron*," in *Variétés pour Marguerite de Navarre 1978-2004. Autour de l'*Heptaméron (Paris: Champion, 2006), 176, and Hermann Wetzel, "Éléments socio-historiques d'un genre littéraire: L'histoire de la nouvelle jusqu'à Cervantès," in *La Nouvelle française à la Renaissance*, ed. Lionello Sozzi and V. L. Saulnier (Geneva: Slatkine, 1981), 41.

32. Navarre, *Œuvres complètes. Tome X: L'Heptaméron*, 1:15; Marguerite de Navarre, *The Heptameron*, trans. Paul Chilton (London: Penguin, 1984), 68.

33. Cazauran, "*L'Heptaméron* face au *Décaméron*," 182.

34. Navarre, *Œuvres complètes. Tome X: L'Heptaméron*, 1:1; Navarre, *The Heptameron*, 60.

35. For Deborah Losse, "there is a strong argument for equating the public narrator with the textual author in the *Heptaméron*." Deborah Losse, "Authorial and Narrative Voice in the *Heptaméron*," *Renaissance and Reformation/Renaissance et Réforme* 11, no. 3 (1987): 225. This reading follows logically from Boccaccio's example, even if the *Heptaméron* does not offer a direct confirmation.

36. Navarre, *Œuvres complètes. Tome X: L'Heptaméron*, 1:17; Navarre, *The Heptameron*, 69.

37. Navarre, *Œuvres complètes. Tome X: L'Heptaméron*, 1:16; Navarre, *The Heptameron*, 69.

38. For an analysis of the relationship between fact and fiction in historical French narratives, see Natalie Zemon Davis, *Fiction in the Archives* (Stanford, CA: Stanford University Press, 1987), 2–3.

39. See Patricia Cholakian for an extensive analysis of sexual violence in the *Heptaméron*, including in tales that this chapter examines, such as 5, 14, and 72. Patricia F. Cholakian, *Rape and Writing in the* Heptaméron *of Marguerite de Navarre* (Carbondale: Southern Illinois University Press, 1991), 61–64, 118–125, 213–214. See also Mihoko Suzuki, "Gender, Power, and the Female Reader: Boccaccio's *Decameron* and Marguerite de Navarre's *Heptameron*," *Comparative Literature Studies* 30, no. 3 (1993): 240.

40. Lyons, *Exemplum*, 75.

41. Ferguson offers additional comparisons of the *Heptaméron* and the *Book of the Courtier* in "Recreating the Rules," 161–163, as does Régine Reynolds-Cornell in "*L'Heptaméron* de Marguerite de Navarre: Influence de Castiglione," *Studi di letteratura francese* 5 (1979): 25–31.

42. Alain Pons, introduction to Baldassare Castiglione, *Le Livre du courtisan*, trans. Alain Pons (Paris: Flammarion, 1991), V–VIII.

43. Pons, "Introduction," VIII.

44. In story 51, the duke of Urbino has a young woman executed for having passed letters between his son and a woman whom he did not want his son to marry. Even the intervention of the duke's wife on the young woman's behalf was not enough to save her. Navarre, *Œuvres complètes. Tome X: L'Heptaméron*, 2:610–611; Navarre, *The Heptameron*, 430.

45. Citations from the *Book of the Courtier* refer first to the sixteenth-century French translation by Gabriel Chappuys (1585), modernized by Alain Pons. Castiglione, *Courtisan*, 19. English citations refer to Baldassare Castiglione, *The Book of the Courtier*, ed. Daniel Javitch, trans. Charles Singleton (New York: Norton, 2002). Castiglione, *Courtier*, 10. Although the Chappuys translation was published after the queen of Navarre's death, the present chapter cites it instead of the 1537 Jacques Colin version because Alain Pons's critical edition of the Chappuys text made the *Courtier* widely accessible to scholars of early modern France.

46. Castiglione, *Courtisan*, 21; Castiglione, *Courtier*, 11.

47. Castiglione, *Courtisan*, 21; Castiglione, *Courtier*, 11.

48. Castiglione, *Courtisan*, 25; Castiglione, *Courtier*, 13.

49. Castiglione, *Courtisan*, 25; Castiglione, *Courtier*, 13.

50. Pons, "Introduction," XXVIII–XXIX.

51. Castiglione, *Courtisan*, 25; Castiglione, *Courtier*, 13.

52. "Castiglione uses a number of discursive tactics throughout the text to exclude woman from a theoretical construction while seemingly including her by assigning her the selection and direction of the conversation." Valeria Finucci, *The Lady Vanishes: Subjectivity and Representation in Castiglione and Ariosto* (Stanford, CA: Stanford University Press, 1992), 31.

53. Castiglione, *Courtisan*, 28; Castiglione, *Courtier*, 15.

54. Castiglione, *Courtisan*, 235; Castiglione, *Courtier*, 151.

55. Stephen Kolsky examines the role of scholastic debate and its accompanying jargon in silencing women, especially during the debate on the ideal *dame*. Stephen Kolsky, "The Limits of Knowledge: Scholasticism and Scepticism in *The Book of the Courtier*," *Parergon* 25, no. 2 (2008): 22.

56. Janet Levarie Smarr, *Joining the Conversation: Dialogues by Renaissance Women* (Ann Arbor: University of Michigan Press, 2005), 2. See Joan Gibson for more on the feminine "virtues" of chastity, silence, and obedience. Joan Gibson, "Educating for Silence: Renaissance Women and the Language Arts," *Hypatia* 4, no. 1 (1989): 10.

57. Navarre, *Œuvres complètes. Tome X: L'Heptaméron*, 1:16; Navarre, *The Heptameron*, 69.

58. As Le Cadet explains, "L'anti-intellectualisme paradoxal de ces intellectuels [les évangéliques] doit se comprendre comme une volonté de distinguer la science et la sagesse." Le Cadet, *L'Évangélisme fictionnel*, 145.

59. Winn shows that Marguerite de Navarre played a major role in shaping the dialogue genre in France. See Colette H. Winn, *The Dialogue in Early Modern France (1547–1630): Art and Argument* (Washington, DC: Catholic University of America Press, 1993), 81.

60. As Philippe de Lajarte notes, the fact that the devisants share a faith exposes in the debates the divergences in perspective resulting from their societal positioning. Philippe de Lajarte, L'Heptaméron *de Marguerite de Navarre: "En bien nous mirant"* (Paris: Honoré Champion, 2019), 331.

61. Navarre, *Œuvres complètes. Tome X: L'Heptaméron*, 1:208; Navarre, *The Heptameron*, 186.

62. Navarre, *Œuvres complètes. Tome X: L'Heptaméron*, 1:209; Navarre, *The Heptameron*, 186.

63. Cathleen Bauschatz examines related themes in "'Voylà, mes dames…': Inscribed Women Listeners and Readers in the *Heptaméron*," in *Critical Tales: New Studies of the Heptaméron and Early Modern Culture*, ed. John D. Lyons and Mary B. McKinley (Philadelphia: University of Pennsylvania Press, 1993), 106–107.

64. Navarre, *Œuvres complètes. Tome X: L'Heptaméron*, 1:209; Navarre, *The Heptameron*, 186.

65. Navarre, *Œuvres complètes. Tome X: L'Heptaméron*, 1:208; Navarre, *The Heptameron*, 186.

66. "Elle doit aussi être plus circonspecte [que le courtisan] et prendre davantage garde à ne pas donner d'occasion de dire du mal d'elle" ("Also she must be more circumspect, and more careful not to give occasion for evil being said of her"). Castiglione, *Courtisan*, 235; Castiglione, *Courtier*, 151.

67. When his opponents cite examples from the Bible to support their negative outlook on women, Julien le Magnifique shifts the conversation "afin de ne pas mêler les choses divines avec nos propos frivoles" ("in order not to mingle divine things with these foolish discussions of ours"). Castiglione, *Courtisan*, 251; Castiglione, *Courtier*, 161.

68. Navarre, *Œuvres complètes. Tome X: L'Heptaméron*, 1:209; Navarre, *The Heptameron*, 187. In their edition of the *Heptaméron*, Cazauran and Lefèvre indicate that "dans le *Courtisan* de Castiglione, la donna di Palazzo doit de même paraître ne pas comprendre quand on lui parle d'amour avec modestie et *copertamente* (L. III, ch. LV)" (881).

69. Navarre, *Œuvres complètes. Tome X: L'Heptaméron*, 1:210; Navarre, *The Heptameron*, 187.

70. For more on the storytellers, see Navarre, *The Heptameron*, 11–13. Betty Davis studies the storytellers in detail and offers an overview of their diverging mentalities on women and sex in particular. Betty Davis, *The Storytellers in Marguerite de Navarre's* Heptaméron (Lexington, KY: French Forum Publishers, 1978), 189–191.

71. Navarre, *Œuvres complètes. Tome X: L'Heptaméron*, 1:69; Navarre, *The Heptameron*, 101.

72. Navarre, *The Heptameron*, 29.

73. Augustine, *The City of God*, vol. 2, ed. Marcus Dods (Edinburgh: T. & T. Clark, 1871; Project Gutenberg, 2014), 99, https://www.gutenberg.org/files/45305/45305-h/45305-h.htm.

74. For Glyn P. Norton, "the will to cross over the barrier, to ascend in faith a strange and treacherous path, places Oisille in the vanguard of Marguerite's elite few."

Glyn P. Norton, "Narrative Function in the *Heptaméron* Frame Story," in *La Nouvelle française à la Renaissance*, ed. Lionello Sozzi and V. L. Saulnier (Geneva: Slatkine, 1981), 442.

75. Charles Fantazzi explains that Vives originally wrote the book for the young Mary Tudor during his time teaching in England but that the recommendations he provides for female education extend to other contexts and stages of life. Charles Fantazzi, introduction to Juan Luis Vives, *The Education of a Christian Woman: A Sixteenth-Century Manual*, ed. and trans. Charles Fantazzi (Chicago: University of Chicago Press, 2000), 1.

76. Paula Sommers, "Feminine Authority in the *Heptaméron*: A Reading of Oysille," *Modern Language Studies* 13, no. 2 (1983): 55.

77. Sommers, "Feminine Authority," 55.

78. Vives, *Education of a Christian Woman*, 301.

79. Thysell argues that women's equal participation in the discussions contrasts with John Calvin's views on gender, according to which women were subordinate in human life. Carol Thysell, *The Pleasure of Discernment: Marguerite de Navarre as Theologian* (Oxford: Oxford University Press, 2000), 48.

80. Vives, *Education of a Christian Woman*, 270.

81. Vives, *Education of a Christian Woman*, 271.

82. Edwin Duval uses the term *travaux pratiques* to describe the storytelling and debates. Edwin Duval, "'Et puis, quelles nouvelles?': The Project of Marguerite's Unfinished *Decameron*," in *Critical Tales: New Studies of the* Heptaméron *and Early Modern Culture*, ed. John D. Lyons and Mary B. McKinley (Philadelphia: University of Pennsylvania Press, 1993), 251.

83. Fantazzi, introduction to Vives, *Education of a Christian Woman*, 1.

84. Leanna Bridge Rezvani views Oisille's insistence on equal access to the scriptures for men and women as the *Heptaméron*'s stand against Catholic traditionalists, who lacked confidence in women's interpretive abilities. Leanna Bridge Rezvani, "The *Heptaméron*'s 67th Tale: Marguerite de Navarre's Humble Heroine Confronts the Querelle des Femmes and Catholic Tradition," *Romance Notes* 52, no. 1 (2012): 46.

85. See chapter 3 for more on the pairing of Word and world in the Augustinian exegetical approach that Marguerite employed. I agree with Margaret Ferguson here that the text invites readers to compare bridge-building and storytelling. Ferguson, "Recreating the Rules," 59.

86. See 1 Corinthians 3:1.

87. On this point, see, for instance, Olivier Millet, "Réforme du sermon et métamorphose du prédicateur (De Surgant à Lambert d'Avignon et Érasme): Témoignage évangélique et fiction romanesque dans *L'Heptaméron* de Marguerite de Navarre," in *Annoncer L'Évangile (XVe–XVIIe siècle): Permanences et mutations de la prédication* (Paris: Cerf, 2006), 367–368; Christine Martineau-Génieys, "La *Lectio divina* dans *L'Heptaméron*," in *Études sur* L'Heptaméron *de Marguerite de Navarre*, ed. Christine Martineau-Génieys (Nice, France: Association des Publications de la Faculté des lettres de Nice, 1996), 22–29; Martineau-Génieys, "La voix de l'évangélisme dans *L'Heptaméron*

de Marguerite de Navarre," in *Mélanges Jean Larmat: Regards sur le Moyen Âge et la Renaissance. Histoire, langue et littérature*, ed. Maurice Accarie (Paris: Belles Lettres, 1983), 386–389; and Catharine Randall, "Scandalous Rhetorics: Preaching Plain Style in Marguerite de Navarre," *Women in French Studies* 13 (2005): 13.

88. Sommers highlights this shift in her analysis of the text's frame. Paula Sommers, "Marguerite de Navarre's *Heptaméron*: The Case for the Cornice," *French Review* 57, no. 6 (1984): 789.

89. Navarre, *Œuvres complètes. Tome X: L'Heptaméron*, 1:10; Navarre, *The Heptameron*, 65. Margaret Ferguson views Parlamente as the ultimate figure of feminine authority in the text. Ferguson, "Recreating the Rules," 187. The present chapter argues that Oisille occupies that role because her focus on education and care presents an alternative to patriarchal authority.

90. Navarre, *Œuvres complètes. Tome X: L'Heptaméron*, 1:11; Navarre, *The Heptameron*, 66.

91. Navarre, *Œuvres complètes. Tome X: L'Heptaméron*, 1:13; Navarre, *The Heptameron*, 67.

92. The frame narrator explains that the abbot does not want to welcome the company; he only does so because he is afraid of offending a powerful aristocrat who is a friend of the storytellers. Navarre, *Œuvres complètes. Tome X: L'Heptaméron*, 1:9; Navarre, *The Heptameron*, 65.

93. Navarre, *Œuvres complètes. Tome X: L'Heptaméron*, 1:10; Navarre, *The Heptameron*, 65.

94. Mary B. McKinley, "Telling Secrets: Sacramental Confession and Narrative Authority in the *Heptaméron*," in *Critical Tales: New Studies of the* Heptaméron *and Early Modern Culture*, ed. John D. Lyons and Mary B. McKinley (Philadelphia: University of Pennsylvania Press, 1993), 150.

95. Historically, 1 Timothy 2:11–12 has been interpreted as barring women from preaching. Many exegetes have noted that the writer's preoccupation with male-only leadership contradicts Paul's commendation of Phoebe, a woman whom he calls a "deaconess" in Romans 16:1, and have therefore argued that Paul did not write 1 Timothy. Warren Quanbeck, "The First Letter of Paul to Timothy," in *The New Oxford Bible with the Apocrypha*, ed. Herbert G. May and Bruce M. Metzger (Oxford: Oxford University Press, 1974), 1440. Nevertheless, given the historical impact these verses had, Oisille's role appears all the more surprising.

96. Navarre, *Œuvres complètes. Tome X: L'Heptaméron*, 1:12; Navarre, *The Heptameron*, 66.

97. Catharine Randall views this exposition as preaching, whereas Paula Sommers considers it a form of religious education. Randall, "Scandalous Rhetorics," 14; Sommers, "Feminine Authority," 54. In either case, Oisille is an instructor and a leader.

98. This project dovetails with the notion of "church" as community rather than institution, as Duval contends. Duval, "'Quelles nouvelles?'" 237.

99. For analyses of the storytellers' increasing interest in Bible study, see Millet, "Réforme du sermon"; Martineau-Génieys, "La voix de l'évangélisme" and "Lectio divina"; Defaux, "De la bonne nouvelle"; and Jan Miernowski, "Le miracle de la

Pentecôte à Sarrance: Cohérence narrative et vérité religieuse dans la septième journée de *L'Heptaméron*," in *Narrations brèves: Mélanges de littératures anciennes offerts à Krystyna Kasprzyk*, ed. Piotr Salwa and Ewa Dorota Zokiewska (Geneva: Droz, 1993), 179–181.

100. Martineau-Génieys, "Lectio divina," 30–35.

101. Navarre, *Œuvres complètes. Tome X: L'Heptaméron*, 2:297; Navarre, *The Heptameron*, 235.

102. Navarre, *Œuvres complètes. Tome X: L'Heptaméron*, 2:517; Navarre, *The Heptameron*, 376.

103. See 1 Corinthians 3:2.

104. "Little children, let us not love in word or speech but in deed and in truth" (1 John 3:18).

105. For more on the biblical readings on which Oisille teaches, see Marie-Madeleine de La Garanderie, *Le Dialogue des romanciers: Une nouvelle lecture de L'Heptaméron de Marguerite de Navarre* (Paris: Minard, 1977), 76–77, and Martineau-Génieys, "La voix de l'évangélisme," 386–391.

106. "But be doers of the word, and not hearers only, deceiving yourselves" (James 1:22).

107. Navarre, *Œuvres complètes. Tome X: L'Heptaméron*, 2:681; Navarre, *The Heptameron*, 476. Miernowski argues that for Marguerite, Pentecost signifies unity in diversity and the relationship between the Word and the ineffable nature of faith. Miernowski, "Le miracle de la Pentecôte," 195. The present study sees this reverence of scripture as coexisting with an action-oriented faith.

108. Navarre, *Œuvres complètes. Tome X: L'Heptaméron*, 2:768; Navarre, *The Heptameron*, 535.

109. Ferguson and McKinley, "The *Heptaméron*," 365–366. See also Thysell, *The Pleasure of Discernment*, 10, 121.

110. Navarre, *Œuvres complètes. Tome X: L'Heptaméron*, 2:561; Navarre, *The Heptameron*, 400.

111. Millet, "Réforme du sermon," 371.

112. Navarre, *Œuvres complètes. Tome X: L'Heptaméron*, 2:486; Navarre, *The Heptameron*, 356.

113. Navarre, *Œuvres complètes. Tome X: L'Heptaméron*, 2:487; Navarre, *The Heptameron*, 356.

114. Navarre, *Œuvres complètes. Tome X: L'Heptaméron*, 2:487; Navarre, *The Heptameron*, 357.

115. This reading of Oisille differs from that of Thysell, for instance, who views the storytellers as equally authoritative during the debates. Carol Thysell, "Gendered Virtue, Vernacular Theology, and the Nature of Authority in the *Heptaméron*," *The Sixteenth Century Journal* 29, no. 1 (1998): 50.

116. Navarre, *Œuvres complètes. Tome X: L'Heptaméron*, 2:487; Navarre, *The Heptameron*, 357.

117. Oisille's approach to spirituality aims to improve material conditions via a reform project and thus bridges the gap between the political and religious readings of

the text that Gérard Defaux analyzes in "Marguerite de Navarre et la guerre des sexes: *Heptaméron*, première journée," *French Forum* 24, no. 2 (1999): 135.

118. Navarre, *Œuvres complètes. Tome X: L'Heptaméron*, 2:561; Navarre, *The Heptameron*, 400.

119. Navarre, *Œuvres complètes. Tome X: L'Heptaméron*, 2:779; Navarre, *The Heptameron*, 543.

120. Navarre, *Œuvres complètes. Tome X: L'Heptaméron*, 2:779; Navarre, *The Heptameron*, 543.

121. Navarre, *Œuvres complètes. Tome X: L'Heptaméron*, 2:779; Navarre, *The Heptameron*, 543.

122. Navarre, *Œuvres complètes. Tome X: L'Heptaméron*, 2:779; Navarre, *The Heptameron*, 543. See James 1:15.

123. "The frame-story's schematic *paragone* on the active and contemplative life sets the tone, then, for the entire work." Norton, "Narrative Function," 447.

124. Navarre, *Œuvres complètes. Tome X: L'Heptaméron*, 1:XXXIV.

125. Umberto Eco, *Role of the Reader: Explorations in the Semiotics of Texts* (Bloomington: Indiana University Press, 1979), 11.

Conclusion

1. Nicolas Le Cadet, *L'Évangélisme fictionnel: Les* Livres *rabelaisiens, le* Cymbalum mundi, L'Heptaméron *(1532–1552)* (Paris: Classiques Garnier, 2011), 15–16.

2. Citton calls the intermediary space of the literary text the *"entre-deux"* or "between the two," which could signify the interaction between reader and text in addition to the conversation between past and present. *Lire, interpréter, actualiser*, 36. Freccero adds the element of queer temporality to this discussion of historical modes of reading: "In its radical disruption of normative temporal continuities, both for what happens and for how we tell what happens, this kind of historical practice that is also a queering of the notion of 'succession' aims to open up sites of possibility effaced, if not foreclosed, by (hetero)normative historicisms" (Carla Freccero, *Queer/Early/Modern* [Durham, NC: Duke University Press, 2006], 195).

3. Lauren Artress, *The Path of the Holy Fool: How the Labyrinth Ignites Our Visionary Powers* (N.p.: Rose Petal Press, 2020), 86–87.

4. Lauren Artress, *Walking a Sacred Path: Rediscovering the Labyrinth as a Spiritual Practice* (New York: Riverhead Books, 1995), 5.

5. Artress, *The Path of the Holy Fool*, 3–4.

6. Artress, *Walking a Sacred Path*, xv; Craig Wright, *The Maze and the Warrior: Symbols in Architecture, Theology, and Music* (Cambridge, MA: Harvard University Press, 2001), 271. Wright explains, for instance, that those who walk the labyrinth in the vein of Artress's movement might receive a feather blessing "'intended to smooth your energy field'" (272).

7. Artress, *Walking a Sacred Path*, 115.

8. Artress, *Walking a Sacred Path*, 13.

9. "About Veriditas," Veriditas, accessed June 25, 2021, https://www.veriditas.org /page-1863725.

10. Artress, *The Path of the Holy Fool*, 25.

11. "Girls' Education," The Malala Fund, accessed August 31, 2021, https://www .malala.org/girls-education.

12. "Let Girls Learn," Obama White House Archives, accessed August 30, 2021, https://obamawhitehouse.archives.gov/letgirlslearn.

13. "Let Girls Learn."

14. "Emma Watson: Gender Equality Is Your Issue Too," UN Women, September 20, 2014, https://www.unwomen.org/en/news/stories/2014/9/emma-watson-gender -equality-is-your-issue-too.

15. "Sandra Muller, France's #MeToo Creator, Fined for Defamation," BBC, September 25, 2019, https://www.bbc.com/news/world-europe-49824683.

16. "French #MeToo Founder Wins 'Historic' Defamation Appeal," *The Guardian*, January 4, 2021, https://www.france24.com/en/france/20210401-french-metoo -founder-wins-historic-defamation-appeal.

17. Zacharek, Stephanie, Eliana Dockterman, and Haley Sweetland Edwards. "The Silence Breakers." Time, December 18, 2017. https://time.com/time-person-of-the-year -2017-silence-breakers/.

18. Gurvinder Gill and Imran Rahman-Jones, "Me Too Founder Tarana Burke: Movement Is Not Over," BBC, July 9, 2020, https://www.bbc.com/news/newsbeat-53269751.

19. "Tarana Burke, Founder," MeToo, August 31, 2021, https://metoomvmt.org/get-to -know-us/tarana-burke-founder/.

20. "Herstory," Black Lives Matter, August 31, 2021, https://blacklivesmatter.com /herstory/.

21. "About #SayHerName," African American Policy Forum, August 31, 2021, https://www.aapf.org/sayhername.

22. Zineb Dryef, "Comment Assa Traoré est devenue une figure de l'antiracisme en France," *Le Monde*, July 3, 2020, https://www.lemonde.fr/m-le-mag/article/2020 /07/03/je-suis-la-pour-raconter-l-histoire-de-mon-frere-assa-traore-au-nom-de-sa -verite_6045035_4500055.html.

23. Lucie Souiller, "Affaire Adama Traoré: Une expertise réalisée à la demande de la famille met en cause les gendarmes," *Le Monde*, March 4, 2021, https://www.lemonde .fr/societe/article/2021/03/04/affaire-adama-traore-une-expertise-realisee-a-la -demande-de-la-famille-met-en-cause-les-gendarmes_6071972_3224.html.

24. bell hooks, "Theory as Liberatory Practice," *Yale Journal of Law and Feminism* 4, no. 1 (1991): 2.

Bibliography

"About #SayHerName." African American Policy Forum. Accessed August 31, 2021. https://www.aapf.org/sayhername.

"About Veriditas." Veriditas. Accessed June 25, 2021. https://www.veriditas.org/page -1863725.

Ahmed, Ehsan. "Guillaume Briçonnet, Marguerite de Navarre and the Evangelical Critique of Reason." *Bibliothèque d'humanisme et renaissance* 69, no. 3 (2007): 615–625.

Alighieri, Dante. *The Inferno*. Translated by Robert and Jean Hollander. New York: Doubleday, 2000.

Artress, Lauren. *The Path of the Holy Fool: How the Labyrinth Ignites Our Visionary Powers*. N.p.: Rose Petal Press, 2020.

———. *Walking a Sacred Path: Rediscovering the Labyrinth as a Spiritual Practice*. New York: Riverhead Books, 1995.

Augustine. *The City of God*. Vol. 2. Edited by Marcus Dods. Edinburgh: T. & T. Clark, 1871; Project Gutenberg, 2014. https://www.gutenberg.org/files/45305/45305-h/45305-h.htm.

———. *De doctrina Christiana*. Edited and translated by R. P. H. Green. Oxford: Clarendon, 1995.

Bauschatz, Cathleen. "'Voylà, mes dames . . .': Inscribed Women Listeners and Readers in the Heptaméron." In *Critical Tales: New Studies of the* Heptaméron *and Early Modern Culture*, edited by John D. Lyons and Mary B. McKinley, 104–122. Philadelphia: University of Pennsylvania Press, 1993.

Beebee, Thomas O. *The Ideology of Genre: A Comparative Study of Generic Instability*. University Park: Pennsylvania State University Press, 1994.

Bideaux, Michel. *Roberval, la demoiselle et le gentil-homme: Les Robinsons de Terre-Neuve*. Paris: Classiques Garnier, 2009.

Blaylock, Joshua. "Intertextual Echoes: Emblems, Rabelais, and *Heptaméron* 13." *L'Esprit créateur* 57, no. 3 (2017): 79–92.

———. "A Skeleton in the Closet: Secrecy and Anamorphosis in Marguerite de Navarre's *Heptameron*." *The Sixteenth Century Journal* 45, no. 4 (2014): 951–972.

Boccace. *Le Décaméron de Messire Jehan Bocace Florentin*. Paris: Imprimerie pour Estienne Roffet, dict le Faulcheur, 1545. *Gallica*. https://gallica.bnf.fr/ark:/12148 /btv1b8600071m/f7.image.

Boccaccio, Giovanni. *The Corbaccio*. Translated and edited by Anthony K. Cassell. Urbana: University of Illinois Press, 1975.

———. *The Decameron*. Translated by Wayne A. Rebhorn. New York: Norton, 2013.

Brock, Theresa. "A Love That Reforms: Improving Gender Relations by Contesting Typologies of Women in *La Comédie de Mont-de-Marsan* and *L'Heptaméron* 10 and 42." *Renaissance and Reformation/Renaissance et Réforme* 43, no. 1 (2020): 51–79.

———. "Subverting Seduction: Gender and Genre in Marguerite de Navarre's *Heptaméron*." *Women in French Studies* 26 (2018): 13–26.

Bromilow, Pollie. *Models of Women in Sixteenth-Century French Literature: Female Exemplarity in the* Histoires tragiques *(1559) and the* Heptaméron *(1559)*. Lewiston, NY: Edwin Mellen, 2007.

Calvin, Jean. *Traité des reliques suivi de l'excuse à messieurs les Nicodémites*. Edited by Albert Autin. Paris: Éditions Bossard, 1921.

Calvin, John. *Institutes of the Christian Religion*. 2 vols. Translated by Henry Beveridge. Grand Rapids, MI: Eerdmans, 1964.

———. *Treatise on Relics*. Translated and edited by Joe Nickell. Amherst, NY: Prometheus Books, 2008.

Castiglione, Baldassare. *The Book of the Courtier*. Edited by Daniel Javitch. Translated by Charles Singleton. New York: Norton, 2002.

———. *Le Livre du courtisan*. Translated by Alain Pons. Paris: Flammarion, 1991.

Cazauran, Nicole. "*L'Heptaméron* face au *Décaméron*." In *Variétés pour Marguerite de Navarre 1978–2004. Autour de l'*Heptaméron. Paris: Champion, 2006.

Cazauran, Nicole, and Sylvie Lefèvre. Preface to *Œuvres complètes*. *L'Heptaméron* by Marguerite de Navarre, VII–CIII. Edited by Nicole Cazauran and Sylvie Lefèvre. 3 vols. Paris: Honoré Champion, 2013.

Cholakian, Patricia F. *Rape and Writing in the* Heptaméron *of Marguerite de Navarre*. Carbondale: Southern Illinois University Press, 1991.

Cholakian, Patricia F., and Rouben C. Cholakian. *Marguerite de Navarre: Mother of the Renaissance*. New York: Columbia University Press, 2006.

Citton, Yves. "Détourner l'actualisation." Fabula (2012), https://www.fabula.org/atelier .php?Limites_des_lectures_actualisantes.

———. *Lire, interpréter, actualiser. Pourquoi les études littéraires?* Paris: Éditions Amsterdam, 2007.

Collins, Patricia Hill. *Black Feminist Thought: Knowledge, Consciousness and the Politics of Empowerment*. New York: Routledge, 2008.

Connolly, Daniel. "At the Center of the World: The Labyrinth Pavement of Chartres Cathedral." In *Art and Architecture of Late Medieval Pilgrimage in Northern Europe and the British Isle Texts*, edited by Sarah Blick and Rita Tekippe, 285–314. Leiden: Brill, 2005.

Cornilliat, François, and Ullrich Langer. "Naked Narrator: *Heptameron* 62." In *Critical Tales: New Studies of the* Heptaméron *and Early Modern Culture*, edited by John D. Lyons and Mary B. McKinley, 123–146. Philadelphia: University of Pennsylvania Press, 1993.

Cottrell, Robert. *The Grammar of Silence: A Reading of Marguerite de Navarre's Poetry*. Washington, DC: Catholic University of America Press, 1986.

Crenshaw, Kimberlé. "Mapping the Margins: Intersectionality, Identity Politics, and Violence against Women of Color." *Stanford Law Review* 43, no. 6 (1991): 1241–1299.

Dallmayr, Fred R. "A War against the Turks? Erasmus on War and Peace." *Asian Journal of Social Science* 34, no. 1 (2006): 67–85.

Davis, Betty. *The Storytellers in Marguerite de Navarre's* Heptaméron. Lexington, KY: French Forum Publishers, 1978.

Davis, Natalie Zemon. *Fiction in the Archives.* Stanford, CA: Stanford University Press, 1987.

Defaux, Gérard. "De la bonne nouvelle aux nouvelles: Remarques sur la structure de *L'Heptaméron.*" *French Forum* 27, no. 1 (2002): 23–43.

———. "Marguerite de Navarre et la guerre des sexes: *Heptaméron*, première journée." *French Forum* 24, no. 2 (1999): 133–161.

DeSilva, Jennifer Mara. "Introduction: 'Piously Made': Sacred Space and the Transformation of Behavior." In *The Sacralization of Space and Behavior in the Early Modern World: Studies and Sources*, edited by Jennifer Mara DeSilva, 1–32. New York: Routledge, 2016.

Devitt, Amy. "Integrating Rhetorical and Literary Theories of Genre." *College English* 62, no. 6 (2000): 696–718.

Doob, Penelope Reed. *The Idea of the Labyrinth from Classical Antiquity through the Middle Ages.* Ithaca, NY: Cornell University Press, 1992.

Duval, Edwin. "'Et puis, quelles nouvelles?': The Project of Marguerite's Unfinished *Decameron.*" In *Critical Tales: New Studies of the* Heptaméron *and Early Modern Culture*, edited by John D. Lyons and Mary B. McKinley, 241–262. Philadelphia: University of Pennsylvania Press, 1993.

Dzero, Irina. "From Exile to Escape: Frame Narratives of the *Decameron* and the *Heptameron.*" In *Topodynamics of Arrival: Essays on Self and Pilgrimage*, edited by Gert Hoffman and Snježana Zorić, 169–183. Amsterdam: Rodopi, 2012.

Eco, Umberto. *From the Tree to the Labyrinth: Historical Studies on the Sign and Interpretation.* Translated by Anthony Oldcorn. Cambridge, MA: Harvard University Press, 2014.

———. *Role of the Reader: Explorations in the Semiotics of Texts.* Bloomington: Indiana University Press, 1979.

Eichel-Lojkine, Patricia. *Marguerite de Navarre. Perle de la renaissance.* Paris: Perrin, 2021.

"Emma Watson: Gender Equality Is Your Issue Too." UN Women, September 20, 2014. https://www.unwomen.org/en/news/stories/2014/9/emma-watson-gender-equality -is-your-issue-too.

Erasmus, Desiderius. *The Education of a Christian Prince.* Edited and translated by Lisa Jardine. Cambridge: Cambridge University Press, 1997.

Estienne, Robert. *Dictionnaire françois-latin.* Paris: L'imprimerie de Robert Estienne, 1549; Geneva: Slatkine Reprints, 1972. *Gallica.* https://gallica.bnf.fr/ark:/12148 /bpt6k4396v/.

Evangelisti, Silvia. "Spaces for Agency: The View from Early Modern Female Religious Communities." In *Attending to Early Modern Women: Conflict and Concord*, edited by Karen Nelson, 128–144. Newark: University of Delaware Press, 2013.

Evans, Joan. *Monastic Architecture in France: From the Renaissance to the Revolution.* Cambridge: Cambridge University Press, 1964.

Falkowski, Wojciech. "The Carolingian *Speculum principis*—the Birth of a Genre." *Acta poloniae historica* 98 (2008): 5–27.

Febvre, Lucien. *Autour de* L'Heptaméron. *Amour sacré, amour profane.* Paris: Gallimard, 1944.

Ferguson, Gary. "Gendered Oppositions in Marguerite de Navarre's *Heptaméron*: The Rhetoric of Seduction and Resistance in Narrative and Society." In *Renaissance Women Writers: French Texts/American Contexts,* edited by Anne R. Larsen and Colette H. Winn, 143–159. Detroit, MI: Wayne State University Press, 1994.

———. *Mirroring Belief: Marguerite de Navarre's Devotional Poetry.* Edinburgh: Edinburgh University Press, 1992.

———. "Puns, Exemplarity, and Women's Sexual Agency: Nomerfide and Oisille, *Heptaméron* 5 and 6." In *Itineraries in French Renaissance Literature: Essays for Mary B. McKinley,* edited by Jeff Persels, Kendall Tarte, and George Hoffman, 25–40. Leiden: Brill, 2018.

Ferguson, Gary, and Mary B. McKinley. "The *Heptaméron*: Word, Spirit, World." In *A Companion to Marguerite de Navarre,* edited by Gary Ferguson and Mary B. McKinley, 323–372. Leiden: Brill, 2013.

Ferguson, Margaret. *Dido's Daughters: Literacy, Gender, and Empire in Early Modern England and France.* Chicago: University of Chicago Press, 2014.

———. "Recreating the Rules of the Games: Marguerite de Navarre's *Heptaméron*." In *Creative Imitation: New Essays on Renaissance Literature in Honor of Thomas M. Greene,* edited by David Quint, 153–187. Binghamton, NY: Medieval and Renaissance Texts and Studies, 1992.

Finucci, Valeria. *The Lady Vanishes: Subjectivity and Representation in Castiglione and Ariosto.* Stanford, CA: Stanford University Press, 1992.

Fish, Stanley. "How to Recognize a Poem When You See One." In *Is There a Text in This Class?: The Authority of Interpretive Communities,* 322–337. Cambridge, MA: Harvard University Press, 1980.

———. "Interpreting the *Variorum*." *Critical Inquiry* 2, no. 3 (1976): 467–468.

Fisher, Adrian. *The Amazing Book of Mazes.* New York: Abrams, 2006.

Foxworth, Laura. "'No More Silence!': Feminist Activism and Religion in the Second Wave." In *The Legacy of Second-Wave Feminism in American Politics,* edited by Angie Maxwell and Todd Shields, 73–98. London: Palgrave Macmillan, 2018.

Francis, Scott. *Advertising the Self in Renaissance France: Lemaire, Marot, and Rabelais.* Newark: University of Delaware Press, 2019.

———. "Marguerite de Navarre, a Nicodemite? 'Adiaphora' and Intention in *Heptaméron* 30, 65, and 72." *Renaissance and Reformation/Renaissance et Réforme* 39, no. 3 (2016): 5–31.

———. "Scandalous Women or Scandalous Judgment? The Social Perception of Women and the Theology of Scandal in the *Heptaméron*." *L'Esprit créateur* 57, no. 3 (2017): 33–45.

Freccero, Carla. "Archives in the Fiction: Marguerite de Navarre's *Heptaméron*." In *Rhetoric and Law in Early Modern Europe,* edited by Victoria Kahn and Lorna Hutson, 73–94. New Haven, CT: Yale University Press, 2001.

———. "Patriarchy and the Maternal Text: The Case of Marguerite de Navarre." In *Renaissance Women Writers: French Texts/American Contexts*, edited by Anne R. Larsen and Colette H. Winn, 130–140. Detroit, MI: Wayne State University Press, 1994.

———. *Queer/Early/Modern*. Durham, NC: Duke University Press, 2006.

———. "Queer Nation, Female Nation: Marguerite de Navarre, Incest, and the State in Early Modern France." *Modern Language Quarterly* 65, no. 1 (2004): 29–47.

———. "Voices of Subjection: Maternal Sovereignty and Filial Resistance in and around Marguerite de Navarre's *Heptameron*." *Yale Journal of Law & the Humanities* 5, no. 1 (1993): 147–157.

Frelick, Nancy. "Female Infidelity: Ideology, Subversion, and Feminist Practice in Marguerite de Navarre's *Heptaméron*." *Dalhousie French Studies* 56 (2001): 17–26.

———. Introduction to *The Mirror in Medieval and Early Modern Culture: Specular Reflections*, edited by Nancy M. Frelick, 1–30. Turnhout, Belgium: Brepols, 2016.

———. "Mirroring Discourses of Difference: Marguerite de Navarre's *Heptaméron* and the *Querelle des femmes*." *French Forum* 32, no. 3 (2017): 375–392.

———. "Speech, Silence, and Storytelling: Marguerite de Navarre's *Heptameron* and Narrative Therapy." *Renaissance and Reformation/Renaissance et Réforme* 36, no. 1 (2013): 69–92.

"French #MeToo Founder Wins 'Historic' Defamation Appeal." *The Guardian*, January 4, 2021. https://www.france24.com/en/france/20210401-french-metoo-founder -wins-historic-defamation-appeal.

Frisch, Andrea. *The Invention of the Eyewitness: Witnessing and Testimony in Early Modern France*. Chapel Hill: Department of Romance Languages, University of North Carolina, 2004.

Gibson, Joan. "Educating for Silence: Renaissance Women and the Language Arts." *Hypatia* 4, no. 1 (1989): 9–27.

Gill, Gurvinder, and Imran Rahman-Jones. "Me Too Founder Tarana Burke: Movement Is Not Over." BBC, July 9, 2020. https://www.bbc.com/news/newsbeat -53269751.

"Girls' Education." *The Malala Fund*. Accessed August 31, 2021. https://www.malala.org /girls-education.

Glidden, Hope. "Gender, Essence, and the Feminine (*Heptameron* 43)." In *Critical Tales: New Studies of the* Heptaméron *and Early Modern Culture*, edited by John D. Lyons and Mary B. McKinley, 25–40. Philadelphia: University of Pennsylvania Press, 1993.

Haraway, Donna. "Situated Knowledges: The Science Question in Feminism and the Privilege of Partial Perspective." *Feminist Studies* 14, no. 3 (1988): 575–599.

Harding, Sandra, ed. *The Feminist Standpoint Theory Reader: Intellectual and Political Controversies*. New York: Routledge, 2004.

Hartsock, Nancy. "The Feminist Standpoint: Developing the Ground for a Specifically Feminist Historical Materialism." In *Discovering Reality: Feminist Perspectives on Epistemology, Metaphysics, Methodology, and Philosophy of Science*, edited by Sandra Harding and Merrill B. Hintikka, 283–310. Dordrecht: Kluwer Academic, 1983.

"Herstory." Black Lives Matter. Accessed August 31, 2021. https://blacklivesmatter.com
/herstory/.

hooks, bell. *Feminist Theory: From Margin to Center.* London: Pluto, 2000.

———. "Theory as Liberatory Practice." *Yale Journal of Law and Feminism* 4, no. 1
(1991): 1–12.

Jeanneret, Michel. "Modular Narrative and the Crisis of Interpretation." In *Critical
Tales: New Studies of the* Heptaméron *and Early Modern Culture*, edited by John D.
Lyons and Mary B. McKinley, 85–103. Philadelphia: University of Pennsylvania
Press, 1993.

Jónsson, Einar Már. *Le Miroir: Naissance d'un genre littéraire.* Paris: Les Belles Lettres,
2004.

Jourda, Pierre. *Marguerite d'Angoulême, duchesse d'Alençon, reine de Navarre
(1492–1549): Étude biographique et littéraire.* 2 vols. Paris: Champion, 1930.

Kelly-Gadol, Joan. "Did Women Have a Renaissance?" In *Becoming Visible: Women in
European History*, edited by Renate Bridenthal and Claudia Koontz, 137–164. Boston: Houghton Mifflin, 1977.

Kem, Judy. "Fatal Lovesickness in Marguerite de Navarre's *Heptaméron.*" *The Sixteenth
Century Journal* 41, no. 2 (2010): 355–370.

Kern, Hermann. *Through the Labyrinth: Designs and Meanings over 5,000 Years.*
Munich: Prestel, 2000.

Klaus, Carrie F. "From *Désert* to *Patrie*: Marguerite de Navarre's Lessons from the New
World." *L'Esprit créateur* 57, no. 3 (2017): 58–66.

Knecht, R. J. *Renaissance Warrior and Patron. The Reign of Francis I.* Cambridge: Cambridge University Press, 1994.

Kolsky, Stephen. "The Limits of Knowledge: Scholasticism and Scepticism in the *Book
of the Courtier.*" *Parergon* 25, no. 2 (2008): 17–32.

La Charité, Claude. "Les Questions laissées en suspens par le *Brief recit* (1545) de Jacques
Cartier et les réponses de la nouvelle 67 de *L'Heptaméron* (1559) de Marguerite de
Navarre." *Œuvres et critiques* 36, no. 1 (2011): 91–109.

———. "Rhetorical Augustinianism in Marguerite de Navarre's *Heptaméron.*" *Allegorica* 23 (2002): 55–88.

La Garanderie, Marie-Madeleine de. *Le Dialogue des romanciers: Une nouvelle lecture
de* L'Heptaméron *de Marguerite de Navarre.* Paris: Minard, 1977.

La Grèze, Gustave Bascle de. *Les Pèlerinages des Pyrénées.* Paris: Jacques le Coffre, 1858.

LaGuardia, David. "Exemplarity as Misogyny: Variations on the Tale of the One-Eyed
Cuckold." In *Narrative Worlds: Essays on the French Nouvelle in 15th and 16th Century
France*, edited by Gary Ferguson and David LaGuardia, 139–158. Tempe: Medieval
and Renaissance Texts and Studies, Arizona State University, 2005.

Lajarte, Philippe de. "Amour et passion dans *L'Heptaméron*: Perspective éthique et perspective pathologique." In *La Poétique des passions à la Renaissance: Mélanges
offerts à Françoise Charpentier*, edited by François Lecercle and Simone Perrier,
369–387. Paris: Classiques Garnier, 2001.

———. *L'Heptaméron de Marguerite de Navarre: "En bien nous mirant."* Paris: Honoré
Champion, 2019.

Langer, Ullrich. "The Renaissance Novella as Justice." *Renaissance Quarterly* 52, no. 2 (1999): 311–341.

Lebègue, Raymond. "*L'Heptaméron*, un attrape-mondains." In *De Ronsard à Breton, recueil d'essais: Hommages à Marcel Raymond*, 35–41. Paris: José Corti, 1967.

Le Cadet, Nicolas. *L'Évangélisme fictionnel: Les* Livres *rabelaisiens, le* Cymbalum mundi, L'Heptaméron *(1532–1552)*. Paris: Classiques Garnier, 2011.

Lefèvre d'Étapes, Jacques. *La Saincte Bible en francoys translatee*. Antwerp: Martin Lempereur, 1530.

Leroy, M. L'Abbé Louis. *Histoire des pèlerinages de la Sainte Vierge en France*. 2 vols. Paris: Louis Vivès, 1874.

Lestringant, Frank. "La Demoiselle dans l'île: Prolégomènes à une lecture de la Nouvelle 67." In *Lire* L'Heptaméron *de Marguerite de Navarre*, edited by Dominique Bertrand, 183–196. Clermont-Ferrand, France: Presses universitaires Blaise Pascal, 2006.

"Let Girls Learn." Obama White House Archives. Accessed August 30, 2021. https://obamawhitehouse.archives.gov/letgirlslearn.

Leushuis, Reinier. "Mariage et 'honnête amitié' dans *l'Heptaméron* de Marguerite de Navarre: Des idéaux ecclésiastique et aristocratique à l'agapè du dialogue humaniste." *French Forum* 28 (2003): 29–56.

Llewellyn, Dawn. *Reading, Feminism, and Spirituality: Troubling the Waves*. London: Palgrave Macmillan, 2015.

Long, Kathleen. "Teaching the Rhetoric of the Battle of the Sexes: Dialogues in and between the *Heptameron* and the *Decameron*." In *Approaches to Teaching Marguerite de Navarre's* Heptaméron, edited by Colette Winn, 181–185. New York: Modern Language Association of America, 2007.

Losse, Deborah. "Authorial and Narrative Voice in the *Heptaméron*." *Renaissance and Reformation/Renaissance et Réforme* 11, no. 3 (1987): 223–242.

Luther, Martin. "Address to the Christian Nobility of the German Nation, concerning the Reform of the Christian Estate." In *Luther's Primary Works, Together with His Shorter and Larger Catechisms, Translated into English*, edited by Henry Wace and C. A. Buchheim, 159–244. London: Hodder and Stoughton, 1896.

Lyons, John D. *Exemplum: The Rhetoric of Example in Early Modern France and Italy*. Princeton, NJ: Princeton University Press, 1990.

Martineau, Christine. "Le Platonisme de Marguerite de Navarre." *Bulletin de l'Association d'étude sur l'humanisme, la réforme et la renaissance* 4 (1976): 12–35.

Martineau-Génieys, Christine. "La *Lectio divina* dans *L'Heptaméron*." In *Études sur* L'Heptaméron *de Marguerite de Navarre*, edited by Christine Martineau-Génieys, 21–42. Nice, France: Association des Publications de la Faculté des lettres de Nice, 1996.

———. "La voix de l'évangélisme dans *L'Heptaméron* de Marguerite de Navarre." In *Mélanges Jean Larmat: Regards sur le Moyen Âge et la Renaissance. Histoire, langue et littérature*, edited by Maurice Accarie, 385–391. Paris: Belles Lettres, 1983.

Matthews, W. H. *Mazes and Labyrinths: A General Account of Their History and Developments*. London: Longmans, Green, 1922.

Maupeu, Philippe. *Pèlerins de vie humaine: Autobiographie et allégorie narrative, de Guillaume de Deguileville à Octovien de Saint-Gelais.* Paris: Honoré Champion, 2009.

Maxwell, Angie, and Todd Shields. Introduction to *The Legacy of Second-Wave Feminism in American Politics,* edited by Angie Maxwell and Todd Shields, 1–18. London: Palgrave Macmillan, 2018.

McKinley, Mary B. "Agony, Ecstasy, and the Mulekeeper's Wife: A Reading of *Heptaméron* 2." In *A French Forum: Mélanges de littérature française offerts à Raymond C. et Virginia A. La Charité,* edited by Gérard Defaux and Jerry Nash, 129–142. Paris: Klincksieck, 2000.

———. "An Ottoman 'Fixer' in Marguerite de Navarre's *Heptaméron.*" *L'Esprit créateur* 53, no. 4 (2013): 9–20.

———. "Telling Secrets: Sacramental Confession and Narrative Authority in the *Heptaméron.*" In *Critical Tales: New Studies of the* Heptaméron *and Early Modern Culture,* edited by John D. Lyons and Mary B. McKinley, 146–171. Philadelphia: University of Pennsylvania Press, 1993.

Michon, Cédric. "Le Rôle politique de Louise de Savoie (1515–1531)." In *Louise de Savoie (1476–1531),* edited by Pascal Brioist, Laure Fagnart, and Cédric Michon, 103–116. Tours, France: Presses universitaires de Rennes and Presses universitaires François-Rabelais, 2015.

Middlebrook, Leah. "'Tout Mon Office': Body Politics and Family Dynamics in the *Verse epîtres* of Marguerite de Navarre." *Renaissance Quarterly* 54, no. 4 (2001): 1108–1141.

Miernowski, Jan. "Le miracle de la Pentecôte à Sarrance: Cohérence narrative et vérité religieuse dans la septième journée de *L'Heptaméron.*" In *Narrations brèves: Mélanges de littératures anciennes offerts à Krystyna Kasprzyk,* edited by Piotr Salwa and Ewa Dorota Zokiewska, 177–196. Geneva: Droz, 1993.

Miller, Tanya Stabler. *The Beguines of Medieval Paris: Gender, Patronage, and Spiritual Authority.* Philadelphia: University of Pennsylvania Press, 2014.

Millet, Olivier. "Réforme du sermon et métamorphose du prédicateur (De Surgant à Lambert d'Avignon et Érasme): Témoignage évangélique et fiction romanesque dans *L'Heptaméron* de Marguerite de Navarre." In *Annoncer L'Évangile (XVe–XVIIe siècle): Permanences et mutations de la prédication,* edited by Matthieu Arnold, 363–380. Paris: CERF, 2006.

Morwood, James, ed., *Pocket Oxford Latin Dictionary: Latin-English,* 3rd ed. (Oxford: Oxford University Press, 2012).

Navarre, Marguerite de. *The Heptameron.* Translated by Paul Chilton. London: Penguin, 1984.

———. *Œuvres complètes. Tome. IV: Théâtre.* Edited by Nicole Cazauran. Paris: Honoré Champion, 2002.

———. *Œuvres complètes. Tome X: L'Heptaméron.* Edited by Nicole Cazauran and Sylvie Lefèvre. 3 vols. Paris: Honoré Champion, 2013.

———. *Selected Writings: A Bilingual Edition.* Edited and translated by Rouben Cholakian and Mary Skemp. Chicago: University of Chicago Press, 2008.

Navarre, Marguerite de, and Guillaume Briçonnet. *Correspondance (1521–1524)*. Edited by Christine Martineau, Michel Veissière, and Henry Heller. 2 vols. Geneva: Droz, 1975.

Nazarian, Cynthia. "Honor and Gender in the *Heptaméron* of Marguerite de Navarre." *L'Esprit créateur* 60, no. 1 (2020): 87–99.

Noonan, F. Thomas. *The Road to Jerusalem: Pilgrimage and Travel in the Age of Discovery*. Philadelphia: University of Pennsylvania Press, 2007.

Norton, Glyn P. "Narrative Function in the *Heptaméron* Frame Story." In *La Nouvelle française à la Renaissance*, edited by Lionello Sozzi and V. L. Saulnier, 435–447. Geneva: Slatkine, 1981.

O'Malley, John W., ed. *Collected Works of Erasmus*. Toronto: University of Toronto Press, 1988.

Pajon-Héron, Marine. "Les aménagements architecturaux et paysagers réalisés par Louise de Savoie au château de Romorantin." In *Louise de Savoie (1476–1531)*, edited by Pascal Brioist, Laure Fagnart, and Cédric Michon, 61–71. Tours, France: Presses universitaires de Rennes and Presses universitaires François-Rabelais, 2015.

Peterson, Nora Martin. "The Impossible Striptease: Nudity in Jean Calvin and Michel de Montaigne." *Renaissance and Reformation/Renaissance et Réforme* 37, no. 1 (2014): 65–85.

———. *Involuntary Confessions of the Flesh in Early Modern France*. Newark: University of Delaware Press, 2016.

Pisanty, Valentina. "From the Model Reader to the Limits of Interpretation." *Semiotica* 206 (2015): 37–61.

Pitkin, Barbara. *What Pure Eyes Could See: Calvin's Doctrine of Faith in Its Exegetical Context*. Oxford: Oxford University Press, 1999.

Planté, Christine. "Femmes exceptionnelles: Des Exceptions pour quelle règle?" *Les Cahiers du GRIF*, no. 37–38 (1988): 90–111.

———. "Genre, un concept intraduisible?" In *Le Genre comme catégorie d'analyse. Sociologie, histoire, littérature*, edited by Dominique Fougeyrollas-Schwebel, Christine Planté, Michèle Riot-Sarcey, and Claude Zaidman, 127–136. Paris: L'Harmattan, 2003.

Plantey, Damien. *Les Bibliothèques des princesses de Navarre au XVIe siècle: Livres, objets, mobilier, décor, espaces et usages*. Villeurbanne, France: Presses de l'enssib, 2016.

Quanbeck, Warren. "The First Letter of Paul to Timothy." In *The New Oxford Bible with the Apocrypha*, edited by Herbert G. May and Bruce M. Metzger, 1440–1443. Oxford: Oxford University Press, 1974.

Rabelais, François. *Gargantua and Pantagruel*. Translated and edited by M. A. Screech. New York: Penguin, 2006.

———. *Œuvres complètes*. Edited by Jacques Boulenger. Paris: Gallimard, 1955.

Randall, Catharine. *Earthly Treasures: Material Culture and Metaphysics in the Heptaméron and Evangelical Narrative*. West Lafayette, IN: Purdue University Press, 2007.

———. "Objects of Desire: Reading the Material World Metaphysically in Marguerite de Navarre's *Heptaméron*." *Quidditas* 19 (1998): 167–195.

———. "Scandalous Rhetorics: Preaching Plain Style in Marguerite de Navarre." *Women in French Studies* 13 (2005): 11–24.

Regosin, Richard. "Death's Desire: Sensuality and Spirituality in Marguerite de Navarre's *Heptaméron*." *MLN* 116, no. 4 (2001): 770–794.

Reid, Jonathan. *King's Sister—Queen of Dissent: Marguerite de Navarre (1492–1549) and Her Evangelical Network.* 2 vols. Leiden: Brill, 2009.

Reynolds-Cornell, Régine. "*L'Heptaméron* de Marguerite de Navarre: Influence de Castiglione." *Studi di letteratura francese* 5 (1979): 25–31.

Rezvani, Leanna Bridge. "The *Heptaméron*'s 67th Tale: Marguerite de Navarre's Humble Heroine Confronts the Querelle des Femmes and Catholic Tradition." *Romance Notes* 52, no. 1 (2012): 43–50.

———. "Nature and Nourishment, Bodies and Beasts: The *Heptaméron*'s Portrayal of Marguerite de Roberval's Marooning." *Dalhousie French Studies* 102 (2014): 3–7.

Rigolot, François. "Magdalen's Skull: Allegory and Iconography in *Heptameron* 32." *Renaissance Quarterly* 47, no. 1 (1994): 57–73.

Rudolph, Conrad, ed. *Pilgrimage to the End of the World: The Road to Santiago de Compostela.* Chicago: University of Chicago Press, 2004.

Rummel, Erika. *Erasmus.* London: Continuum, 2004.

"Sandra Muller, France's #MeToo Creator, Fined for Defamation." BBC, September 25, 2019. https://www.bbc.com/news/world-europe-49824683.

Saward, Jeff. *Labyrinths & Mazes: A Complete Guide to Magical Paths of the World.* New York: Lark Books, 2003.

———. *Magical Paths: Labyrinths & Mazes in the 21st Century.* London: Mitchell Beazley, 2002.

Silvas, Anna M., ed. *Gregory of Nyssa: The Letters. Introduction, Translation, and Commentary.* Leiden: Brill, 2007.

Smarr, Janet Levarie. "Introduction: A Man of Many Turns." In *Boccaccio: A Critical Guide to the Complete Works,* edited by Victoria Kirkham, Michael Sherberg, and Janet Levarie Smarr, 1–20. Chicago: University of Chicago Press, 2014.

———. *Joining the Conversation: Dialogues by Renaissance Women.* Ann Arbor: University of Michigan Press, 2005.

Snyder, Susan. "Guilty Sisters: Marguerite de Navarre, Elizabeth of England, and the *Miroir de l'âme pécheresse.*" *Renaissance Quarterly* 50, no. 2 (1997): 443–458.

Sommers, Paula. "Feminine Authority in the *Heptaméron*: A Reading of Oysille." *Modern Language Studies* 13, no. 2 (1983): 52–59.

———. "Marguerite de Navarre's *Heptaméron*: The Case for the Cornice." *French Review* 57, no. 6 (1984): 786–793.

———. "The Mirror and Its Reflections: Marguerite de Navarre's Biblical Feminism." *Tulsa Studies in Women's Literature* 5, no. 1 (1986): 29–39.

Souiller, Lucie. "Affaire Adama Traoré: Une expertise réalisée à la demande de la famille met en cause les gendarmes." *Le Monde,* March 4, 2021. https://www.lemonde.fr /societe/article/2021/03/04/affaire-adama-traore-une-expertise-realisee-a-la-deman de-de-la-famille-met-en-cause-les-gendarmes_6071972_3224.html.

Stephenson, Barbara. *The Power and Patronage of Marguerite de Navarre*. New York: Routledge, 2004.

Suzuki, Mihoko. "Gender, Power, and the Female Reader: Boccaccio's *Decameron* and Marguerite de Navarre's *Heptameron*." *Comparative Literature Studies* 30, no. 3 (1993): 231–252.

"Tarana Burke, Founder." MeToo. Accessed August 31, 2021. https://metoomvmt.org /get-to-know-us/tarana-burke-founder/.

Telle, Émile. *L'Œuvre de Marguerite d'Angoulême, reine de Navarre, et la querelle des femmes*. Toulouse: Imprimerie Toulousaine Lion, 1937.

Tetel, Marcel. *Marguerite de Navarre's* Heptaméron: *Themes, Language, and Structure*. Durham, NC: Duke University Press, 1973.

Thompson, Emily. "Playing with Fire: Narrating Angry Women and Men in the *Heptaméron*." *Renaissance and Reformation/Renaissance et Réforme* 38, no. 3 (2015): 161–175.

Thysell, Carol. "Gendered Virtue, Vernacular Theology, and the Nature of Authority in the *Heptaméron*." *Sixteenth Century Journal* 29, no. 1 (1998): 39–53.

———. *The Pleasure of Discernment: Marguerite de Navarre as Theologian*. Oxford: Oxford University Press, 2000.

Tinguely, Frédéric. *L'Écriture du Levant à la Renaissance: Enquête sur les voyageurs français dans l'empire de Soliman le Magnifique*. Geneva: Droz, 2000.

Ullyatt, Tony. "'Gestures of Approach': Aspects of Liminality and Labyrinths." *Literator* 32, no. 2 (2011): 103–134.

Usher, Phillip John. *Errance et cohérence: Essai sur la littérature transfrontalière à la Renaissance*. Paris: Classiques Garnier, 2010.

Vance, Jacob. "Humanist Polemics, Christian Morals: A Hypothesis on Marguerite de Navarre's *Heptaméron* and the Problem of Self-Love." *MLN* 120, no. 1 (2005): S181–S195.

Vives, Juan Luis. *On Assistance to the Poor*. Translated by Sister Alice Tobriner. Toronto: University of Toronto Press, 1999.

———. *The Education of a Christian Woman: A Sixteenth-Century Manual*. Edited, and translated by Charles Fantazzi. Chicago: University of Chicago Press, 2000.

Wetzel, Hermann. "Éléments socio-historiques d'un genre littéraire: L'Histoire de la nouvelle jusqu'à Cervantès." In *La Nouvelle française à la Renaissance*, edited by Lionello Sozzi and V. L. Saulnier, 41–78. Geneva: Slatkine, 1981.

Williams, Wes. *Pilgrimage and Narrative in the French Renaissance: "The Undiscovered Country."* Oxford: Clarendon, 1998.

Winn, Colette H. *The Dialogue in Early Modern France (1547–1630): Art and Argument*. Washington, DC: Catholic University of America Press, 1993.

———. "'Trop en corps': Marguerite de Navarre and the Transgressive Body." In *Renaissance Women Writers: French Texts/American Contexts*, edited by Anne R. Larsen and Colette H. Winn, 99–114. Detroit, MI: Wayne State University Press, 1994.

Woods, Joshua. "Comment Assa Traoré est devenue une figure de l'antiracisme en France." *Le Monde*, July 3, 2020. https://www.lemonde.fr/m-le-mag/article/2020/07 /03/je-suis-la-pour-raconter-l-histoire-de-mon-frere-assa-traore-au-nom-de-sa-verite _6045035_4500055.html.

Wright, Craig. *The Maze and the Warrior: Symbols in Architecture, Theology, and Music.* Cambridge, MA: Harvard University Press, 2021.

Zacharek, Stephanie, Eliana Dockterman, and Haley Sweetland Edwards. "The Silence Breakers." *Time*, December 18, 2017. https://time.com/time-person-of-the-year-2017 -silence-breakers/.

Zegura, Elizabeth Chesney. *Marguerite de Navarre's Shifting Gaze: Perspectives on Gender, Class, and Politics in the* Heptaméron. New York: Routledge, 2017.

———. "What the Monk's Habit Hides: Excavating the Silent Truths in Marguerite de Navarre's *Heptaméron* 31." *Renaissance and Reformation/Renaissance et Réforme* 38, no. 2 (2015): 53–92.

Index

About the Author

Theresa Brock is Assistant Professor of French Studies at Smith College. She received her PhD from The Pennsylvania State University and has published articles on women writers, literary genre, and religious studies in the early modern era, with particular emphasis on the sixteenth century. She is currently at work on a second book that examines the influence of gender and religion on hermeneutics of the natural world in texts by early modern French writers.

Printed and bound by CPI Group (UK) Ltd, Croydon, CR0 4YY

09/06/2025

14685738-0001